HOW TO BUY
(almost anything)
SECONDHAND

The essential A-to-Z covering more than
150 items large and small, common and
unusual.

Entertaining to read and full of surprising
snippets of information, this book tells you
where to look, how to locate unusual sales
and how to bid at auction. The entries
show how to pinpoint faults and assess
whether cheap repairs are possible and how
to restore your purchases to good condition
when you get them home.

'Guides bargain-hunters through the pros
and cons of buying anything from a private
airliner to a house-hold broom.'
Daily Mirror

ACKNOWLEDGEMENTS

Hundreds of people contributed their ideas and experience to this book. Manufacturers, dealers, trade associations, enthusiasts' clubs, specialist magazines, menders and friends were all enormously generous with both their time and their knowledge. I happily acknowledge my debt to them. I am especially grateful to a few patient people who were repeatedly consulted: Marion Giordan of the Electricity Consumers' Council; Cassandra Kent and her colleagues at the Good Housekeeping Institute; Nora Riddington of the Electrical Association for Women; Chris Rogers of the Institute of Trading Standards Administration; the staff of the British Standards Institution and the Office of Fair Trading. Particular thanks must also go to Mike Solomons of London Sound, Geo Clark of Brunnings, Michael Cross of EMI, Gerry Dorey, Dorothy Gillies, Stuart Gillies, Derek Halfpenny of Wedgwood, Lynn Hardy-Smith, John Heritage, Paul McAlinden and Gerry Murray. Peter Campbell supplied a constant and encouraging flow of ideas and information: he also designed the book.

Above all, my thanks go to Margaret Crowther of Astragal Books, who edited the manuscript and oversaw the entire

project; without her constant interest, ceaseless encourage-
ment and stunningly practical suggestions, the book would
certainly have foundered.

Caroline Evans worked with me throughout the project,
and it would be hard to exaggerate her contribution to the
content and style of the book. She suggested, researched,
organized and checked a large part of the material, always
original when all around was secondhand. Many of the best
and most curious ideas in this book are unquestionably hers.

HOW TO BUY
(almost anything)
SECONDHAND

Richard Ball

CORGI BOOKS
A DIVISION OF TRANSWORLD PUBLISHERS LTD

HOW TO BUY ALMOST ANYTHING SECONDHAND

A CORGI BOOK   0   552   12013   8

Originally published in Great Britain by the Architectural Press Ltd.

PRINTING HISTORY
Architectural Press edition published 1981
Corgi edition published 1982

This book is set in Times Roman 10 on 11 pt.

Corgi Books are published by Transworld Publishers Ltd., Century House, 61–63 Uxbridge Road, Ealing, London W5 5SA

Made and printed in Great Britain by
Cox & Wyman Ltd., Reading, Berks.

CONTENTS

To Margaret, with love

SECONDHAND ADVICE

"It's NEW!" The advertising industry loves to launch a product with the ancient claim for novelty. There's still a strong sales appeal in this very temporary virtue, which vanishes as soon as the goods are sold. Time after time the innovative consumer has paid dearly for a novelty product, only to see prices tumble as production volume grows. He is left only with the memory of the brief prestige brought by being among the first owners of a new product. As each new development is seized on by the wealthy and enthusiastic, excellent appliances may be discarded onto the secondhand market, where the shrewd consumer waits, muttering his guiding principle: the less you pay, the less you stand to lose. In a world where people pay for novelty, secondhand prices will be low.

The secondhand market is not entirely free from a longing for novelty. Sellers introduce the hallowed quality by labelling used goods "nearly new". They dislike the term "secondhand" which conjures up a tawdry vision of junk shops and jumble sales, auction rooms and pawnbrokers. This image seriously underestimates the extent and sophistication of the secondhand society. The market in used but sophisticated machinery, for example, runs smoothly and internationally, with secondhand technology moving from the West to the countries of the Third World. While the booming Indian film industry buys up redundant cameras from the British movie makers, beautiful old European steam locomotives still trundle over the Third World. A market in secondhand computers has begun to flourish; international airlines fly secondhand aircraft around the world; and at a more intimate level the country's most skilled surgeons join forces with western technology's most advanced instrumentation to transplant secondhand hearts on the National Health Service. Even secondhand footballers are advertised and sold on an international scale: a good runner in his early twenties with no nagging injuries was valued at over a million pounds in England in 1980.

The price of a secondhand football international is of course of less direct interest to the average consumer than price movements in the market for secondhand cameras or cars. The typical car's value plummets as it is driven out of the showroom door, though Rolls Royce cars remain a notoriously good investment, with secondhand prices higher than retail. The Rolls is the exception which proves the basic rule of the secondhand world: secondhand goods are cheaper than new ones. It is this factor which rules out of the secondhand category such aberrations as the profitable black market in tickets for the Centre Court at Wimbledon or the FA Cup Final, and it is this same factor which places antiques beyond the scope of this book.

Up-to-date knowledge of prevailing prices is vital to the secondhand buyer. Money can be wasted by jumping into the secondhand market without checking out the price of comparable brand-new goods. Technical innovation, changing market conditions and the rise of the discount warehouse have recently played havoc with the price of used cameras, calculators, records and audio equipment.

Advertisers traditionally consider qualities such as dura-

12

bility and ease of repair to be far weaker selling points than
novelty. These are the matters of greatest concern to the
buyers of secondhand goods. They have no prejudice against
the unfashionable looks of last year's model, as long as it
works well and it is cheap. They know that manufacturers
regularly change their range merely by sticking last year's
innards in a redesigned box, and that where such a superficial
view of novelty dominates the market, bargains are easy to
find.

Even at rock bottom prices, some items remain largely
unwanted. Demand for used socks, mattresses, medicine and
film is slack. There's something practically biological about
the revulsion many parents-to-be feel for secondhand prams.
Yet few items find no buyer. Beyond the jumble sale lies the
obsessive end of the secondhand spectrum, where buyers are
willing to spend infinite time and trouble rather than open the
purse wide enough to buy anything new. These are the people
who seek out old calendars whose time has come round again,
pencilling in a new batch of bank holidays, religious festivals
and phases of the moon.

Movements of the moon are of little help in deciding the right
time to buy secondhand, but prices do move with the seasons.
Skis are cheaper in June when the snow has melted, while
the price of old tents falls with the autumn leaves. Motorbikes
grow in popularity with the length of the days each spring.

Secondhand prices also follow long-term trends. Any object will eventually cross the artificial divide between cheap
junk and valuable antique if it lasts long enough. The antique
category has recently expanded enormously, to embrace many
everyday objects. Old tools now feature in museums and
country pubs, as well as in private collections. Any farm
auction has its ancient wheelbarrows riddled with woodworm,
and bidding is always brisk. Cunning farmers are now storing
away useful old engines still in working order in the hope of
selling them as industrial antiques before they turn to rust.

There is a time and a place for everything secondhand, and
the ideal occasion is often an unlikely one. Buyers know they
will find what they need in a specialist shop, whether it is

jewellery, cameras, paintings, cars or furniture. Prices here are consequently high, reflecting demand and convenience. However, if you find a modern painting in a sale of agricultural machinery, or a used typewriter in a carpet sale, you could have found a bargain, as competition from other bidders will be minimal. The secondhand buyer is always alert.

The vultures of the secondhand world descend to pick clean the depressed areas of the country, where sudden redundancies force people to sell off their belongings to pay the bills. Those who find it unsavoury to exploit the unfortunate will have a harder hunt for bargains. Certain parts of the country are best avoided. For example, the south east is generally expensive. Ancient kettles and water heaters are rarely worth buying in hardwater areas, as they may be clogged up with mineral deposits. The hardest water comes out of the taps in parts of north and south-east Scotland, East Anglia, parts of Essex, Gloucestershire, Hampshire, Kent, parts of Lancashire, London, West Midlands, Sussex, Wiltshire and parts of Yorkshire.

The public views secondhand dealers with well-founded suspicion. Too many dealers are eager to exploit public ignorance. The psychology of the successful dealer is uncomfortably close to that of the criminal. Some dealers repent and turn to God. In 1980 there was a mass "conversion" of traders at Haywards Heath, Sussex, when it was learned that Seventh Day Adventists could trade on Sundays.

Some dealers are skilled in buying cheap, others are good at getting a top price when they resell, and the two skills are not necessarily combined in the same person. The shrewd buyer can allow himself a good profit and still sell cheap.

General dealers who advertise a "houses-cleared-for-cash" service rarely give fair prices to the unfortunate seller, and their claim to clear houses completely is often inexact: they drive away their van loaded with the most saleable items and fail to return for the rubbish. However, such men are saints compared to the men "on the knocker", whose claim that "we pay high cash prices" is mind-bogglingly false. Brighton is the centre of the British knockers, and addresses on the south coast usually feature on the advance warning handouts pushed through the public's letterboxes, announcing that a buyer will soon be knocking on the door, cash in pocket. Their golden rule is "never make an offer"; they prefer to force the victim to name a price, usually an absurdly low one; in this way they legitimise outrageous exploitation of the elderly and ignorant.

Junk dealers insure themselves against their own ignorance. They are often incapable of telling a good item from a bad one, so they balance the risk of missing a gem by overcharging for undesirable rubbish. For example, if they know that good tin toys fetch a high price, they are tempted to put the same high price tag on the rustiest and most squashed toys they find. Collectors often discover that specialist dealers are cheaper for the item in average condition, as specialists are less likely to overcharge for junk. Specialist dealers also offer properly reconditioned goods with worthwhile guarantees.

Some dealers like to hide their true professional identity behind a private address in a newspaper small ad, despite a law forbidding the practice since 1977. They can betray themselves to alert readers who notice that the same telephone number appears in several ads. Other dealers wander the streets pretending to collect stuff for charity. This is also illegal. The genuine charity shops are a good source of secondhand goods.

Charities differ from the dealers in that the law stops them buying anything for resale. Those which haven't set up registered trading companies rely entirely on gifts to stock their shops. Some welcome donations of junk and jumble in almost all its forms. Others seek it out. The worthy People's Dispensary for Sick Animals (PDSA), for example, has about thirty shops scattered around the country, plus three large jumble depots, in London, Birmingham and Nottingham. The PDSA vans tour these cities on a junk hunt and return to the jumble base loaded with furniture, paper, prams, lawnmowers, broken kettles and brollies and cast-off hats. The vast London warehouse in Liverpool Road is a cathedral of jumble, where astonishing mountains of brollies and chairs sit next to the baling machine which prepares woollens for re-cycling in Yorkshire. When activity in the antique trade is sluggish, the depots are thrown open to the public.

In large cities, the Salvation Army may sell cheap sec-ondhand furniture to the public. The junk business is used as part of the Army's rehabilitation programme, and will be manned by the men in the hostels. They are often rather grumpy alcoholics whose commitment to the work is slight, and they can give an unprepared customer a rough but often rewarding ride.

Some extraordinary objects can be put to use by inventive voluntary organisations. Milk bottle tops are still turned into guide dogs for the blind, as the aluminium content can be sold to the scrap metal smelters for an average 15 pence per pound (1980 prices) by individual volunteers all over the country, who then forward the proceeds to the central charity. Aluminium is welcome in all its forms, whether pull-rings from beer cans, take-away food trays or yoghourt carton tops. Charitable links with the scrap metal business are extensive. Brass and steel are saleable, and very decorative old kettles and brasswork find their way to the metal dealers.

Oxfam runs more shops than the illustrious Marks and Spencer, and in every one there's a green bin where milk bottle tops—preferably clean—can be dropped, together with any other aluminium object. Every Oxfam shop should also have a little black box for used stamps. Secondhand stamps have become a significant money-spinner for enter-prising charities. A used ten pence stamp may rank among the most boring objects in Britain, but somewhere in the world someone needs one for the collection, especially if it is a commemorative picture stamp. The stamps collected by Oxfam or the PDSA are sorted by a philatelist; some are then packaged and sold through their own shops, others are sent abroad. The Save the Children Fund (SCF) sends the most undesirable secondhand stamps by the ton to the United States. In 1980 the bulk price was £1.50 per kilo for the rubbish, the price rising with the desirability of the stamps. The SCF claims to throw nothing away, but they have no use for secondhand Christmas cards, bottle tops or silver paper.

16

The long list of wanted objects includes coins, medals, postcards, cigarette cards and beer mats.

Oxfam's Huddersfield-based "Wastesaver" project developed a thriving button-recycling scheme. When a really tatty garment comes into a shop and is declared too nasty to wear, it is sent to Huddersfield, where the buttons are snipped off. The attractive buttons are packeted and sold through the Oxfam shops, while the buttonless garments are sold to the rag merchants.

Torn and worn garments and sheets traditionally provide the nation's charitable ladies with the raw materials for patchworks and collages, but voluntary organisations can make money from selling unwearable clothes. The fabric is recycled by the rag industry and turned into brand-new furnishing material, roofing felt, industrial padding or wipes.

Small ads in local newspapers are a popular method of selling off unwanted property. If the item is cheap enough, the advertisement can often be placed free of charge. Classified ads can be an excellent source of secondhand items, as both the article and the owner can be examined. As the sale normally takes place in the seller's own home, appliances can often be seen working before you buy. If a telephone number is given, the advertiser's locality can be traced. To locate London numbers, check the code in the directories under "London telephone exchange codes and districts served".

The unchallenged king of the classified world is *Exchange and Mart*, an august weekly magazine which dropped its editorial content during the wartime paper shortage and never looked back. *Exchange and Mart* remains supreme, although it has been joined in the all-ad arena by several rivals operating at both national and local level, and by the local radio swop shops. At local level, buyers should keep their eyes on the cards in the Post Office and the newsagent's window.

Specialist magazines are a steady source of equipment for sale. Just choose your interest, buy your magazine, and look in the back pages. *Practical Self-Sufficiency,* for instance, has a strange range of classified ads: the same issue may have on offer a wind pump, bee hives, a Jersey cow, a milking machine, butter churns and assorted goats, pigs and poultry. The fading of the first flush of enthusiasm sometimes shines through as disillusioned smallholders put their entire life style on sale in a small ad.

A specialist organisation may help in the hunt for something specific. For example, the English Vineyards Association is often informed if a used corking machine is up for sale, while the Photographers' Gallery in London has a crowded notice board covered with cards offering cameras for sale.

Buying from street markets can lead to problems. If goods turn out to be broken, the law allows you to have your money back, but disgruntled buyers often hump broken goods back to the market only to find the stallholder has vanished. This is because some market traders sublet their stalls on a daily basis. The council's street trading licence is not normally granted to the market but to the individual trader, and licenses are not normally transferable, nor can the type of goods on the stall be changed without the approval of the council's street trading committee. Unlicensed street traders are a running feature in the magistrates' courts. No licence is needed to trade on private land, where many markets operate. Information on the time and place of markets can be supplied by the local council. Expect few bargains from famous street markets such as Portobello Road.

The streets of any city are to some extent a rich and unpredictable source of discarded articles. There is usually a filing cabinet standing somewhere in the city of London at night, while cloth offcuts litter the streets north of Oxford Street on an average evening, and empty film reels roll down Wardour Street. They are all free.

Taking rubbish could be theft. The law allows the scavenger to take anything from a skip in the street if he or she genuinely believes that the person who put it there would have no objections. It is often possible to ask. Lifting things from dustbins is equally permissible, as long as you believe the council would not object. In practice it is risky to take anything with a large scrap value, but tatty household items are fair game. If you want to make door-to-door collections you may need a free licence under the House to House Collections Act 1939.

An interesting form of exchange operates in Holland. Every few weeks, the council invites the citizens to put their large unwanted items out in the street. During the night, people on the lookout for free furniture scurry through the city and gather what they want. The council collects up the remnants in the morning.

Jumble sales are a prime source of secondhand clothes, cutlery and small kitchen equipment, all washed down by cups of tea. However, it is too difficult to examine any complex appliance amid the flailing elbows of determined and vigorous old ladies on a Saturday afternoon, so rely on nothing you buy. The true bargains vanish in the first few frantic minutes, so it is wise to be in the queue when the doors open. Everything has to be shifted in a single afternoon, so prices are very low, and the cause is often a good one. Jumble sales are normally announced in the local press.

A refined alternative to the Saturday afternoon jumble sale, complete with refreshments stall, is the "antique fair", where dozens of dealers assemble to sell. Each dealer hires a stall to display a selection of his or her stock. Items are not necessarily antique, but prices are generally too high to be classified as "secondhand". However, bargains are there late in the day, as dealers pack up after a bad day; as in food markets, they would rather sell cheap than wrap. Fairs are advertised in *Exchange and Mart* on Thursdays.

Three golden balls still dangle outside the pawnbroker's shop. Pawnbroking is an ancient trade, and in all likelihood the same balls hung over the present pawnbroker's father and grandfather, who took pledges before him. The pattern of modern pawnbroking was set by the Pawnbroker's Act in 1872, after which pawnbrokers were licensed by the local authority until the arrival of the Consumer Credit Act 1974. Now the pawnbroker needs a Consumer Credit licence from the Office of Fair Trading. In theory a pawnbroker can take anything as a pledge, but most of today's pawnbrokers are specialist jewellers, watchmakers or furriers. Clothes are considerably less common. Whenever a pledge is taken, and a loan made, a specially printed ticket changes hands. Loans are divided into three categories: under £2 they are known as Lows, from £2–£5 as Auctions and from £5–£50 as Special Contracts. If a Low or Auction pledge is unredeemed after six months and seven days, the pawnbroker can sell it. Lows can be sold in the shop, but Auctions and Special Contracts must go to public auction, properly advertised and complete with printed catalogue. The pawnbroker will often bid for the lots himself, to resell them at a higher price in the shop. The original owner can redeem the pledge at any time until the hammer falls.

Auctions can be cheap, but when bidding fever grips several people simultaneously, prices can be astonishingly high. A bed mass-produced in the Midlands in the 1930s and originally sold for £5 fetched nearly £24,000 when Sotheby's sold it in Monte Carlo fifty years later. Unless the tubes were stuffed with heroin, the price is hard to explain. Auctions are usually cheaper than antique shops—after all, the dealers stock up in auction rooms and they have to allow themselves a large mark-up. They may sniff arrogantly around the auction room looking quite intimidating, but they can't stop anyone bidding, nor can they bid as high as a private buyer. A discount of about one third on shop prices is normal at auctions dominated by the trade buyers. For this discount, the buyer loses the protection of the Sale of Goods Act 1979, though the Trade Descriptions Act still applies.

Stories of "The Ring" should alarm no-one except the auctioneer, as this is merely a conspiracy to keep prices down. Several dealers join forces, with only one bidding; the ring of dealers then hold a second auction among themselves later, sharing out the profit.

Almost anything can be bought at auction, from carpets and furniture to cattle and reusable building materials, cars and standing straw to job lots and dead men's shoes. "The property of the Deceased" often pulls in the crowds at country auctions, especially if the sale is held in the funereal atmosphere of the deceased's own home.

Several hundred auction houses operate in the UK, and each auctioneer has his or her own terms of business, generally listed in the catalogue. There is no standard form for these conditions, and they vary a lot. A typical catalogue warns the public that "the lots are sold 'as they lie' with all faults and errors or mis-statements of description, measurements, weight, quantity, quality, number or otherwise." The dull but important small type continues: "the purchaser should be deemed to have inspected the lots he buys and if he buys without previous inspection he shall do so at his own risk." A laborious checking procedure is sometimes unavoidable, for example whenever a set of anything is offered for sale. There's not much point in buying an incomplete pack of cards or a chess set with a missing bishop. The cost of a successful bid can be raised surprisingly if the conditions impose a buyer's premium. VAT can also affect prices. If VAT is payable on a lot, it will be marked in the catalogue, normally with an asterisk. Catalogues usually state that a deposit is demanded, but this condition is rarely enforced.

Catalogues are cheap for all but the prestige art auctions. They are on sale on viewing day, when the lots are laid out for public inspection, usually on the day before the auction. The catalogue lists the lots in the order in which they will be sold, normally starting with the less desirable items which get the typical sale under way. The lot numbers are marked in the catalogue and on the articles themselves. Catalogue descriptions are often informative at the major sales, seldom deliberately misleading even at the smallest auction, though they may be very basic. The letters "a.f." ("as found" or "all faults") normally mean that the article is damaged. Auctioneers will not necessarily bring bidders' attention to faults, and the reason for sale is not usually revealed. Proper inspection is an essential means of self defence. It is also part of the fun; digging through mysterious boxes of odd unclassified junk is one of the joys of the auction. Jewellery and other small items with thief-appeal are displayed in locked glass cases. The porter will always open them up for inspection.

A free leaflet from the Incorporated Society of Auctioneers and Valuers explains *Buying and Selling at Auction*. It is available from 3 Cadogan Gate, London SW1X 0AS. Auctions are enjoyable—even exciting—events but bidding for the first time can be terrifying. A practice try may reduce the terror. Visit a few auctions to see how they run before you try to buy. Most people bid by raising their catalogue, though the brave just shout out. The auctioneer will choose the steps in the bidding. Typically he will start at £1 and move up in one pound stages to £20, then by leaps of £2, £3, £3, £2 up to £100, where the stakes are raised to £5. The law says that once the hammer comes down, the lot becomes the responsibility of the last bidder, who must pay. Avoid being carried away by the thrill of the chase: decide on your top price before the sale begins, and stick to it. Talk to one of the porters; they know the reserve price on any lot and can often give accurate forecasts of the bidding.

The whole process of viewing, bidding and carrying the goods away can take three days. Planning can save time. If you want to bid for just one item late in the sale, calculate the time it will come under the hammer. Each lot lasts on average 30–40 seconds, making 90–120 lots per hour. If you can't go to the auction, leave your bid with the auctioneer's office or the porter. There is no charge for this service, but tips are welcome following successful bids. A possible drawback in the system is that the goods may disappear before you can collect them or suffer damage at the frustrated hands of failed rival bidders.

Delivery charges can increase costs, and buyers must move their lots fairly fast to avoid accumulating storage charges. Transport can often be arranged by the auctioneer. You may need a supply of boxes and wrapping materials to move your own things. Goods may be transported in secondhand tea chests, still with tea dust in the bottom. Household removal companies use them routinely. Chests can cost a lot to buy unless you can get to the tea importers without using gallons of expensive petrol. The lids are often missing from used tea chests. Packing large chests in small cars can prove impossible.

There is a list of "Auction Rooms" in the *Yellow Pages*. Prestige art auctions are advertised in the *Daily Telegraph* on Mondays and *The Times* on Tuesdays. The property section of local newspapers carries news of forthcoming local auction sales. Specialist interest auctions are advertised in the specialist press. Auctions of plant and machinery, for example, may be announced in *Machinery Market* or the *Building Trades Journal,* while the *Draper's Record* and *Jewish Chronicle* carry news of clothing auctions. *Art and Antiques Weekly* and the monthly magazine of the Antique Collectors' Club have an auction calendar.

Nearly every week the Home News pages of the Department of Trade magazine *British Business* carry announcements of government auctions in the coming month. These intriguing auctions are held all over the country, and anyone can attend. The Ministry of Defence auctions carry large amounts of new or little-used equipment, often sold in small lots. Private buyers can bid against the dealers for government surplus furniture, from card tables, chairs and roll-top desks to bookcases, bedroom suites and tea trolleys. Tools, clothes, kitchen equipment and cars are regularly on offer. The catalogue announces that "the goods have been examined for explosive material, but no guarantee that they are free from such material can be given". For legal reasons, "all crested buttons, insignia and badges must be removed before resale: the buttons and insignia must be mutilated and disposed of as scrap."

Incidentally, not everything in "government surplus" stores is government surplus. Much of it is just manufactured to the same patterns but using inferior materials. Genuine ex-service material can be recognised by the arrow mark, the letters "WD" or the year of manufacture and the initials (not the full name) of the manufacturer.

Lost property from British Rail and unclaimed mail from the Post Office are auctioned off after a decent delay. Anything

23

left in trains belongs to British Rail. After "a reasonable length of time" (usually about a week) in the station's lost property office, an item will go to join the regiments of forgotten umbrellas in the regional lost property office. If no owner has emerged some three months later, lost property is publicly auctioned. Auctions are held several times a year by Anstey Horne & Co. in BR's Harrow Road, London W2 warehouse. The catalogue makes surreal reading.

Lost property from the British Airports Authority, British Airways and Air France is sold by West London Auctions of Sandringham Mews, London W5 on alternate Saturday mornings. This is clearly the place to find a suitcase, brief-case, camera or umbrella. Umbrellas and gloves are the most frequent arrivals in London Transport's lost property office in Baker Street. Lost items are—with the sensible exception of perishable goods!—kept in Baker Street for about three months before going to auction. About two thirds of the property handed in remains unclaimed and is auctioned monthly by Greasby's of Tooting. The proceeds of the auction help towards the costs of the lost property operation, which runs, appropriately, at a loss.

There are bankrupt stock specialists in the big cities, who organise auctions on behalf of the liquidators. In central London, Frank Bowen auctions off large quantities of office furniture at 15 Greek Street on alternate Thursdays.

Beware of the shady one-off, one-day auctions held in hired halls and hotel rooms. A 1979 code issued by the Office of Fair Trading has not stamped out the practice of distributing leaflets advertising radios for one penny and televisions for a pound. Prices are manipulated by professional buyers planted in the room. Bargains are non-existent, and unhappy buyers are often manhandled.

Buyers in a hurry are easily cheated. Enthusiasm and naivety are the two prime conditions for a rip-off. If you need a thing urgently, it may save money to buy it new and guaranteed. Alternatively, hire it. Hire companies have appeared in all the major cities and towns in the UK, and the range of goods is impressively wide. If hired goods don't work, they are

24

easy to return to the dealer. Hire companies and retailers may also deliver and install appliances free of charge. These two services are rarely thrown in with a secondhand buy, and when you have to pay for the transport, a secondhand bargain may begin to look pricey.

Even a well-informed buyer cannot examine all secondhand goods in enormous detail, on the principle that only the demolition man gives a house a thorough survey. However, it is prudent to remember that the most "genuine reason for sale" is that an article is utterly useless or impossibly expensive to run. Electricity and gas boards publish free leaflets giving comparative fuel consumption figures for various types of domestic appliance, but individual models deviate from the average. Restoration costs can also push up the overall price astonishingly, as the buyers of Brighton's old West Pier discovered. A long period of neglect led to a £3 million repair bill on top of the "giveaway" price.

Sale of domestic appliances may be prompted by a lack of spare parts. Spares starvation is used by manufacturers as a classic marketing device in the growth economy. In the words of a 1970s advertisement for razors, "instead of changing blades, you just throw the whole thing away". Consumers are meant to consume, not to "make do and mend" in the wartime spirit.

Inbuilt obsolescence is the enemy of the secondhand buyer. Superficial design obsolescence—a metal box instead of a teak effect veneer, for example—is of no importance, particularly at times of anarchic fashion. A lack of functional spare parts is more serious. Stocks of spares may be deliberately destroyed by a manufacturer. Scrap metal merchants were selling suspiciously large quantities of spares for British Leyland cars in the late 1970s at ludicrously low prices. Accidents can also destroy spares. In January 1980 fire wiped out the entire stock of aircraft spare parts at British Aerospace in Surrey. Luckily, further stocks were held at Dulles Airport, Washington.

Cannibalising spare parts becomes the only practical way of keeping some old equipment going. This involves ripping a wanted part out of another broken machine of the same type.

The electrical appliance manufacturers' association, AM-DEA, has recommended that important spares should be kept by the manufacturer for several years after the end of the production run, but this still leaves the earliest appliances irreparable. Commercial manufacture of gas began in 1806, and electricity has been produced for over a century; many ancient appliances from these pioneer days still lurk in attics, junk shops and the homes of the very old. Spares will be found only in museums.

If manufacturers' literature is hard to find for an aged appliance — perhaps because the manufacturer sank in the last depression — it may be hard even to understand the way the thing should work. Consumer reports on old models can sometimes be found by looking in specialist magazines of the period. These can be traced through the local library. Many old test reports will be of doubtful objectivity, as the magazines may have hesitated to offend valued advertisers, but some of the information is often handy. For objective consumer reports, consult back issues of the Consumers' Association magazine *Which?*.

The British Standard Kitemark can also help in the hunt for quality secondhand goods. The kitemark is not necessarily a safety mark but it does show that the thing was adequately designed and made. Some 350 standards cover consumer goods, with some unlikely candidates among them, such as BS 5709 for stiles, bridle gates and kissing gates. A British Standard describes how a product must be made in order to be fit for the purpose. Most are voluntary, but some have the force of safety regulations. In 1975 a safety mark was introduced. If the BS number appears on the product without the kitemark, this is merely the manufacturer's claim that it conforms. Imported goods can carry the kitemark.

Metrication may cause incompatibility problems between old appliances and new systems. Oven temperatures can be marked in degrees centigrade or Fahrenheit, and kitchen scales may give both metric and imperial weights, which is handy for using a variety of recipes old and new, British and continental. Metric weights can be bought for old pan scales. Central heating and plumbing pipes have gone metric in recent years. There is no change in the size of lead and iron/steel pipes, but copper sizes have changed. All metric capillary fittings and certain metric compression fittings will need an adaptor to fit them into an imperial system. Adaptors are easy to buy. Pipe fittings using screw threads are unchanged.

Damaged articles are often extremely cheap because professional repair services are not. Careless buyers waste money by failing to spot damage before they buy and being forced to pay later for a repair or to discard the whole thing. However, shrewd buyers with repair skills can pick up real bargains.

The necessary skills can be acquired at evening classes, where the teachers may also be a good source of information on where to buy the tools and materials needed for tricky repair jobs. Teachers may even know of secondhand equipment for sale. The variety of courses on offer remains impressive, although financial pressures have forced the price of courses up dramatically in certain areas.

Local libraries can provide details of local courses. In London, the annual *Floodlight* booklet covers evening classes and part-time day classes in inner London. Students can spend an evening learning how to repair clocks, watches, books, furniture, bicycles, shoes, harness, hi-fi, cars, pianos, plates, tools or scooters. Traditional crafts are also well represented among the evening classes.

Competition for the one-evening-a-week classes comes from the growing selection of "craft centres" run by the education authorities. Students spend a weekend in a very grand country house learning about their chosen craft in a setting most would prefer to the schools or technical colleges where evening classes usually run. Information about craft courses is available from the Information Officer at the Crafts Council, 12 Waterloo Place, London SW1Y 4AU (tel: 01–839 1917). The Council also maintains a geographically-arranged register of craftsmen in England and Wales: the list can be invaluable to anyone looking for an expert to repair a broken buy.

SECONDHAND LAW

The law protects the buyer of secondhand goods, especially from the professional dealers. Whenever a secondhand dealer is at work, whether in a fully-fitted junk shop or just in his front room at home, anything he sells in the business is covered by the basic rules of the Sale of Goods Act 1979. Although a buyer can't in fairness expect old, used and secondhand goods to be in flawless condition, this law declares that a buyer has every right to expect the goods to be capable of doing the job they are normally intended to do. The law refers to this as "merchantable quality", and it means, for example, that a record player should spin records and a spin drier should spin wet clothes. You can't expect any sympathy from the law if the dealer told you an appliance was broken or faulty before you bought it. When it comes to the legal crunch, a court will take the price you paid into account.

In 1965 the illustrious Lord Denning pronounced: "A buyer

should realise that when he buys a secondhand car defects may appear sooner or later, and, in the absence of an express warranty, he has no redress. Even when he buys from a dealer the most he can require is that it should be reasonably fit for the purpose of being driven along the road." The car should be usable, but it need not be perfect.

If you examine the goods before the sale, you can't complain later about faults you ought to have noticed during that particular examination. A cracked cabinet or missing knob are obvious to anyone. However, if the faults are hidden away inside the machine, or even if you are content to rely on the dealer's judgement and therefore don't bother to examine the goods at all, the law says you are entitled to compensation if the thing you buy doesn't work. In a curious sense, you have better legal protection if you make only a superficial examination and buy on trust. However, there's a vast difference between being in the right and getting satisfaction! In practice it is far more satisfactory to make every effort to buy an article in working order, as litigation consumes time, energy and perhaps money.

The law considers what the dealer says to be very important. Any description of the goods has to be accurate. Furthermore, if you tell the dealer you want the goods for a particular purpose, however bizarre, they have to be fit for that purpose, otherwise you can have your money back. So, for example, if you ask the dealer if an old bedstead would make a suitable trampoline for your grandmother and he tells you it would, the bedstead must not collapse the first time she leaps.

It is wise to ask why the goods are being sold and if there is anything wrong with them. If the answers are dishonest, the trader may fall foul of the Trade Descriptions Act should the local council's Trading Standards Department find out. Such legal revenge under criminal law might give you a glow of satisfaction but it would not automatically lead to compensation. Your case is strengthened by a witness; take a friend and write down what the dealer says as soon as possible, ideally while you are still in the shop. A friend can also give useful moral support in confrontations with dealers.

There is an unfortunate and constant risk of secondhand goods turning out to be stolen, and nervous buyers fear the sound of policemen smashing through their doors at dawn with a warrant for their arrest on charges of handling stolen goods. Alarm is unnecessary. You would not be breaking the law, as long as you acted in good faith. A buyer has every right to believe that the seller is the owner of the goods he is selling. Nevertheless, you will almost certainly have to give the goods back to the rightful owner and then try to get your money back from the dealer, who may of course be penniless. Some people have circumvented the problem by paying in cash and not revealing their name or address to the seller.

Cunning buyers have used the same anonymity to avoid future problems with outstanding hire purchase payments. Remember that until the final payment is made, the goods still belong to whoever supplied the credit, whether that's the trader or a finance company. The local Citizens' Advice Bureau or Consumer Advice Centre can check whether there are payments outstanding on used cars. You have to fill in a form which is then forwarded to the HP Information service, and a reply comes back in about a week. This is usually too late to be useful, so it is fortunate that secondhand cars are the major exception to the rule obliging return of HP goods to the finance company. If you buy a used car in good faith, you can keep it, even if it is still on HP. There is an odder exception. This concerns the "market overt" and declares that from sunrise to sunset on market days in established markets in England, or in any shops in the city of London, you become the rightful owner of anything normally sold there that you buy in good faith. However, if you have a shrewd idea that the goods are stolen, you risk fourteen years in prison for handling stolen goods.

Secondhand shops often try to take away your rights by hanging warnings on the wall declaring "no money refunded". Such signs are meaningless, as the Unfair Contract Terms Act 1977 ensures that nothing a dealer says can take away a consumer's basic rights under the Sale of Goods Act. You can still get your money back if the goods are defective. "No refunds" signs are illegal and can be reported to the local Trading Standards Department.

Guarantees are often valueless. Remember that your basic rights are to be found with the retailer, quite independent of the manufacturer's guarantee, and no guarantee can reduce these rights. A worthwhile guarantee will cover every part of the appliance, free repairs (both parts and labour) and return postage; it should allow anyone to use the goods and last for at least three months.

Buyers need extra vigilance when the seller is a private individual rather than a professional dealer. The Sale of Goods Act 1979 offers very limited protection in both private sales and auctions. Any description of the goods has to be accurate, but if a private seller keeps his mouth shut, there is little to stop him selling broken, useless, even dangerous goods to the innocent buyer. Obviously the Trade Descriptions Act will not apply in private deals. This Act makes it a criminal offence to make false claims, such as describing an ex-hire car as having spent its life with "one careful lady driver". If the seller induces you to buy by a false statement, you may have a claim under the Misrepresentation Act. If you are physically injured by dangerous goods, you may have a common law claim for negligence and for breach of contract.

Because of the private seller's extra freedom to rip people off, some dealers try to pass themselves off as private individuals. A common practice is to place a misleadingly innocent advertisement in the classified section of a newspaper, giving a private address. This could lead the buyer to the dealer's own home or a friend's front room. A 1975 survey by the Office of Fair Trading found a long list of articles being sold all over the country by this tricky ploy. Electrical appliances, guitars, typewriters, bicycles and camping equipment featured in the enormous list of goods on offer by hidden dealers.

Following the survey, the Business Advertisement (Disclosure) Order 1977 tried to flush disguised dealers out of the classified columns: now, the law says, they must declare that they are dealers, although many of them still don't. Consumers tend to be more sympathetic to a supposedly private seller's explanation of why the goods are being sold and are less likely to ask awkward questions about the state of the goods.

Buyers should be careful about pretending to be dealers in order to get a trade discount price for secondhand goods. The Sale of Goods Act doesn't automatically protect dealers, and that includes phoney dealers, whom the law considers should be able to look after themselves. You can also lose the protection of the Act if you buy something exclusively for use in your business from a dealer.

It is perfectly normal to beat down the price of anything on offer secondhand, whether you are a dealer or not. There is no fixed price. The market price is what someone will pay, and production costs are nil. The usual opening ploy in the haggling game is to look at the desired object as if it were slightly offensive, asking "what can you do me that for?" or "what's your best price for that?"

It is an offence under the Consumer Protection Act 1961 and the Consumer Safety Act 1978 to sell certain dangerous goods in the course of business. The law applies to both British and foreign goods. However, it does not cover auctions or private sales. Secondhand or used goods are not specifically excluded, however old they are, but there is an exclusion clause for goods sold for scrap and goods damaged by fire or flood and sold to a person in the business of buying damaged goods for repair or reconditioning. If such goods are resold to the public, they must comply with the regulations made under these Acts.

It does not matter whether it is the dealer's *main* business to sell goods covered by the safety regulations, as long as it is *part* of his business. Items covered by the safety regulations are carrycot stands, nightdresses, cooking utensils, electric blankets, the colour of electric flexes, heating appliances, pencils and graphic equipment, toys, glazed ceramic ware, electric equipment, children's hood cords, vitreous enamel-ware, oil heaters, babies' dummies, cosmetics, prams and pushchairs, oil lamps and aerosols.

The regulations are really only of use to the consumer as

a deterrent. **Once dangerous goods are in the house, the law is of little help.** A legal remedy is no consolation when the family and the house have been consumed by fire. The trader will pay a fine if found guilty, but the money will not be yours. You will have to bring a separate civil action for damages.

The Office of Fair Trading investigates unfair trading practices, but doesn't deal with individual complaints or act as a referee in disputes. They publish a lot of handy free leaflets in the *For Your Protection* series on shoppers' rights on faulty goods. These are available from Trading Standards departments, Citizens' Advice Bureaux, Consumer Advice Centres, or the Office of Fair Trading, Room 310, Field House, Bream's Buildings, London EC4A 1PR (tel: 01–242 2858).

The OFT encourages various trade organisations to introduce codes of practice spelling out the way in which members should handle consumer complaints. These codes do not have the force of law. One useful code covers the length of time manufacturers should maintain stocks of spare parts for discontinued electrical appliances.

Laws are broken, codes of practice are ignored, and mistakes are made. If something you buy secondhand from a dealer goes wrong unacceptably soon, you can return it to the dealer and ask for compensation. Obviously it is hard to take back goods bought in a remote town to which you never need return. Moreover, any court action will probably have to be taken in the court covering the dealer's home or business address, which may not be convenient for you. Care in buying secondhand goods should therefore increase with the distance from home.

Bear in mind that the definition of "faulty" will become less exacting as the goods grow older and cheaper. A dealer may try to avoid legal responsibility by claiming that a broken or unsafe article was sold merely as a decorative object and was never meant to be in working order. This is quite a common defence with articles which are old enough to be sold as "antiques". To have a good chance of compensation, the buyer needs to prove he would never have bought the thing if he had been aware of its real condition.

If the dealer turns awkward and refuses to accept his responsibility, don't break up the shop or the dealer's glasses; best results are obtained by a firm and calm approach. Take a friend for moral support and as a possible witness in court. If the dealer refuses to co-operate, ask your local Trading Standards Department or Citizens' Advice Bureau for help. The addresses are in the 'phone book.

No law says you can't have your money back if you have no receipt. Nevertheless, it is a great help to have one as a record of the deal. Do not let the dealer keep the receipt when you complain—it could be evidence in court.

You can accept a repair if you want, and you may decide this is the simplest solution, but nothing forces you to take a repair rather than a refund. If you let the repair go ahead, write a note to the dealer saying that the repair does not prejudice your rights under the Sale of Goods Act, so you can still get your money back if the repair is unsuccessful. There is absolutely no reason to accept a credit note if you don't want one. In fact it is probably better not to accept a credit note. Many have a time limit, and they force you to buy from a shop which has already proved unsatisfactory.

Some secondhand dealers will be amazed to learn that you think you have any rights at all and will give you a crude brush-off. Do not despair. Write to the dealer explaining what's wrong with the dud goods, remind him of his legal obligations, tell him that you formally reject the goods and cancel the contract, ask for your money back and threaten him with court action if you don't get your money back in fourteen days. Keep a copy and post the letter recorded delivery.

Even if you win your court case, experience shows that you are not very likely to get your money back from a begrudging dealer straight away. There could be more legal dealings before you are recompensed. The whole process can drag on so long that your anger and enthusiasm have dwindled to nothing. There is very little joy in winning a court case if your opponent has disappeared or has no money. The law can't make anything work, it can only give you compensation. Legal action is therefore only worth trying after you have written off the article completely.

The mere menace of legal action is enough to make most dealers pay up, but some will call your bluff. If the prospect of the courts appals or scares you, take some free advice from your local Citizens' Advice Bureau, Consumer Advice Centre or Trading Standards Department. The Consumer Advice Centres came under attack from cost-conscious government in 1980, when £4 million of funding was withdrawn. Over half the centres closed immediately, others being saved by emergency local authority action, often surviving in dingy offices away from public view.

Trading Standards Departments are the modern version of the old weights and measures inspectors, and they can be found by telephoning the town hall. The department deals increasingly with criminal offences under the Trade Descriptions Act, which makes it an offence to give false descriptions in the course of a business. The maximum penalty is a £1000 fine.

The Citizens' Advice Bureaux, Consumer Advice Centres and neighbourhood law centres can normally supply copies of a free booklet from the Lord Chancellor's Office called *Small claims in the county court,* which explains how to sue without a solicitor. The booklet is available by post from the Lord Chancellor's Department, Page Street, London SW1. Copies are also available from the county court itself, which is where any action you bring is likely to be heard. They are usually listed in the telephone directory under "Courts". The staff in the court office should be able to explain how you take out a summons for a claim involving under £500, which can be dealt with without solicitors.

The claim normally goes before the registrar, who acts as arbitrator. The atmosphere is not particularly formal, though registrars vary from area to area in the degree of sympathy they offer to the layman struggling to represent himself. A legal representative can be employed, but to discourage their use the party who wins is rarely able to recover the costs from the other side.

No professional legal representatives were allowed in two highly-praised experimental courts in Manchester and London. Formality was minimised: smoking was allowed during the hearings and tea or coffee would be served to all concerned. These Small Claims Courts were used when both sides in a dispute agreed to have their problems aired before and judged by volunteer panels of lawyers and technical experts. The verdict was binding on both parties. The court would happily meet in private houses, to settle a washing machine dispute for example. The London court was handling 500 cases a year when it became a victim of economic cutbacks in 1979.

SECONDHAND A-Z

Reliable secondhand goods can be hard to find: this survey of the secondhand world is a consumer's guide to sources of secondhand goods. Once buyers have located the thing they want in the secondhand market, the key to success is a careful pre-purchase examination. The Secondhand A–Z provides the information needed to make a practical and thorough check designed to find the faults in each individual item. The simple tests will reveal most major problems to the average buyer with no specialist knowledge. It identifies the trouble spots which should consign appliances to the scrap-heap and steers the buyer away from those high-risk items which rarely reach the secondhand shop before they need a very expensive repair. The possibilities of economical repair—both professional and diy—are also detailed.

A

AIR CONDITIONERS

The worldwide effort to keep hot buildings cool consumes more energy than the attempt to heat cold buildings up. In Britain the balance is reversed, and there is regrettably little need for domestic air conditioning equipment. Some conditioners also act as humidifiers, though few British homes need added damp.

An air conditioner is basically a fridge with its back stuck outside the house and a fan forcing warm air through it. The air conditioner consequently combines the problems of the fan and the fridge, adding some of its own. Buyers of secondhand conditioners need to be certain their purchase needs no reconditioning. A breakdown may simply be due to a blown fuse, a loose wire or just a wrongly-set thermostat, but do-it-yourself repairs are rarely possible. Discontinued equipment is a poor gamble.

The machine must be clean: filthy coils work at reduced efficiency and increase both running costs and the risk of problems. Dirty filters cut the flow of air over the coils. Dirt may be covering rust, which develops when moisture-laden water condenses inside the conditioner.

Installation costs should be taken into account when calculating the true cost of a secondhand appliance. Running costs can also be significant; make sure the conditioner is the right capacity for your room.

AIRCRAFT

There's a lively international market in used passenger aeroplanes, a fact revealed to the bewildered traveller by such bizarre clues as the Spanish language instructions printed inside a certain Middle Eastern airline's fleet. British Airways occasionally buys secondhand as a stopgap measure while waiting for delivery of a new mammoth. They sell off old planes by tender, often to small charter airlines. Sales to overseas airlines may be arranged by agents dealing in secondhand aircraft.

For the private buyer, choosing a secondhand flying machine should be less nerve-wracking than buying a used car. Every aircraft must, by law, have a full record of its past, and this should include reports of any accidents. The law also lays down a maintenance schedule and specifies times when essential parts must be replaced, whether worn or not.

The practices of the nastier car dealer, who resurrects lifeless parts just long enough for a sale to go through, are therefore ruled out. The rogue dealer is further deterred by the strict supervision which makes "clocking" (turning back the mileage) impossible.

The Civil Aviation Authority (CAA), proudly claiming the strictest safety requirements in the world, soon shoots down the flying sharks.

Every aircraft must have the CAA's Certificate of Airworthiness (C of A). Unlike a car's MOT certificate, the C of A can last from one year—normal length for privately maintained small aircraft—to three years or even more for the fleets of large international airlines with approved maintenance systems.

There is no published guide to prices of used aircraft, and although flying lemons are seldom sold, buyers can be grossly overcharged if, like many private pilots, they don't understand aeroplanes. Expert advice is vital during a pre-purchase examination. Before looking at individual aircraft, buyers should decide on the most suitable type of aircraft for their needs and pocket, bearing in mind that budgeting for future maintenance schedules and certificates is of prime importance.

During examination, it is vital to check on the number of hours left before the engine and propeller will have to be replaced, the number of hours flown for purposes of airframe overhaul and the expiry date of the C of A. The type and quantity of avionics (radio communications and navigational equipment) will also influence price. As with a used car, it would be senseless to buy without a trial.

Nervous buyers can be helped by companies such as R. McMillan Aviation of

Teddington, who can work out the customer's needs and acquire a plane to match them. They offer a warranty on all aircraft sold.

Flight International and other magazines are useful sources of information and classified advertisements for secondhand aircraft, parts, resprays etc. *Flight Directory,* the yearbook of *Flight International,* has a useful address list.

AMPLIFIERS *see* Audio Equipment

AUDIO EQUIPMENT

At the budget end of the hi-fi market, the flood of new Japanese equipment is cheap enough to make a second-hand market almost redundant. Doubts about the long-term reliability of cheap hi-fi equipment further restrict secondhand sales. Experts advise against buying budget Japanese equipment after its fifth birthday. At the top end of the market, on the other hand, twenty-year-old units may still be selling strongly.

Hi-fi prices vary oddly from year to year, and it is wise to check out the price of new products before buying anything secondhand.

Prices and specifications of all new equipment are given in *What Hi-Fi?* magazine, which also prints a small section on discontinued equipment. Old copies of the hi-fi magazines can be dug out of local libraries if you want to consult test reports on old lines. A look through the hi-fi pages in half a dozen copies of *Exchange and Mart* will provide a good idea of current second-hand prices. If a particular model is often on sale, you can get a precise idea of prices and can be reasonably confident that the model is repairable. Decide on your top price before you enter the market.

Hi-fi is a world most buyers enter with fear, expecting to be humiliated by glib and devious salesmen. In fact no secret knowledge or complex vocabulary is needed to check out a piece of hi-fi equipment. Making allowances for the fact that a system can sound different in a shop and in your own room, the rule to follow is that if the sound pleases you, that's the right sound for you, even if a costlier system sounds nearer to perfection. The very nervous buyer can take along a knowledgeable friend. The average hi-fi fiend loves choosing a system for someone else and helping to spend other people's money.

It is essential to try all audio equipment before buying it. If you buy from a hi-fi dealer who has proper listening facilities, this should present no problem. In such conditions the secondhand buyer may be offered a better test than those who buy new equipment from the discount warehouses, where the goods are normally sold in sealed boxes. Some dealers take equipment in part-exchange, but there are few regular full-time dealers in secondhand hi-fi. The dealers' prices are generally higher than those in private sales, partly because the dealer offers guarantees and overhauls the equipment on a test bench before selling it. If a dealer has no repair facilities, the extra charge is usually not worth paying, although the dealer's guarantee may be of value. Most dud equipment will fail within the first few weeks, so look for guarantees lasting three months at least.

Audio equipment is often sold in general secondhand shops, where test facilities are non-existent and each piece is usually sold in isolation. In such circumstances, it should at least be possible to plug the unit in, and that is enough to carry out a few simple tests to establish whether it works, although not to judge the quality of performance. The tests differ in detail for each part of a stereo system, and they are explained in the following sections of this book.

The equipment needed for the tests is easy to find and easy to use. You will need a pair of stereo headphones, an insulated mains-test screwdriver, some paper clips, a stroboscopic speed disc to check a turntable, a home-recorded (not pre-recorded) cassette tape to play on a tape deck, and perhaps a portable radio with an external speaker socket to check loudspeakers. Most radios have such a socket, usually a miniature jack plug, but the plug and cable to fit have to be bought separately. You may have to supply and fit your own plug, which calls for an electrician's screwdriver. Meters and lights should work on every item you test. Only the electrically qualified buyer should consider removing the outer case to expose the works inside without disconnecting the equipment from the mains.

Problems will probably be mechanical, as modern electronic circuitry wears out very slowly. However, circuitry is unpredictable, and cannot be guaranteed to last for five minutes after the test. The simpler units in a stereo system will tend to last longest.

Loudspeakers are overall the most reliable items, followed by record decks; next come tuners, amplifiers, receivers (tuner and amplifier combined), reel-to-reel tape recorders and, least reliable of all, the mechanically complex cassette recorders and music centres.

An instruction manual is a useful aid to setting audio equipment up at home. If you are inexperienced, assembly can be almost impossible without it. The original protective packaging is worth having in case the equipment has to be sent away for repair. Avoid equipment offered without a serial number or in boxes with the manufacturer's label removed. These are signs of stolen goods. If you buy a stolen stereo in good faith, you commit no crime, although you may have to return the equipment to the rightful owner if you are traced. Always ask for a receipt. In general the major UK manufacturers will supply spares for equipment as much as twenty years old, but spares for imported equipment over five years old are not automatically available. General spares can usually be had for newer units. If possible, check out spares availability with the manufacturer or importer before you buy. Even better, identify the model immediately before the one that interests you, and ask the manufacturer/importer for a special spare for it—a front panel or a tuning knob for example. This will test the manufacturer's spares policy. If the part has to come from abroad, ask how long it will take to arrive. To locate the distributor of foreign equipment, find an advertisement: the distributor's address is normally featured.

Some manufacturers run subsidised servicing departments, while others pay for all their work under guarantee by charging over the odds for all their non-guarantee work. The best repairer is often the individual who has just set up in business and is eager for work. The ideal is an individual recommended by the manufacturer. Wherever you take broken equipment, ask for an estimate before work begins. Charges can be high.

Britain's top repair specialists include Bristol Hi-Fi Consultants of 28 Upper Maudlin Street, Bristol; Sound Distinctive, 28 The Broadway, Mill Hill, London NW7 3LL; Mike Solomons of London Sound, 266 Field End Road, Eastcote, Ruislip, Middlesex, a specialist in British equipment who has a passion for making broken things work.

AMPLIFIERS

The amplifier is the heart of a hi-fi system, and a good one should last the three score years and ten of the average human heart. A bad one will collapse and die in four years because of weaknesses built in by manufacturers using poor materials in the battle to keep prices down. Some experts warn buyers off secondhand Japanese equipment, claiming its life is brief compared to the best of British such as Quad, Leak, Armstrong and Rogers. New Japanese amplifiers give good value, but some of the superficially glamorous amps are useless secondhand. Manufacturers may change ranges yearly, and there can be bad problems getting spares or service for old imported gear.

The only way to tell if an amp works properly is to put it through its paces. Even this test run may not reveal the irritating intermittent fault which mysteriously cuts out one channel on alternate Fridays. Buyers face the problem inherent in all electronic equipment, that no test can guarantee that any amplifier will continue to work for five minutes more. On the other hand, the well-prepared buyer can check the main features of a secondhand amplifier merely by plugging it in and carrying out a few basic tests. The only equipment needed is a pair of stereo headphones (external speakers are even better), a few paper clips and a mains test (insulated) screwdriver. The complete test routine involves fiddling with the connections at the back of the amplifier. The typical arrangement is not complex, but it can be confusing, even dangerous. It is therefore crucial to familiarise yourself with the tests using your own or a friend's disconnected amplifier before attempting them under the hostile or nervous eye of a seller.

With the headphones plugged into the appropriate socket on the amplifier, a paper clip is pushed into one of the input sockets and the amp is switched on. The standard inputs are for a gramophone pickup (sometimes marked "PU"), a tape recorder (marked "Tape"), a radio tuner and a spare or "Auxiliary".

As long as you hold the clip, your body acts as an aerial and you should hear the hum through the headphones.

The test can't tell you how good the amplifier is, but it does establish whether it works. Test each channel on every function (tape, tuner etc.) in turn, with the channel selector on the front panel turned to the right input and the volume down. Some makes will blow a fuse if used without speakers; indeed there may already be a blown loudspeaker fuse stopping sound from one speaker. As there is a slight risk of

blowing a fuse, make sure the seller agrees to the test.

With equipment that has been misused there is a danger of hitting a live socket, and it is therefore prudent to make a preliminary probe with a mains test screwdriver. If the neon light comes on, look for another amp. Check that the plug is earthed.

If the amplifier has DIN sockets rather than the simpler phono, each hole will have to be tried in turn, as at least three are just earth. Neither socket type is inherently superior—there are good and bad models of both. DIN sockets are more easily damaged by abuse.

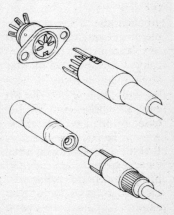

DIN plug and socket (*top*), phono plug and socket (*bottom*)

Next try the treble and bass controls—there should be a noticeable response even on background hiss. Turn each channel up and down to check the balance, and swing the balance to each end of its travel to make sure each channel is the same. Switch to mono to check that the sound is identical through each speaker. If there are any filters, set them at zero and turn them up to check that they cancel out the hiss.

If the amplifier is still connected up in a complete system, examination is easier. Using either speakers or headphones, and with the volume control at zero, listen for any undesirable background crackle or hum. Sample the sound quality at both low and high volume, as some faults will not appear at both levels. Finally turn the volume control back to zero to check whether the hum/crackle has grown any worse. Noisy manual controls normally just need cleaning, but they should bring the price down. To clean controls, unplug the amplifier, remove the casing and squirt proprietary cleaning fluid or cigarette lighter fuel (not gas!) on the point

where the wires enter the controls, working it back and forth for a few minutes. Remember that lighter fuel can damage some plastics. Allow fifteen minutes for the fuel to evaporate before switching the amplifier back on.

Valve amplifiers Valve amplifiers over ten years old enjoy a steady secondhand sale to a minority of enthusiasts who recognise their superiority over some very expensive transistor equipment. Valve amplifier breakdowns are rare, though components can burn out if, for example, a short-circuited amplifier is left switched on. They don't like being run with the loudspeakers disconnected—this can damage the output valves.

There are a few specialist repairers, and manufacturers will overhaul even a twenty-year-old amplifier. Quad, Leak, Armstrong, Radford and Rogers are names the enthusiasts speak with awe. Valves, capacitors and resistors can be replaced in twenty-year-old equipment at present, but a day could dawn when repairs become impossible, when valve manufacturers decide that valves are uneconomical and so stop

making them. If valves or condensers have failed, output could be reduced or distorted. If an output transformer has failed and has to be replaced, the repair can be very dear.

Repair costs vary with labour time, and this varies with the model. For example, the transformer in the Armstrong 100–200 series is virtually inaccessible, whereas in a Leak, Quad or Radford it would be much simpler to replace. There can be problems buying a replacement transformer.

CASSETTE DECKS

Modern stereo cassette recorders are extremely complex. They can be short-lived, unpredictable and very expensive to mend. Overall this is the riskiest piece of audio equipment to buy secondhand. Heavy use can easily kill most off inside four years.

However, cassette deck technology has improved in recent years, and mass production has brought prices down without impairing quality. New stereo recorders are almost invariably a better buy than old. It is unwise to pay more than a few pence for a secondhand portable cassette recorder. A lot can go wrong with these machines; don't expect a secondhand one to last more than three months.

The first signs of normal wear and tear will be audible at the beginning or end of a tape, and not necessarily both. The most basic test will therefore involve taking along a tape you know well, and playing a couple of minutes at the start and a similar section at the end, plus a couple of minutes from the middle for comparison. Your chosen test cassette should not be irreplaceable, as a worn machine can damage tapes. Music is better than words for test purposes as it has a wider dynamic range and a greater frequency response. Sustained single notes will show up any machine-induced warbling or speed variations. There should be some blank sections on the cassette tape, to be used for test recordings. One of your own records is the ideal subject for a test recording. Listen out for poor treble response, which is usually an indication of a worn head.

The "erase" head will be

checked by recording something loud, erasing it and replaying the cleaned tape at maximum volume. If the tape has not been wiped clean, don't buy the recorder. The problem could be just a dirty erase head, but it could be very serious.

Head wear is common in secondhand cassette recorders. Worn heads should be replaced, as they impair sound quality and can crinkle the tape edges. A new head can cost between a quarter and half the price of a complete new machine. A worn head is easy to diagnose: just run your fingernail lightly over it, feeling for the telltale ridge indicating wear. The head should be completely smooth. Clean all finger grease off the head after feeling it for wear.

A dirty head will not play well but it is easily put right by a wipe with a cotton bud soaked in cigarette lighter fuel or the officially recommended isopropyl alcohol. Too much vigorous cleaning will wear heads out. Purpose-made "cleaning cassettes" are useful for enclosed recorders with inaccessible heads, such as those fitted in cars, but cleaning by hand is better whenever possible. A cleaning cassette can leave a ridge of filth at the edges which can eventually hold the tapes you play subsequently away from the head and stop them playing. Certain Akai heads can actually be harmed by cleaning cassettes, as the abrasive cleaner acts as a file.

Dirty pinch rollers can cause irregular tape transport, even breakages. Petrol damages rubber, so it is wiser to use alcohol to clean the rubber pinch wheel. Let it evaporate for fifteen minutes before switching the machine on.

The cassette recorder can be professionally adjusted to record on the tape type of your choice, but competent adjustments are expensive. It is cheaper to beg, borrow or steal a selection of tapes and see if one is suitable.

There is little point in paying much for a recorder without the desirable Dolby noise reduction system or some equivalent, designed to reduce hiss on recordings. The Dolby system can be tested by recording something at a given level and seeing whether it replays at the same level. An error of 1dB or VU division is acceptable. If the VU

meters or any other indicators are broken, avoid the recorder. The tape counter should also be in working order. A microphone and instruction book are useful additions.

A cheap tape deck can often be examined without any other part of the stereo system. A test under these conditions establishes whether it works, but will not reveal much about the machine's quality. If there are no external speakers to test a tape deck, you need a pair of headphones to listen to your chosen tape. Not all decks have a headphone socket, and of course the test doesn't prove that the signal would reach an amplifier.

After checking that the fast forward, rewind and pause functions work, listen to your tape, then switch the machine to "record" and let it run in silence over a blank section of tape. When you play this section back through the headphones there should be no sound.

With the aid of a couple of paper clips, confidence and caution, you can test further functions. Still on "record", put a paper clip into each input channel and re-

cord for a few seconds, keeping hold of the paper clips. Still recording, remove one of the clips, so only one channel is being tested, then move to the other. When you play this section of the tape back, and listen through the headphones, there should be a faint hum, first in stereo then on each channel in turn.

Despite the very real drawbacks of secondhand cassette recorders, they are normally a more sensible investment than the reel-to-reel systems. Most secondhand reel-to-reel tape recorders are either old and feeble relics of the 1960s or expensive machines designed for professional use.

Four-track recording has been standard on reel-to-reel tape recorders since the 1950s, when mono sound still ruled. Modern machines can offer stereo or even quad sound, but the main attraction of reel-to-reel is the possibility of tape editing. Uher portable reel-to-reel machines, as favoured by radio correspondents, are very popular secondhand. Uhers are good for location work and have been proved to last well, unlike their less illustrious cassette equivalents.

HEADPHONES

It is not worth travelling in search of secondhand headphones, as the saving will rarely justify the journey.

However, headphones may be thrown in as part of a larger hi-fi deal. This particular gift horse should certainly be scrutinised, as imperfect secondhand headphones will be worthless.

Even if all seems well on first hearing, tweak and waggle the leads, listening for the spluttering which indicates an intermittent connection. Such a fault often develops after repeated tugging. If the speakers appear to be unbalanced, one of your ears could be waxy, so turn the headphones round and try again. If the sound still seems low in the same ear, see a doctor.

Headphones of the highest quality are no pleasure if they feel uncomfortable. The sound quality should also be pleasing.

LOUDSPEAKERS

A top quality secondhand loudspeaker can be a bargain, as good loudspeakers are designed to last. Indeed, some sound critics claim that they actually improve with age, as the cabinet matures. However, when speakers fail, repair costs are depressingly big, usually at least half the price of a brand-new speaker.

Overloading is the main cause of damage. When too much current is pushed through the speaker, a voice coil can burn out behind a speaker cone—the speaker "blows". A speaker can have two, three or even more cones ("units") to guarantee good sound reproduction over the whole range of sounds from deepest bass to top treble. If only one unit has blown, the speaker will not be completely knocked out. It is therefore important to establish that every cone is responding. This can be done even when speakers are sold in isolation, with no other part of the audio system and no available power supply. The test requires a small battery—one from a portable radio is adequate—and two pieces of wire a few inches long. When the wires are connected to the battery terminals at one end and the terminals at the back of the speaker are touched with the other ends, the speaker will make a very audible click if it works. Some of this noise should be coming from each unit if all is well.

If the portable radio battery is left inside the radio, this can be used for a slightly fuller workout of the speakers, as long as the radio has an external speaker socket. Most do. The socket normally takes a miniature jackplug. Connect the jackplug to a piece of wire, leaving the other end free. Connect this end to the terminals of the speaker. Switch the radio on, and you should hear it through the speaker. This doesn't test the quality, but it shows whether the speaker works.

A burn-out due to overload need not be sudden and dramatic. The wires in a speaker which is only slightly but repeatedly overloaded can overheat, melt the glue and

break loose over a period of months before the speaker finally fails. Unfortunately voice coils are not visible even if the back of the speaker is removed. However, by taking off the grill on the front of the speaker, damaged cones can be seen. The grill is usually held in place by Velcro and will pull off easily; some are held by screws. If a speaker has been played at too high a volume the cones may have torn. This will not stop the speaker working, but it will seriously impair the quality of sound. Slightly displaced coils will cause a rasping, buzzing sound. If the seller will let you, you can very gently push each cone, listening for

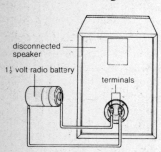

testing a speaker in isolation

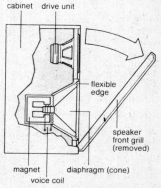

inside a typical speaker

the grating sound which indicates a displaced coil in need of expensive replacement.

British speaker manufacturers can usually repair a single unit, whereas the whole lot will often have to be replaced on an imported speaker.

If the speakers are connected up to an amplifier, try them out. If one speaker appears faulty, swop the leads over at the amplifier—if the fault moves over to the other speaker, the fault lies in the amplifier. If the same speaker stays out, check the cable connections before rejecting the speakers. If all seems well, put the speakers side by side, well away from walls, turn the amp to "mono" and listen to each speaker in turn by turning the balance control. With the balance control set at the half-way point, listen to the hiss coming from the "tweeter" (physically the smallest of the two or three speaker units, and the one which responds to the highest frequencies). The volume of hiss should be the same on both speakers. A poor quality of sound could be remedied very simply if the speakers are just out of phase, due to an elementary—and instantly repairable—mistake by the owner in wiring up the speakers. Put them facing each other about nine inches apart. If the bass response is feeble, switch the wiring around on one of the speakers. Bass response can be affected by the surrounding room; heavy furniture, curtains and carpets all emphasise bass. Speakers may sound very different in your own room. Sound quality can be improved by putting the speakers on a stand.

A scratched cabinet is nothing to worry about, but it can bring down the secondhand price considerably. Cracked wood, on the other hand, is more serious, as it will affect the resonance.

Speakers can be posted off to the manufacturer for a check-up, but this is a costly performance. Speakers are cumbersome to pack and pricey to post.

MUSIC CENTRES

A typical music centre consists of a record player, cassette deck and radio tuner all in the same box, with a couple of external speakers and perhaps a digital clock to complete the system. This combination has the virtue of tidiness, but it is an awkward mixture of items which last a long time and items which don't. The tuner can be expected to keep on tuning long after the cassette recorder has died. Broken items cannot usually be replaced.

Even a simple repair can be enormously expensive, simply because of the time it takes to gain access to any damaged part. Interconnecting leads between the items are out of sight inside the box, so the repairer cannot just waggle the leads around to help locate a loose terminal; he has to dismantle the box, and this takes time, which costs money. The repairer will probably spend some time—and charge some money—checking over all the perfectly good parts of the music centre, as he doesn't want a dissatisfied customer returning with a quite different fault and demanding a free repair. A hidden "safety precaution" charge will often be added to the repair bill to protect the repairer in case he is forced to carry out a further repair free of charge. The more complex the equipment, the higher this insurance charge, and music centres are very complex indeed.

Secondhand music centres are not without their advantages. The only item which could possibly be missing is the speakers, and these can be replaced. A buyer should have every chance of checking out every element and control in the system before buying it. A pair of headphones makes a good substitute during the examination. The speakers supplied with a music centre are rarely excellent, and new speakers could improve it considerably. However, better speakers will show up bad systems, revealing hidden hums and hisses. The music centre's amplifier may not be powerful enough to get a loud sound out of large speakers. A secondhand music centre with a broken cassette recorder may be worth buying if the price is low enough, as this should not impair the performance of the rest of the system.

RECEIVERS

A receiver—also known as a tuner-amplifier—combines the functions and problems of the tuner and the amplifier in a single box. There is no good technical reason to object to the combination, but buyers of secondhand receivers should test them thoroughly and reject any faulty equipment, as repairs to receivers are normally more expensive than the same job on a separate tuner or amplifier. The higher costs reflect the increased access and diagnosis problems facing the repairer.

RECORD PLAYERS

Nostalgia for the early days of rock and roll can breed a longing to give the 45s from the 50s a spin in glorious substandard mono on a genuine old record player. This is the only valid reason for seeking out a secondhand record player. New ones are very cheap and carry a guarantee. However, a ludicrously cheap old machine that works well on every speed is worth buying.

Play a selection of records you know if possible. The records should not be irreplaceable, as the cartridge on any old record player will almost certainly have to be changed, and a blunt or chipped stylus harms grooves. Reject the machine if it crackles: a new stylus might solve the problem, but there may be a fault in the speaker or the amplifier.

The test records should have long single notes which will show up speed variations. A cheap strobe disc from a hi-fi dealer will also show up inconsistencies of speed under artificial light. A worn rubber idler wheel can cause speed fluctuations. An idler wheel is easily replaced and can be seen by prising off the circlip holding the turntable down and lifting the turntable off the spindle.

Rumble is a common problem with record players. With the machine switched off, spin the turntable by hand and listen out for a grumbling sound from the centre bearing. Don't buy a rumbly record player. The bearings are normally sealed, making lubrication tricky, but a little oil dripped down the spindle may ease a sluggish turntable. Oil will destroy rubber components, so keep it away from belts and wheels.

The point where the arm drops automatically onto the record can be altered by adjusting a screw under the arm at the pivot. If the autochange or reject mechanism will not work at all, don't buy. Noisy controls can be cleaned. A bent turntable ranks high among the reasons to turn a machine down, as it will have to be replaced. A plastic turntable is not even worth looking at, as it will soon stick even if it is free when you buy it. Dud switches and burnt-out motors are also too much trouble to repair in an old record player, but a loose flex connection should not condemn an otherwise satisfactory machine.

Lock the pick-up arm in position and immobilise the turntable during transit, or it could be wrecked.

TUNERS

Modern solid-state stereo tuners need little or no maintenance, but when faults develop, repairs are expensive. A broken tuner is not worth owning, but a good quality secondhand tuner in working order should be cheap enough to be a bargain. In a good reception area even a fifteen-year-old tuner fitted with a good aerial should be only marginally inferior to today's best. The aerial is a key factor affecting performance, and it is vital for adequate FM reception. However the flat ribbon or wire dipoles which some tuners contain should be able to pick up enough signal to establish whether the tuner works; otherwise, poke a short piece of wire into the aerial socket. The cost of buying and installing a proper roof or loft aerial should be taken into account.

You will need an amplifier to check the tuner's performance. In the absence of external speakers, wear headphones to test the tuner. Before switching on, check that the tuner has the features you need—FM for stereo broadcasts, and AM. Short wave appeals to keen listeners; long wave is almost essential in the UK. Modern tuners without long wave came onto the secondhand market in large numbers when the BBC shuffled their transmission wavelengths in November 1978.

Switch the tuner on and check that it receives all the stations you may want to hear. Try all controls and preset buttons. Be sure to test the stereo function; some secondhand tuners which appear to be stereo units are mono, as a stereo decoder was an optional extra on some early models. If the tuner crackles when you tap it (or preferably drop it one inch), forget it. A buzz on AM will probably be caused by a nearby fluorescent light or a similar source of interference. Serious internal defects can produce background hiss, which is often worse on stereo than mono.

Test the tuner for as long as possible, leaving it on during any discussions you have with the seller, as faults can take time to show up.

TURNTABLES

A turntable's only job is to turn at the right speed, without wavering or vibrating. Outward appearances will not prove a turntable works, so if you can't try it, don't buy it. It should at least be possible to plug it in and watch it spinning, even if there is no handy amp or speaker. In these limiting conditions, you will need a cheap strobe disc, which can be bought from any hi-fi shop, and an electric light, preferably a fluorescent one. Switch the light on, place a record on the platter, put the strobe disc on the record, switch on and play the record, even if you can't hear it. The disc will tell you whether the turntable is

working correctly at every speed—if the wheel of lines seems to turn anticlockwise, the turntable is running slow, clockwise and it is too fast. More seriously, the test will help to diagnose "wow", an irritating fault caused by changes of speed and pitch. If the wheel wavers, wow is there.

A turntable must be cheap to be worth buying without deeper investigation. A much better idea of the turntable's quality comes after playing a record, listening to a minimum of five minutes' music at each speed, and listening also for background noises in the blanks between the tracks. This test must involve records you know well. The best records for revealing wow are those with long single notes which should remain perfectly steady. Operatic records are often ideal.

"Rumble" is the other symptom of disease in turntables, indicating damage to the centre bearing or drive system. Sometimes the damage can be "felt" by rotating the platter gently by hand, feeling for any rough spots, or "heard" by switching the deck off and spinning the platter, with your ear over the centre spindle—a scuffing noise means trouble in the bearings. A rumbling turntable may be worth buying if it is cheap, as lubrication can often improve performance remarkably. All bearings benefit from lubrication with clean oil.

On traditional rim-driven turntables, such as the admirable old Garrards (never the best but impressively durable), a worn idler wheel can increase rumble. These are cheap and easy to replace. After long periods of idleness, an idler wheel can develop a permanent depression, which causes a thumping sound as the table turns.

Belt-driven systems should give less rumble trouble, as the motor vibrations are isolated from the turntable. Drive belts are easy to spot and will often need replacing, as they wear, stretch and develop a permanent kink if left unturned for a long time. Oil can spoil rubber belts and idler wheels. The newer direct-drive turntables are free of such problems, but their circuitry is so complex that they cannot be confidently recommended secondhand. Famous names on old turntables include Dual, AR, Garrard, BSR and Thorens.

Deck shapes change, and there is little chance of finding a replacement for a missing plastic cover. A scruffy, scratched cover can lower the price and can be cleaned up with Brasso. Rub gently to avoid melting the plastic and grinding in the polish; follow up with a dose of spray-on furniture polish, wipe both off and repolish. Do a test spot first.

A bad arm can destroy records. The arm's job is to keep the stylus at the correct angle in the record groove. Light weight is desirable and only the cheapest arms have an integral cartridge. In the absence of other information, four wires emerging from the cartridge indicate stereo.

After testing the basic mechanisms on an automatic arm by moving it to the centre of the platter and seeing what happens, finer tuning can be checked. The arm must move freely over its bearings: movement can be tested by pushing the arm gently towards the centre with a piece of flimsy paper—any points of resistance will soon be felt.

It is safe to assume that the cartridge on any secondhand arm will need replacing, and this additional cost should be taken into consideration when haggling over the price. There is no easy way to check the state of the stylus before you buy it, and the stylus regularly represents half the cost of a complete cartridge.

A stylus can be checked by a dealer equipped with a suitable microscope, and Shure of Maidstone will inspect their own products free of charge. Where possible, it is wise to use your own, known, undamaged cartridge during the test.

B

BALLS

see Rackets

BARBECUES

When summer rain sends a barbecue party scuttling indoors, the abandoned barbecue may be left in the garden to rust. As the weeks pass, the familiar, simple cast-iron barbecue soon develops a thick and offputting rust coat for the winter. This is easily removed by an electric drill fitted with a wire brush attachment. However, rust can rapidly eat right through thin metal air vents and their mountings, and it may also have weakened the grill supports. Toxic chemical rust removers should be cleaned off grills before food is laid on them, and it is safe to assume any rust-free secondhand barbecues have been treated. Brittle cast-iron barbecues should be looked over carefully for signs of cracking, caused by cold water being poured on to put out the fire.

A full trial run from cold charcoal to hot kebabs is seldom possible before buying, as the charcoal takes a good half hour to warm up before any cooking can begin. However, it is worth going through the motions to check that nothing essential is missing.

It is obviously important to have the correct grill, and a set of skewers will save future outlay. Cook's tools such as long tongs and fork are also useful but are cheap to buy separately. Small items are easily mislaid as people rummage in junk shops, and it is worth hunting briefly for any odd skewers separated from their barbecue.

Simple do-it-yourself barbecues are easily improvised using a construction of secondhand bricks and a grill salvaged from a discarded oven. No mortar is needed. The Brick Development Association publish a straightforward design for such a system, which is easily adapted to any surroundings.

BATHROOM FITTINGS

Baths Today's interior designers often plan bathrooms as period pieces echoing the age of the house, and this trend has pushed up the price of the original Victorian and Edwardian ornate cast-iron baths, together with the more angular models of a later period. Before the price rises, demolition men would smash up even the finest old baths, selling the pieces to a scrap metal dealer. Smashing is

still common, and anyone who has tried to carry a cast-iron bath downstairs from a fourth floor bathroom will sympathise with the destruction. If you want a bath from a demolition job, alert the foreman at an early stage, and wherever you buy a secondhand bath, be sure to take into account the cost and trouble of transporting it home.

The Vitreous Enamel Development Council awards its seal of approval to certain bath cleaning products. One effective treatment for drip stains, rust marks and hard water deposits on old white enamel is a dose of "RB70", which is a very strong chemical, to be used only according to instructions. Homekraft's Bath Stain Remover is a jelly-like alternative for all colours of baths, sinks and wcs.

Renubath Services of 596 Chiswick High Road, London W4 5RS (tel: 01–995 5252) will retouch chipped enamel or carry out a complete reenamelling job. Bath Services, 26 Romilly Street, London W1 (tel: 01–437 8238) operate a similar service, as do New Look Bath Services of Nantwich,

Cheshire. Results are normally good, but the job can cost more than a new acrylic bath.

The Plastic Bath Manufacturers' Association recommend Ajax Liquid and Cleen-O-Pine Liquid to clean baths; abrasive cleaners and scouring powders can damage the surface. Light scratches can often be rubbed off plastic baths with liquid silver polish. Minor marks caused by cigarette burns or nail varnish spills may be removed by glass paper followed by silver polish. The colour does not go right through a glass fibre bath, so treatment can be tricky. Hard water deposits often come off with a lemon. Be sure any plastic bath is sold complete with supporting frame and adjustable feet.

Taps Brass taps have become the province of the dealer in pricey architectural antiques, but less grand models are usually readily available from scrap metal dealers and, increasingly, in junk shops. All the working parts of the tap can be replaced, but the job is lengthy and uneconomical. However, washers will almost certainly need renewal. Washers are sold — often given away — by plumbers' merchants and diy shops. Replacement of worn washers is straightforward as long as the tap has not seized up inside.

WCs The technological magic of the 20th century has left the loo untouched, the pattern being set by Thomas W. Twyford's one-piece loo in 1880. No old wc should present a plumber with a fixing problem, as long as it is completely crack-free. Old wcs can be used with new cisterns, even modern low-level ones. Unclean loos are poor buys, as they are extremely tough to clean. The condition of the seat hinges is less important, though these will, for obvious reasons, often be seriously rusty.

BED SETTEES

It is very useful if room-to-room delivery is included in the price of a secondhand bed settee. Moving a primitive Put-U-Up convertible bed settee is good training for a fairground strong man. The thing's extreme weight makes it essential to check a secondhand settee's condition carefully before you take it home and risk horrible revelations which will force you to carry it back to the shop: this operation can break your heart in prospect and your back in practice. Bed settees last many years and are often an excellent secondhand buy, with sellers unaware of the very high cost of new models. Where space in a secondhand shop is too restricted to allow full extension of a put-u-up, this should put-u-off buying. The frame and section hinges could be distorted or rusty, and rust can stain bed clothes. The frame's springing may be damaged or missing. The mattress presents the same possible problems as those on other beds.

The major point to examine is the state of the upholstery; buyers without upholstery skills and plenty of spare time would be buying only trouble with a shabby, tattered settee. Professional upholstery services are expensive and often booked up for months. Any fabric covering lightweight foam units must be fireproof.

BEDS AND BEDDING

A 1979 Gallup survey found that one person in every four spends the night in a second-hand bed. The under-25 age group seems especially prone to the habit. Most second-hand beds are free, mainly inherited from generous relatives, but one person in twelve pays for a used bed.

The survey results naturally horrified the National Bedding Federation (NBF), who consider old beds a hazard to health and business. They approve of those furniture retailers who burn any used beds they find no matter what their apparent condition. No manufacturer, the NBF say, will take a used bed into any part of his premises where new beds are made.

Summarising the official attitude, the Federation asks "Would you buy or use second-hand underwear?" And they have the answer: "Of course not. And underwear can be washed." Mattresses can't be washed. No member of the Association of British Launderers and Dry Cleaners will touch them, though many used to. A clean mattress cover is nevertheless of doubtful value—it could hide some truly squalid stains and severe tears. Be sure to look inside a cover and to examine both sides of any mattress for dirt and damage, bearing in mind that Dunlopillo mattresses can only be used one way up.

An expensive hair mattress could be remade, in which case the hair would be sterilised, but this would almost certainly cost more than a new mattress.

Old beds display gruesome faults, from lumps, damp and broken springs to dust, "stains", bacterial infestation and even the sturdy bed bug, which can stay alive for a year without food. Add to that the possibility of inheriting a mattress from one of Britain's million-strong lice carriers or half million scabies sufferers, mix it with the accumulated rot of the 1¼ pints of moisture which the average body sweats out each night, then add a pound of skin a year, and that's a pretty disgusting picture.

Despite such horror stories, a good quality bed should last about 15 years. This means beds from the mid-60s should be laid to rest, but more recent ones can still have useful life in them. As an aid to dating, a smooth top means the mattress was made after 1960. Before this date, all mattresses were tufted or buttoned. As time goes by, an old mattress develops dips and hollows and offers the sleeper less support. A mattress should "give" at the hips and shoulders when you lie down, but should take its shape again once you get off it. Brand-new mattresses can be tried out in furniture shops to get the feel of things.

Problems of finding a mattress the right size for an old bed have been complicated by metrication.

Manufacturers understandably argue that there's little point in buying a new mattress for an old base. Sagging divan bases spoil new mattresses. A divan base should be sound and solid, with a smooth surface. Any wobbles or creaks or springs protruding through the surface mean the base is not offering the mattress enough support.

The divan now rules supreme, and new metal-based bedsteads are virtually unobtainable. Lovers of the traditional big brass bed must look for secondhand ones, which are normally overpriced or in need of very expensive rebrassing. The wooden part of a bedstead should be sound, and springs on an old base should be checked over for breaks—by pressing each one individually. Squeaky springs spoil sleep. Test the tautness of a diamond mesh. The head and feet of any bed come under quite considerable strain and may well have worked loose. Check that they can be tightened up, and don't pay much for any bed without seeing it fully assembled.

Spring mattresses come in three types. The most expensive have pocketed springs, followed by continuous wire—introduced in the 1960s—and the humble open springs. On the whole, the more springs the better. Mattresses should never be bent. Don't buy any mattress which has been folded up in the shop, attic or auction room. And having made sure you are buying a flat mattress, don't spoil your luck by rolling it up or bending it to stuff it into the back of the car while you take it home.

Blankets The spread of the continental quilt has increased the number of unwanted blankets. The most public-spirited have always given their surplus blankets to emergency relief appeals, but many still come up for sale secondhand.

Most old blankets can and must be washed before use, and many will still carry the maker's washing instruction label. No blanket should be cleaned in a coin-op dry cleaning machine, as dangerous solvent fumes get trapped in heavy articles. Non-washable blankets, together with very old ones and those without a label, can be sent to a dry cleaner with a special blanket service. Names of suitable establishments can be given by the Drycleaning Information Bureau. Two drying tips—white wool blankets turn yellow if left in direct sunlight; striped blankets should hang on the line with stripes running vertically to limit dye-bleeding. Blankets can be dyed—the Drycleaning Information Bureau can provide details of local cleaners prepared to tackle the work.

If blankets are "felted" (matted), there's no point in buying them for use on the bed, as this process can't be reversed. Felted blankets will have lost their warmth, because once the fluffiness has gone, air can no longer be trapped between the fibres.

However, they could make cheap and effective interlinings for curtains.

It is hard to tell what a blanket is made of. The Woolmark was introduced in 1964 to label pure new (not recycled) wool. Without the guidance of the Woolmark, there's no simple test for wool except burning! The idea is that wool burns slowly and goes out easily, leaving a brittle gummy residue. It melts before it burns and gives off a nasty acrid smell like burning hair. If possible, put a few fibres through this test. In general, natural fibres burn and char, whereas true synthetics melt and burn with a small flame, leaving a black globule.

Textile experts use the burning test to distinguish between the very similar burning habits of cotton, linen and viscose rayon, but it's a tough challenge for the layman without a microscope and a lot of knowledge. This is particularly true with blended materials.

More reliable tests will be even more unacceptable to the seller than the burning test, as they involve wetting the fabric, staining it or even dissolving it.

Pillows It is all but impossible to tell in advance how much cleaning a secondhand article will stand without disintegrating. In the case of pillows, both the buyer and the cleaner are faced with particular problems. No cleaner wants an irate customer demanding compensation because his pillow has been destroyed, and neither does he want his shiniest machines clogged up with feathers from a rotten pillow. For this reason pillows are often refused by nervous cleaners, although the Drycleaning Information Bureau can trace a few stout firms who will take the job on. Feather pillows are better washed than dry-cleaned, and a launderette is a good alternative to the domestic washing machine for laundering them. The launderette's heavy-duty machines can stand the wet weight of pillows better than the feebler domestic machine.

No pillow filling is really improved by washing, just made more hygienic. First step with any dirty pillow is to try sponging marks off with warm soapy water and then to air it. Night creams and skin oils can attack foam-filled pillows, and the problems could be aggravated by dry cleaning solvents. Laundering is a better way for both foam and polyester-stuffed pillows. The less widely used kapok filling will go lumpy whatever method is chosen, which may explain such a pillow's presence in the secondhand market.

BEER BARRELS

Aluminium beer kegs mysteriously vanish from the back of pubs in large numbers, like after-hours drinkers in a police raid. The explanation is found not in sabotage by militant real-ale enthusiasts, but in the kegs' high scrap value, which has stimulated a large and illegal steal-and-smelt business. Some are used as mooring buoys for boats, but most are melted down over a bonfire made of used car tyres and sold to scrap dealers. According to the British Scrap Federation, beer kegs never become legitimate scrap, as the breweries just don't get rid of them.

The traditional wooden barrels are more likely to interest the average law-abiding citizen, for these can be both decorative and useful in the garden. A complete secondhand barrel can be put out to grass as a pleasantly flavoured water butt, while half-barrels are popular plant-tubs.

The essential element in an old barrel is not the wooden bodywork but the iron. As long as the hoops are not corroded or working loose, the barrel is likely to be sound. The bunghole can be filled in with a tap or a cork, available from home brewing suppliers.

Garden centres sometimes sell 25-inch diameter secondhand half-barrels, at prices fluctuating with area and fashion. The price rises if the barrels are varnished and painted—often badly—before sale.

A few breweries still use wooden barrels but they are an unreliable source of secondhand ones. Coopers offer lower prices and a better chance of success. Coopers often sell half barrels as plant tubs, and they are the main source of complete old barrels for use as water butts. Not all coopers sell old barrels, as some deal only in metal and plastic. Local coopers can be traced through the *Yellow Pages* under "Coopers and Cask Makers" or "Drums and Kegs".

The market in secondhand rum barrels suddenly took off when the Navy stopped its traditional issue of rum to HM's sailors. At that time a wily seadog in Portsmouth suggested selling off all the redundant wooden barrels. After nostalgic naval tipplers had bought their souvenir barrel, the rest were sold on the open market. Like all rum barrels they hold 40 gallons and are made in seasoned oak with black iron hoops. Ordinary rum barrels cost perhaps one third of the new price, but the Navy barrels have a particular antique value. Barrels can make awkward car passengers, so bear possible delivery charges in mind.

BEES and HIVES

"Considerable caution should be exercised by the beginner in buying a secondhand bee hive", according to the Ministry of Agriculture, Fisheries and Food. Caution is also counselled by the century-old British Beekeepers' Association (BBA), who devote a sentence of their very brief introductory leaflet to advising against buying "any secondhand equipment or any bees before seeking the advice of an experienced beekeeper". It seems that despite the generally benign nature of people in the bee world, you can still get stung.

Joining the local branch of the BBA is a wise move for anyone in the market for a secondhand hive. Members often know of any hives for sale locally and can advise on both hives and the type of bees found to flourish in the area. The official BBA journal *Bee Craft* has advertisements for secondhand hives and equipment. Bee-related ads also feature regularly in the magazine *Practical Self Sufficiency*.

All the hives in an apiary should be of one type, to make parts interchangeable. Wise buyers therefore select British Standard hives, in models still being made. Since the British National Hive was standardised in 1960 by BS 1300, it has had interchangeable units and should be a safe buy. Buying cheap hives of mixed types is false economy. A small number of secondhand National hives, complete with bees, is on sale annually at Maisemore

Apiaries, Old Road, Maisemore, Gloucester, GL2 8HT. Hives may be on the market for dubious reasons beyond the knowledge of the newcomer to beekeeping. Informed advice from an experienced beekeeper can be invaluable. A careful examination usually reveals any structural problems. Signs of woodworm attack should be viewed with suspicion, since the proprietary woodworm killer fluids can also poison bees. Protecting the hive's woodwork with paint is ill-advised, as this often leads to condensation in the hive. Any secondhand hive should be sterilised before it is restocked with bees. A blow-torch flame played over the hive body is a good disinfectant.

Best time to buy is early summer, usually during May. The winter is a risky time to buy, as bees may be dead rather than just sleeping. Attempting to move active bees during a busy summer is madness. At normal times a good beekeeper will help you move the bees to their new home and advise on hive siting.

If a hive is being sold with vacant possession, ask what became of the bees which lived there. They may have died of terrible diseases still lingering in the frames. They may have just been sold separately, in which case the frames will have gone with them. Empty frames in the hive make beekeepers nervous, as they may harbour the spores of the disease Nosema, or be under attack from the wax moth, which can ruin honeycomb.

Don't buy bees before they have been given an official clean bill of health unless the seller offers a warranty that they conform to the British Standard specification. You can — or you can ask the vendor to — kill a sample of about 25 bees with a drop of petrol or carbon tetrachloride, and post them in a labelled box to the County Bee Adviser or the Ministry's Bee Adviser, with a note asking for tests for adult bee diseases. These worthies will send a report giving your new bees the all-clear or telling how to treat their ailments.

Protective clothing is vital for beginners' confidence, and novices should take the bee veil. Check it carefully for potentially disastrous holes. Other equipment may also be on sale from the person who sells you a hive and bees.

For further background information, secondhand bee books are sold by "Bee Books New and Old", Tapping Wall Farm, Burrowbridge, Somerset.

BICYCLES

As car running costs rise, the bicycle is making a major comeback. The new wave of cyclists has been collectively horrified at the price of today's new machines, and many have turned with varying degrees of success to the cheaper secondhand market. Most people can balance on a bicycle, but dealers confirm a low level of basic technical awareness among buyers of secondhand bikes, who often ignore even the simplest tests to reveal a bicycle's roadworthiness.

A bicycle, as most people know, has two wheels. The first check on a used bike is to lift each wheel off the ground and spin it, to see if it runs true and freely. A tiny wobble can be rectified by a repair shop or just ignored, but bad buckling means new wheels are needed, and these are phenomenally expensive.

Look the tyres over—if the tread has gone, you will need new ones.

A bicycle, as most people also know, is stopped by brakes. There should be two. Try each one separately by spinning the wheel in the air and applying the brake. The wheel should stop instantly, and the brake should release the wheel when you relax your grip. Now take the brakes on a road test if the seller will allow you to ride the bike away, which he almost certainly won't allow in an auction or market. Before you mount the machine, make sure the saddle and handlebars are securely fixed. Work up a good speed and brake suddenly. Worn brake blocks are no problem—they are cheap to buy and easy to fit. With the front brake applied, try to rock the bike backwards and forwards to reveal undesirable play in the brake mountings or steering head bearings.

A bicycle, as most people know, has two pedals and a chain. The chainwheel teeth should not be worn into a hook shape. Swing the entire pedal assembly (the chainset) round; it should run freely and smoothly. This tests both

69

the chainset itself and the back wheel cog. Then try to move the chainset from side to side to test for play. The result of this test is slightly hard for the beginner to judge, but basically there should be no movement. An even harder test for the beginner to master comes with an examination of the geometry of the frame, which will establish whether the frame is bent. This is obviously an important matter. Look at the bike from the side: if the forks have been bent the bike probably has a head-on crash in its past. Bends may also show in the crossbar of a man's bike and the bar leading from the handlebars to the chainset on any bike. Considerable damage shows up as a bend where the tubes join the headset.

If the bicycle passes all these tests, the chances of its being mechanically sound are good. Cosmetic features really are unimportant. Rust does not matter in the slightest unless there are actual holes in the wheel rims rather than mere brown marks on brakes, handlebars and frame where paint and chrome have lifted. Elbow grease and steel wool will clear rust, as will rust remover if you have more money than elbow grease. Rusty bicycles are usually very cheap, even if mechanically very sound.

Very few bicycles are beyond repair, but expert advice is needed to estimate the value of a bike in need of extensive repairs. Many small cycle shops sell secondhand parts for obsolete bikes, and a friendly approach usually brings a sympathetic response. Most have rare bits tucked away that they will not admit to in public. Spare parts for old-fashioned bicycles are still manufactured by W. R. Pashley of Stratford-on-Avon: although they cannot deal direct with the public, they may be able to direct you to your nearest stockist.

The retail bicycle shop is rarely a good source of secondhand machines, although many have a regular supply of part-exhanged machines on sale. Few shops recondition bikes before reselling them, and the price is usually high. The alternatives are hardly more enticing. Auctions can be very cheap, but the opportunity to ride the bike before the bidding is over is usually denied, and auctions carry no guarantee if things begin to fall to pieces as soon as the bike touches the road. It is vital to examine the machine at the viewing day before bidding.

General Auctions Ltd of 63/65 Garratt Lane, London SW18 (tel: 01–874 2955) hold bicycle auctions every Monday, with viewing on the previous Friday and just before the sale. The lots may be bikes found by the police (these are chained together, making examination tricky), or privately-entered bicycles which can be checked quite extensively, though not ridden. The auction may also be a source of spares, as the police will enter odd frames they find abandoned in the street. Dowell, Lloyd and Co. of 4 Putney High Street, London SW15 sell bikes on behalf of the Metropolitan Police every three months. Once again, bikes can't be ridden, but they are not chained together.

You can't ride the bikes even at the enterprising London Bicycle Market and Auction, operating from Bay 49 of the Westway Flyover in Ladbroke Grove, London, where up to 100 bikes are auctioned each Saturday afternoon from 14.00, with viewing from 9.00am. Prices since 1978 have ranged from 10 pence to £350. The non-polluting, health-inducing bicycle combines economic and ecological appeal, making it the perfect form of transport to attract alternative enterprise. The Market and Auction is such an enterprise, planned as a sort of country horse market in central London, with repair facilities available all week and secondhand spares on sale.

Street markets can usually boast a few secondhand bicycles, some of them looking slightly stolen and sold by furtive dealers: such markets will be cheaper than shops. Advertisements for secondhand machines appear in the cycling press, for example in the weekly *Cycling,* but their classified section is dominated by expensive racing machines.

Private sales are often arranged through advertisements in the newsagent's or Post Office window. Prices are often low, but there is no guarantee of quality.

Buyers with limited funds to invest in two wheels should remember that the law demands lights, and movement demands a chain. If these are missing from a cheap old machine, they could easily add a third to the overall cost of the bike.

BILLIARD TABLES

The billiard table owned by snooker champion Joe Davis was sold at Sotheby's in December 1979 for £10,000. At that time this was roughly four times the price of a brand new table. The Davis table clearly has special appeal to any player, and its quality can be guaranteed, but secondhand tables with far less illustrious pedigrees regularly cost more than new ones too.

The quality of old billiard tables is both hugely variable and very difficult to judge. The amateur snooker player who is looking for a table for the spare room but is lacking the technical knowledge to match his enthusiasm should not spend even £5 on a secondhand table without getting specialist advice. This normally means avoiding both auctions and private sales and seeking the relative safety of the specialist shop selling reconditioned tables. The dealer can advise on the depth of slate (which may vary from ½ inch to 2½ inches), the quality of cloth and cushion rubber, and other technical matters. Perhaps the dealers' major contribution to successful secondhand buying comes with their delivery and installation services. Slate is horrendously heavy and easy to break, and is certainly not suitable for the unskilled to transport from auction room to private home in the back of the family Mini. Once the hundredweights of slate have been humped into their new resting place, even a skilled table fitter is faced with a four-hour job to set the table up, fit the cloth and make the fine adjustments. Without the fitter's attention, the table will almost certainly provide an unsatisfactory playing surface. There is no universally accepted standard table size, though there is an official template to judge championship pocket-sizes.

Bar billiard tables are benefitting from the upsurge of interest in traditional pub games which has accompanied the growing consumption of real ale. Nevertheless, ill-informed pub landlords still evict these remnants of the days of public bars and no piped music. They are pounced on by private buyers who find such tables more convenient in the home than the mammoth full-sized snooker table. As this is also a game which it is easy to play badly, the price of secondhand tables has soared.

Tables will have been punished during their pub life by spilt beer, smouldering cigarettes and drunkenly intense players. They are rarely found in good condition before an expensive overhaul. Tables are occasionally advertised in *Exchange and Mart*.

BINOCULARS and OPERA GLASSES

Used binoculars can be hard to judge, as the superficial signs of damage are much less important than the state of the binoculars' insides. Scratched paint and chipped plastic on the bodywork don't harm the workings; more surprisingly, scratches and even chips on the lenses themselves need not impair performance. However, external damage could point to a careless owner, suggesting the binoculars have suffered a damaging series of drops, knocks and severe shakings.

It is crucial that the binoculars' two optical systems should be precisely parallel, and abuse can destroy the alignment, meaning an expensive repair which only the manufacturer may be able to undertake.

The test for proper alignment is to look through the binoculars at a distant object — there should be only one image, and no binoculars showing identical twin objects are worth paying much money for. The very high price of major repairs is only worth paying for a good pair of binoculars. Binoculars are protected from physical shock by their case, which can be an expensive item to replace, well worth having included in the price. The quality of cases varies from the luxury of rigid, lined leather cases to cheap plasticised cardboard. This variety reflects the huge differences in prices and quality among the various manufacturers' binoculars. Before seeking out secondhand binoculars, a quick survey of current new prices is advisable. In the absence of better information, the manufacturer's name is a reasonable guide to quality. Many experts remain snooty about the quality of Korean binoculars.

It is sensible to decide before buying on the type of

binoculars you need. Eight × 30 is often recommended as the best balance, the first figure giving the magnification (in this case eight times), the second giving the diameter in millimetres of the objective lens, which is the one furthest from your eye. Binoculars with a magnification greater than ten times will exaggerate any trembling of the average user's hands and also restrict the field of view in much the same way as a telephoto lens on a camera.

Bad binoculars have inbuilt faults which can be spotted by the careful buyer. They often make straight lines look bent and can surround the objects you are looking at with a halo of colour. These faults grow more noticeable towards the edge of the field of view.

It is important to test the binoculars out of doors, to avoid any interference from the glass in a shop's window. Pay attention to the feel of the binoculars, especially if you wear spectacles, as these can make viewing very uncomfortable.

The focusing system must be manipulated to test for play. The centre wheel needs to turn smoothly.

Problems with the focusing mechanism could be due to poor manufacture, but dirt is a more common cause of trouble. A certain amount of dust is almost certain to have penetrated old binoculars. Dirt inside the optical system can be spotted by turning the binoculars the wrong way round, holding them up to the light and looking through each lens individually for signs of filth. Most dealers can clean the optics inside.

Binoculars can suffer badly after the combined onslaught of sand and salt air at the seaside, grinding away the threads and clouding up internal lenses. Most binoculars are made of die-cast aluminium, but in very rare cases you may find ordinary untreated aluminium, which will quickly be destroyed by the sea air. Bracing Skegness is not the ideal spot to look for secondhand binoculars.

A more reliable source for the average buyer is a specialist dealer selling secondhand binoculars taken in part exchange. There are several such shops in London, including the impeccable Brunnings of 133 High Holborn, WC1, who sell all manner of new and secondhand optical instruments, besides running a reliable repair service at fair prices. The most obvious advantage of the specialist dealer over the junk shop is the possibility of comparing the performance of a secondhand instrument with a new one. The specialist may also offer worthwhile guarantees, even a trial period. Secondhand camera shops usually have a few secondhand binoculars in stock.

Secondhand opera glasses sell well around Covent Garden Opera House, and prices are high. Besides the inlaid mother-of-pearl glasses worthy of the Royal Box, there is the occasional red plastic pair looking remarkably stolen from a West End theatre. These are cheap, but usually cost a lot more than the five pence in the slot which released them from behind the seat in the circle.

BIRDS *see* Pets

BLANKETS *see* Beds and bedding

BOATS

Prestige yachts fit for Cannes harbour are monstrously pricey, even secondhand. Only the expert can feel safe in judging the soundness of a large yacht and a client's investment. When boats cost as much as houses, a professional survey is a wise preliminary to secondhand buying, although over half the transactions go through without a surveyor's intervention.

The buyer of any boat should study the market closely to get an up-to-date idea of prices and those points—often minor ones—which push up value. Any prospective buyer can make a revealing preliminary boat examination armed only with common sense, a penknife, a torch and a mirror for looking into a boat's many awkward corners. If all seems well, call in a surveyor for a second opinion.

A surveyor may admittedly be unfit to examine anything more seaworthy than a rubber duck, and incompetent ones wisely protect themselves against future legal proceedings for negligence by let-outs in their reports. You can maximise the chances of satisfaction by choosing a chartered engineer of the Royal Institute of Naval Architects who belongs to the Yacht Brokers, Designers and Surveyors Association. The buyer of a new yacht will typically take out a marine mortgage much like a house mortgage, with a deposit being followed by monthly or quarterly repayments over a period of perhaps five years. Secondhand boats, like old houses, can also be financed this way, the mortgage covering some 50 or 60 per cent of the purchase price. Since UK Exchange Control Regulations were abolished in 1979, buyers have been able to repay in any currency they choose.

Mortgages can be arranged through the High Street clearing banks or City merchant banks and finance houses. There are also specialist marine consultants, and yacht brokers can often find finance for boats bought from them. Whatever the source of finance, they will want proof of your ability to keep up the payments.

Yacht brokers are often compared to estate agents. They have a very similar function, bringing buyer and seller together and charging about eight per cent to the seller. The service is free to buyers. The buyer has no Sale of Goods Act protection if the broker points out that the seller is a private individual. Members of the Association of Brokers and Yacht Agents and/or the Yacht Brokers, Designers and Surveyors Association should abide by the "British Boating Industry Code of Practice for the Sale of Used Boats". This reduces the risks. Such brokers will also be able to advise on surveyors (they receive no commission), sources of finance and contracts.

If you buy your boat from a builder who belongs to the Ship and Boat Builders National Federation you have, as well as their admirable code of practice, the protection of the law if things go wrong. Reputable dealers can be genuinely helpful with advice to the uninformed.

Buying privately avoids the broker's hefty commission, but unfortunately many owners have absurdly inflated views of the value of their own craft. Class yachts do tend to be cheaper in private sales, but of course there's not the protection of the Sale of Goods Act. However, buyers knowing both the market and their needs and without fear of contracts can buy confidently without a broker's advice.

On a sail boat the buyer should inspect the hull for structural damage caused by the trailer and, if the boat is GRP (glass fibre), look for outbreaks of cracking in the glaze which may mean an expensive repair. As with all boats, the handy owner can cope with repairs above water level, but it is better to rely on professionals for work which is to be submerged. Rotten planks on clinker hulls can be replaced, although this is a job for the professional boatbuilder if the piece is curved. All signs of rot should be sniffed out on timber-built boats; rot is betrayed by dark, soft wood and often lurks in the still air of lockers or under deck planking.

Obvious repainting could merely be covering scratches, but might be hiding a recent repair or deterioration in the gel coat. Blistering and lifting paint is probably covering rotten timber, and if the top layer of plywood is beginning to lift, rot may have a grip inside—replacement is probably needed.

On a cabin sail boat, minor points like leaking windows with rotted rubber settings could mean trouble, as could a poor joint between deck and hull, but these minor details are of most use to the prospective buyer as indicators of more general neglect. Perhaps the best clue to the boat's condition is found in the sailing gear, especially the mast and spars and both the standing and running rigging. If it is rusty or worn, the chances are that the rest of the boat is in similar condition. Further information about the general standard of maintenance and servicing can be gleaned by checking the small blocks and winches and by a visual examination of the lavatory.

Man-made fibre sails are very durable, but even the most modern fabrics can fall prey to mildew. If the boat has been sailed in salt water, sails should have been washed down before being stored away for the winter. Oddly enough, salt water is less damaging for timber than fresh water, as it disinfects the wood by killing fungi spores.

Engines, on the other hand, like salt water less, and prices for outboard motors used predominantly at sea should be at least five per cent lower than for comparable motors subjected only to fresh water.

Even buyers to whom the internal combustion engine remains an impenetrable mystery should stare at the engine long enough to see if it is clean. Cleanliness is a good sign of care. If the engine is inboard, it should have been drained down in winter against frost damage. Outboard motors should be free of signs of corrosion and should never have been totally immersed. Ask about this.

If an outboard motor needs replacement, buyers may find the well-established, trade-oriented *Threestokes Guide* of use. This is a comprehensive guide to the valuation of secondhand outboard motors, giving both trade-in and retail prices for all outboard motors up to ten years old, sold in quantity in the British market. Although circulation is theoretically restricted to marine trade and insurers, the publishers—C and D Partners of 145/147 High Street, Kelvedon, Essex—will usually supply private enquirers. The guide appears in January and June.

Depreciation of good quality outboard motors is extremely slow, with demand characteristically exceeding supply in the lower and middle sizes. The better motors should be covered by a few months' warranty.

The boat may be moved around by trailer. The trailer's wheel bearings should be checked for wear to avoid pricey disasters during delivery, and both braking and lighting systems should comply with any legal requirements.

Whatever type of boat is being sold, it is both important and tricky to discover if the seller is really the owner. Traders should have a list of stolen engine numbers, but unless the boat is registered there's little conclusive evidence to be found.

Buyers should beware of outstanding hire purchase obligations giving a hire purchase company the right to whisk the boat away.

The boating magazines available from any newsagent have classified advertisements of boats for sale. Specialist magazines include *Rowing,* with advertisements for sculling boats, *Powerboat and Waterskiing* with ski boats, and *Waterways*

World with canal cruisers. A useful book is Dave Gannaway's *Buying a Secondhand Boat*.

BOOKS

Despite the constant welter of new titles and reprints pouring from the presses of Britain, supplies of many excellent old books are exhausted without any reprint being ordered, and the eager reader must fall back on the local library service or the secondhand market. Some love the world of books for its own sake, sharpening their elbows each Friday in preparation for battle at the weekend's jumble sales. Many book bargain hunters are excited by the musty smell of the chase, the rotting books in damp, unventilated, back rooms of secondhand bookshops, where the silverfish, woodworm and book lice live. Others buy secondhand merely to save money.

Secondhand book sellers are a generally sympathetic breed, allowing customers to browse unharassed for hours. This makes the nation's secondhand bookshops a great refuge on wet holidays, as visitors to Hay on Wye— where secondhand bookshops abound—have discovered. Hardier readers haunt the open-air stalls such as the few in Farringdon Road, London, where the remnants of a once-thriving market can be seen each weekday. A buyer merely wanting to read a book rather than collect it for its formal beauty and rarity should find bargains, particularly on the shelves loaded with nondescript editions of the classics, which hold no appeal to collectors. Serious collectors of old books often spurn book club editions, so these can be cheap secondhand. The first edition is the one with collector-appeal, but it is often of less use to the reader than later editions which may contain revisions following outraged letters from readers of the first and incorrect edition. Collectors tend to concentrate on one tiny field of interest, and dealers too may limit their activity to such matters as motoring, cinema or military books. Chances of locating a particular title will be higher at the specialist shop, though most dealers will hunt out any title for a client.

Regular or specialist buyers of secondhand books would soon recover the cost of buying one of the directories of book dealers. The Sheppard Press publish a periodically revised guide to *Dealers in Books,* a directory of dealers in secondhand and antiquarian books in the British Isles. The ninth edition contained details of some 1300 dealers. Sister publications cover Europe, North America and the Indian subcontinent. These directories open up the world of the many private dealers operating from home by catalogue. It is useful to be on the mailing list of dealers in the relevant area of interest. Any book collector or book hunter can get into print, with a free entry in Trigon Press' *International Directory of Book Collectors,* revised every two years. It's a useful link with like-minded collectors and the dealers. Trigon are at 117 Kent House Road, Beckenham, Kent, BR3 1JJ.

It is hard to determine a fair price for old books, as so much depends on fashion. However, the original cost and current availability of both hardback and paperback editions will influence price. The condition of the book will also be important. Original dust jackets are loved by collectors, as are illustrations, and it is always wise to check against the table of illustrations that none is missing. Many old books have been mutilated in the interest of profit, their plates torn out, framed and sold separately. Less profit-oriented mutilations can bring the price down, such as the crayon scribblings of children, which are very hard to remove. Even the humble thumb print can be permanently ingrained. A soft rubber can remove surface dirt, and a ball of soft white bread is the standard tool to rub away dirt and grease. Any crumbs left in the book will grow mouldy.

Books attacked by insects can be fumigated clean. Damp can encourage mildew and the brown stains known as "foxing" as well as insects. Bleaching can clear foxing, but valuable books are best left to an expert. Bookbinders are listed in the *Yellow Pages.* Adhesive tape should not be used for any repair— its lifetime is short, the glue stains the paper and also leads to brittleness. Torn pages are better repaired by

PVA adhesive, with or without the reinforcement of thin strips of tissue paper.

Specialist book auctions hold few bargains, as they are frequented by the most knowledgeable dealers, and lots tend to be large. The annual *Book Auction Records* has thousands of entries giving an international picture of prices at the specialist auction rooms over the previous year. Although designed for dealers, it can be a useful price guide for the avid private collector. Auctions of house contents may be more fruitful than specialist sales, though you may be forced to buy a whole heavy crate of books to get just one or two wanted titles. At least this should be cheap, and rummaging through the crates is fun. The unwanted can be sold.

Selling to dealers is fairly straightforward on the continent, where a simple pricing system operates widely for recent titles—they pay half the cover price and sell at two thirds. Things are more chaotic here, although some dealers buy quite literally by the foot. Most dealers finger through boxes of books brought to them by spring cleaners and executors of wills as if there were something very nasty in there. The seller is always asked to quote his price before bargaining begins. When quoting a price, leave some leeway for bargaining. The usual mark-up runs at some 300 per cent on buying price.

Certain shops limit their book sales to paperbacks and old magazines, with a hard core of soft porn monthlies keeping turnover ticking. These "popular book centres" are a useful source of recent paperbacks, especially in the western and war story areas. There are other operations piled high with cheap paperbacks across the country, from Bath's splendid central market to the Charing Cross Road, but the heart of the book hunter remains in the dust and damp of the general secondhand bookshop.

BOTTLES

Every rise in the price of a bottle of bad wine forces more drinkers to take up home brewing. A regular supply of empty bottles is crucial to the enterprise, to such an extent that Boots find it possible to sell empty wine bottles for about the same price as a half pint of beer. Using secondhand bottles will save huge sums, for they are free. Your local restaurant will probably be delighted to unload its empties on you, as they can present quite a disposal problem. Those too embarrassed to ask for them, who don't know what time of day the restaurateur should be approached, which door to go in by or who to talk to, could just pick the bottles up when they are piled outside to await the refuse collectors.

Old bottles have to be sterilised before reuse to prevent the wine being tainted. Cleanliness is vital, and wine supply shops stock the chemicals to keep bottles germ-free. Bottle cleaning brushes can also be bought, along with corks in a vast range of sizes. Homebrew shops should stock plain and bored corks and cork bungs with diameters going up in quarter inch steps from an inch to 4¾ inches. Conservationists would like to see the returnable bottle making a major comeback. Manufacturers soberly point out that returnables have to be made stronger than throw-aways to stand up

to a lifetime of rough treatment.

The United States is traditionally the throw-away society, but a dozen states have followed the example of Oregon, whose "Bottle Bill" led the crusade to wipe out the one-journey bottle by completely outlawing non-returnables. Opposition to the bill was strong at first, but the obvious benefits have silenced many grumblers: the scheme has created jobs in collection and transportation, cut litter and saved energy. The secondhand bottle has proved to be a beneficial economic force.

In Britain the campaign against the non-returnable bottle has been led by the Friends of the Earth, who rallied support around the call "Don't let them Sch...all over Britain." The Glass Manufacturers' Federation reacted to the slur by introducing "bottle banks" in 1977. Skips are placed prominently in public places, and people are invited to bring along their empties and sling them in. The local authority arranges for the skips to be emptied in a bay and carried in bulk to the bottle manufacturers, who buy them to clean up and melt down in the furnace. Oddly enough, many "deposit-paid" bottles land on the glassy bank. The success of the pilot scheme in four local authority areas led to banks being set up in over 200 towns and cities in 1981. Buckingham Palace boasts its own royal bank of bottles.

The rising cost of raw materials and fuel for the furnace makes glass recycling increasingly viable for the manufacturers. It takes less heat to melt old glass ("cullett") than fresh sand; every tonne of cullet saves 30 gallons of expensive oil.

Local authorities have benefitted in different ways. Reading proved to be the most commercially successful of the first wave, with the bottle bank profits being spent on a kidney machine. Newquay and St Austell make a loss because Cornwall is so remote from the furnaces, but the environmental benefit of reduced litter makes the bottle bank worthwhile. Many authorities are short of tipping space for refuse, and bottles account for some ten per cent of the rubbish in the average domestic dustbin.

Visitors to the Ideal Home Exhibition and similar events usually witness an artful demonstration by the "Bottle Chopper" salesman. He wields this inexpensive and inelegant device with great skill, producing a wondrous range of drinking glasses, vases, ashtrays, candle holders, "art works" and containers of all kinds, all from the humble secondhand bottle. Like most demonstrations, it is not quite as easy as it looks, and first home efforts tend to leave little slivers of glass around the kitchen; but the dedicated achieve good results quite quickly. Thick glass is easier to work with. UK distributors of choppers are A. T. Lee & Co. Ltd, PO Box 530, Chester Street, London SW1X 7BH.

One admirable attempt to put old bottles to new use was pioneered by Alfred Heineken of the famous Dutch brewery. He was so appalled by the litter of potentially useful lager bottles covering the poor countries of the Third World that he set a team of designers to work on a bottle which could, when the contents had gone, be used as a building brick. The result was the WOBO, or

"World Bottle", but a fickle world failed to respond. The project ceased.

BOWLS

Casual players of bowls need no expensive equipment, since both bowls and mat can be hired for the occasional game in the park. However, all serious players own their personal set of "woods" for championship use. The price of good bowls has risen dramatically, and a new set can cost a month of old-age pension payments. Not surprisingly, many newcomers to the game are examining the cheaper secondhand market.

Bowls are traditionally made of a tropical American hardwood, *lignum vitae*, but modern composition bowls are steadily replacing wood on the greens of Britain. Composition bowls are heavier than wood, and their performance is less affected by the elements. Damp can only be kept out of wooden bowls by a protective coat of varnish, and poorly maintained woods can warp. Misshapen bowls are useless, as the all-important bias will be affected, making the behaviour of the entire set of four un-predictable. A set of bowls with any damaged or missing items is never worth buying.

Chipped or split bowls are ruined and irreparable. All four bowls in a hardwood set for flat green bowling would be made from the trunk of the same tree, and their bias performance would be carefully matched. It is all but impossible to make up an incomplete set. Today, bowls may be manufactured in batches of 200–300, but they are still matched up in sets, and dealers will be unwilling to break an unsold set. The three remaining bowls could lie around the shop for years before another customer came in looking for a missing bowl.

Bowls for championship use must be bias-tested and marked "B.I.B.C." (British Isles Bowling Council). The bias test lasts for fifteen years, and the date of expiry will be marked on the bowls; for example, a wood marked "A94" expires in 1994. The "A" refers to the approved tester who carried out the test. Bowls can be retested, and some old ones could therefore carry two or three test marks. A set can be bias tested for about £5.

There is a bias difference

between bowls for flat green bowling and those for crown green. Differences in the arc the bowl makes from a test line are marked in code numbers. A flat green bowl may be marked "3" or carry no bias mark at all. Bowls for the crown green game, confined to parts of the North of England, the Midlands and Wales, vary in weight, whereas flat green bowls come in different diameters from 4¾ to 5 1/16 inches.

BRACES *see* Tools

BRASS

The old brass bedstead once symbolised the most worthless junk, and was often pictured half submerged in muddy canals or making a climbing frame for bindweed on the railway embankment. Now old bedsteads are antiques commanding high prices, but they may be very bad secondhand value indeed.

Where there's brass, there's muck, and filthy brass may prove impossible to clean, whatever a dealer may say. Cleaning solid brass is a straightforward job for a strong arm and a proprietary polish, but anything larger than a door knob is unlikely to be made of solid brass. The combination of polish and elbow grease may rub away the thin brass top coat from tubular brass to reveal dull steel beneath. Once the steel begins to show through on "brass" bedsteads, curtain rails and fenders, rebrassing is the only solution, and it is very expensive. Moreover, few firms now take the work on. The "Brass Founders and Finishers" listed in the *Yellow Pages* are the likeliest lads. Relacquering can often rejuvenate a faded piece of brass, and by protecting the surface from further tarnishing, lacquer can cut the drudgery of endless polishing. The old lacquer must first be lifted off by rubbing with fine steel wool dipped in methylated spirits, and at least two coats of clear lacquer are then painted on. Diy lacquering rarely lasts long, but stoved lacquer can have a ten-year guarantee.

A home attack on tarnish can be mounted by immersing the brass in non-toxic Unibond Biox liquid, but a slice of lemon dipped in salt is often a strong enough rubber to shift light tarnish. The juice should not be left for long on the brass before washing it away, or dark marks can develop.

BRICKS *see* Building materials

BRUSHES

Old brooms and brushes are rarely worth buying, and should only be considered at low, low prices or for very temporary employment on dirty jobs. Connoisseurs may spot the rare real-bristle brush secondhand, highly prized by brushers and expensive when new. However, if the bristles are bent by the brush being stored on its head, the brush's life is over. A wash and comb should restore dirty bristles, and cheaper pvc or nylon brushes are also easily washed clean unless clogged with concrete. New heads and handles are available at low cost from hardware stores for almost any brush.

Mops with a squeezing mechanism to remove excess water have to be soaked to test the squeezer's efficiency; in time the squeezers become bent and can lose their grip. Spare heads are theoretically available but may prove hard to track down.

Good paint brushes make decorating easier, and although cheap new paint brushes are easy to buy, secondhand ones may offer higher quality for the same price. The very best brushes are made of pure hog's bristle grown on the backs of Northern Chinese pigs who roam free for four years in the sub-arctic wastes with this excellent bristle to keep them warm. Southern Chinese bristle is relatively thin, and the ginger South African type is positively feeble in comparison.

Hog bristle brushes are often marked "pure bristle", but the mark may be hidden under layers of encrusted paint. In such cases, bend the bristles back: they should be strong yet springy, and the brush must be thick. Look out for traces of moth damage—moths like bristle brushes!

Bristles are held in position by a central plug, and this system is open to abuse, as a very large plug can be used to minimise the bristle content. The result is a gaping mouth in the brush, especially noticeable when the bristles are wet.

Nylon and cheap horse-hair brushes have a bad reputation for holding too little paint and for leaving streaky brush marks on painted surfaces. However, a recently introduced American nylon from Du Pont appears to be a vast improvement.

An encrusted stock may be hiding a rusty or loose ferrule; both conditions make a brush a bad buy. Proprietary brush cleaners and paint strippers such as Polyclens or Nitromors will clean up a paint-clogged brush in time, and will even cut through solidified impact adhesive, but several days and several applications could be needed before any cleanser reaches the root of the trouble in the brush stock. Powerful cleansers don't distinguish between paint you want to move and paint you don't, and they can make a bad mess of plastic handles.

BUILDING MATERIALS

A new market for second-hand building materials has grown up in recent years. The demolition men have become aware of the profit to be made from satisfying the significant demand for such humble building materials as bricks, joists and doors. Well-stocked demolition yards are appearing all over the country, all willing to deal direct with an eager public wanting small-scale supplies for domestic use. Specialist shops are also spreading at the antique end of the business, and building materials are increasingly likely to figure in the catalogues of country auctions.

In January 1977 the *Architect's Journal* suggested that needless destruction could be reduced by setting up a clearing house to link people with salvage to sell and those in need of particular old items for use in their building project. As a result, "Architectural Salvage" was set up in April 1977 and thrives still, regularly finding good homes for parts of old buildings. "Our prime consideration", the organisers state, "is conservation", and in pursuit of this aim they track down and save both humble and glamorous items which could be used in rehabilitation work. They keep an index of items wanted and for sale and play snap with the two lists until a match is found. Input comes from architects, demolition contractors, local authorities and above all private individuals. Odd items such as bank counters and band stands, bollards and bars, street lamps and cider presses appear on the register, but the bread and butter comes from the constant demand for used bricks, timber and slates.

It is exceptional to buy materials direct from the demolition site, but certain items will normally be thrown away unless a buyer appears on site before demolition begins and asks for them to be salvaged. These include architraves, skirting boards and bannisters.

Members of the public are usually welcome to approach the site foreman but will seldom be allowed to rip out the wanted materials themselves. This work is reserved for the contractor's own employees, for insurance reasons. It is not legal to enter an unoccupied house and tear things out. Neighbours or the local council's rates office will be able to identify the owner, who should be approached before a salvager risks prosecution through unauthorised entry.

Bricks Old bricks became valuable with the fashion among planners and public alike to insist that new brickwork for home extensions or complete new buildings should match the old. Reusing a brick also represents a huge energy saving over manufacturing a new one. The secondhand brick market has been running for centuries—the cathedral tower at St Albans incorporates Roman bricks salvaged from nearby Verulamium. Today the trade is international, with used British bricks being shipped to the USA.

Matching sizes rarely presents a problem. A large mortar joint will usually span any gap between the old imperial brick and the slightly smaller metric equivalent.

Chimney pots Old chimney pots are lovely, but since they became popular as patio flower pots the price has gone through the roof.

Fireplaces Badly-renovated fireplaces are common: it is wise to buy from established specialist shops such as Mr Wandle in London. The Solid Fuel Advisory Service's technical officers will advise free of charge on fitting old fireplaces; they can be located through the district office. The officer may point

88

out quite correctly, that modern fires are considerably more efficient burners of fuel than old open grates. However, if you want an old style, buying secondhand gives good value compared to the astonishing price of reproduction fireplaces.

Slates New slates are often in short supply, and secondhand ones consequently in demand. The main difficulty is normally in matching up sizes accurately, though old slates can grow useless when they begin to flake. Fifty years is considered an average life for slates.

Staircases Spiral staircases have become fashionable as people try to find elegant solutions to access problems when a loft is converted into a habitable room or a house is converted into flats. The price of old ones is high, and professional advice is probably needed if the danger of buying an ill-fitting staircase is to be avoided. Any staircase is a tricky item to manoeuvre, and proper advice is worth taking.

Timber Dirty but cheap secondhand wood can be cleaned up using a hired belt sander or, for small areas, a sanding disc on an electric drill. The disc will leave score marks across the grain which are very hard to remove. A more serious problem than dirt is the voracious woodworm. Before buying, check the timber for woodworm flight holes and check the price of new timber— secondhand prices should undercut new by at least half.

Floorboards, joists and timber suitable for wooden frame wall construction can be bought at almost any demolition yard.

Most demolition jobs generate a large number of cheap and serviceable doors. A door can easily be reduced in height by sawing off the bottom edge, but cutting a piece from the side can be exhausting and difficult. A good plane is the best tool for those taking up the challenge. Check doors for warp. Warped window frames are not worth buying unless you want the glass. Cutting a broken or oversized piece of glass to size is not too tough for the amateur armed with a cutter. Score the glass surface with the cutter and snap the glass over a batten. Check that an old window frame will not contravene modern building regulations.

BUILDINGS

Without moving from site to site, unwanted buildings can find odd uses in inventive new hands. When Wandsworth council in London decided to close down a rather elegant underground lavatory in Lavender Hill as part of their 1980 cost-chopping operation, a local rock band began negotiating enthusiastically for the lease. Their plan was to turn it into a recording studio.

As the heavy metal music moves into London's lavatories, the heavenly choirs are on the run from disused churches. When congregations have drifted away drastically, a church may become religiously redundant, and close. Hundreds have been converted since a piece of legislation called the Pastoral Measure was passed in 1968, allowing the Church of England to dispose of redundant buildings. Churches have witnessed their final conversion into squash courts, houses, museums, ware-houses, community centres, arts centres, and even, like the Wandsworth loo, into recording studios. A good secondhand crypt could make an excellent nuclear fall-out shelter.

The redundancy process is long. After a diocese decides it has no further use for a church, the bishop tells the Church Commissioners and the Advisory Board for Redundant Churches. Proposals flit between the bodies, and after the final thumbs-down three years elapse while attempts are made to find an alternative use: otherwise it's a demolition case. Bits and pieces are sold off individually. Individual buyers interested in spare parts from old churches, such as windows, pews, stone blocks or statues, should contact the local c of e diocese. Each diocese has its own furnishing officer.

You can buy a takeaway building secondhand from Vic Cooper Secondhand Buildings, Waddon Station Goods Yard, Purley Way, Croydon (tel: Burgh Heath 59166). Mr Cooper sells complete buildings bought from building sites and sold to the public for use as garden sheds, workshops and playrooms. Stock varies weekly and visit is by appointment, although the yard is open every Saturday morning.

BURGLAR ALARMS

The best-protected people in the burglar alarm business are not the nation's alarmed householders but the manufacturers of alarm systems. A 1977 Price Commission report complained that competition was undesirably absent from the business, and that the insurance companies were just making matters worse. Insurers almost invariably insist on their clients installing alarms approved by the National Supervisory Council for Intruder Alarms (NSCIA), which in effect means conformity with British Standard BS 4737. This Standard is limited to alarms maintained by the installer, who doesn't sell the system outright, but prefers to receive regular rental from the householder. If the householder tires of the system, the rental company could just take it back without compensation, reuse whatever parts it can and sell the rest for scrap. The effect of this is to restrict the number of secondhand systems almost to nothing.

Do-it-yourself alarm systems, on the other hand, are the property of the householder, who is free to sell them secondhand. Diy installations are traditionally unacceptable to the NSCIA and hence to the insurance companies. As it would be all but impossible to find an "insurance-approved" installer willing to fit and maintain a secondhand system, used alarms are no use if you are buying one to keep your insurance company happy. However, if you are more concerned with deterrence than insurance, even a disconnected and empty bell box fixed obtrusively on an outside wall may be enough to deter the kids and the amateurs who are behind most of Britain's burglaries.

Even diy systems are a rarity on the secondhand market. If you come across a desirable and complete diy alarm system, it is very important to have the instruction manual, as this explains step by step how to install it. Copydex, manufacturers of diy systems, will try to supply replacement instruction manuals for their systems. The result of poor installation is unprovoked bellringing, followed perhaps by visits from annoyed policemen. This problem makes complete secondhand alarm systems a bad risk. If the system goes off for no good reason, you may fall foul of the Control of Pollution Act 1974, which considers owners of noisy burglar alarms to be almost as bad as burglars and lands them with large fines.

Stealing burglar alarms seems an unlikely crime, but a confused customer could try to sell a system secondhand which isn't his to sell. The problem was highlighted by the 1977 Price Commission report which expressed sympathy with customers who didn't understand their contracts with manufacturers/installers/maintenance men. It is often not clear from the contract whether the customer has bought the system or just taken it on hire.

Buyers of secondhand alarms should be very cautious. After all, a "genuine reason for sale" could be that the system has proved incapable of keeping out even the clumsiest bunch of burglars.

BUSES

You need never again be left standing at the bus stop on wet mornings if you have your own double-decker waiting in the garage. However, rebellious commuters are less common buyers of secondhand buses than clubs and playgroups, as few domestic garages have the headroom for a double-decker, and houses surrounded by low bridges could be inaccessible. Single-deckers are a more popular buy, and their price is consequently higher.

Before buying any bus, garage facilities should be arranged. The local transport authority is often willing to let space in its own garages to private owners, and may also be prepared to undertake maintenance and servicing. It is always sensible to buy a bus similar to those in use by the local bus service, as servicing and spare parts will almost certainly be simpler to arrange for widely-used types. The transport authority itself may sell buses direct to the public, but they normally offload redundant buses via a specialist dealer.

Secondhand London buses are popular worldwide. They

carry tourists to Niagara Falls and still ply their old route over the old London Bridge in the Arizona desert. Others tour round Europe in private hands, and large numbers are bought by British bus companies, who repaint them and put them to work for a few more years on rural routes which are less arduous than London's roads.

London Transport recently sold off the last of their famous RT buses, but the Routemaster is still on the roads. Converting an RT could be complicated by the curious design which allows access to battery and dipstick only by lifting the floor; this means a permanent floor cannot be fitted. Choice of a suitable bus will depend largely on the purpose it is going to serve. If it is intended for use as a playbus, the local fire service should be consulted before plans are made. The town hall's social services department may have something to say about toilet facilities and heating. Stationary buses are often heated by catalytic gas heaters burning bottled gas without a flame. Controls for the gas containers must be located outside the bus.

Many of the regulations governing bus conversions are adapted from caravan regulations. Both caravan dealers and boat dealers offer equipment and ideas for maximising use of space, fitting cupboards and incorporating cooking and washing facilities. They will also have the means of securing everything firmly to the bus floor before a bumpy ride.

A private driver may not need a Public Service Vehicle (PSV) licence to sit at the wheel of a secondhand bus. As long as the bus-driving fantasy stops short of charging passengers for the ride, the bus ceases to be a public service vehicle. However, double-deckers may make a HGV licence necessary.

Old buses should have their own long-term variation on the MOT certificate: a seven-year COF (Certificate of Fitness) is given to a new bus. After seven years, it is reexamined and given an extension of between one and seven years depending on condition and type. The examination is carried out by area traffic vehicle examiners. An EEC directive requires PSVs to be tested annually from 1983. The certificate is no guarantee of a mechanically sound machine.

The average passenger-turned-buyer is not qualified to examine a bus, and the AA can unfortunately offer no formal help similar to their examinations of secondhand cars. However, members would probably glean useful information from the motoring organisations' local technical staff, who know their area well and could no doubt name a nearby garage with a mechanic qualified to examine PSVs. Secondhand buses are sold through the classified advertisements section of the weekly magazine *Commercial Motor*. Spare parts and conversion companies can be traced through the same magazine.

C

CAMERAS

The thriving market in used cameras crashed in 1980, when over-production in Japan combined with a strong pound and a small number of shrewd entrepreneurs to slash the price of brand new cameras. While the price of almost everything else continued to move skywards, the cost of quality cameras plunged. Several established secondhand specialists disappeared under the eye of the official receiver. The moral is clear: it is unwise to buy any used camera before checking out the dealer's ads for new cameras in the photographic magazines. The new camera could be cheaper and is quite likely to be superior. Lens quality has improved steadily over the last decade. Following the Olympus lead, manufacturers are making cameras smaller, lighter and simpler to use. Built-in exposure meters are commonplace and even automatic focusing is on offer.

Older cameras may be good investments as antiques, but

they can cause headaches for the photographer. Nearly all new 35mm "slr" (single-lens reflex) cameras have a bayonet fitting for interchangeable lenses, but lens mounting systems have never been standardised. Incompatibility problems between cameras and lenses of different makes are notorious; it may even prove impossible to fit a manufacturer's latest lenses to their own old cameras.

Film may no longer be available to load an old camera, and no-one would recommend buying secondhand film. Even 16mm film can be tough to track down. While serious and well-equipped photographers will buy a larger size of film and cut it down to size, this is too much trouble for the average amateur who just wants a souvenir snapshot of baby's first steps. Some old cameras are not designed to take advantage of the fastest modern films. A film speed setting of 1600ASA is the maximum most people need.

High cost of film rather than unavailability is the drawback with instant picture ("Polaroid") cameras. Caustic chemicals are used to produce instant pictures from cameras using the peel-apart system, and corrosion can cause trouble in used cameras. Examine the rollers carefully. Cameras using a dry process are simpler.

Secondhand instant picture cameras have the great merit of offering instant proof of their performance, though you may not want to waste expensive film on shots taken from the door of the camera shop. Few instant picture cameras are sold with cases, and they are highly vulnerable to being splashed by beer at jolly parties or by the Mediterranean on family holidays. Broken cameras are bad buys, old ones particularly so. Repairs to any camera over twenty years old can be hard to arrange unless the camera was manufactured by one of the prestigious old firms such as Hasselblad. Even the best importers normally stop handling spare parts ten years after a camera's production run ends. Owners of older cameras are in trouble.

The better cameras are normally more expensive to mend. Slr cameras are bafflingly complex, and the arrival of electronics has complicated matters considerably.

Any camera with an electronic fault is best avoided.

All repairs are pricey, for good reason. It can take a skilled person a whole day just to clean a lens. Scratches can be polished out of lenses but this is almost invariably a waste of money.

In the 1950s lens performance was improved by coating, which gives the lens a typically purple cast. Worn lenses can be recoated, but once again the price is usually too high.

Routine owner maintenance is almost impossible, and repair calls for special tools. Do-it-yourself repairs are normally more trouble than a broken camera. They should be systematically avoided. Diy bodges may show up as damaged screw threads or chipped paintwork where parts have been separated. A routine service is a good investment if there is any reason to suspect that a previous owner was negligent. Servicing involves removal of the top plate and relubrication of the moving parts with pencil lead and other costly lubricants.

The perfect prelude to purchase of a used camera is to take it to a specialist repair shop for a bench test and report. This will test the accuracy of the shutter speed to one millionth of a second. Shutter speeds are never truly exact, but they grow worse with age and use as the spring tension changes. The resolution power of the lens will also be checked. Lens problems may be built in because of the formation of the glass or may develop when a thousand natural shocks send the lenses out of parallel. Camera Care Ltd of 30 Tottenham Street, London W1 offered a bench test for under £6 in 1980, and would push it through in half an hour for a hurried customer.

If the seller quite understandably refuses to let the camera out of his/her sight, buyers are still not helpless. A film can be shot off, developed and printed to test the camera's performance. In major cities, rapid processing services are regularly turning films around in an hour or two. The test film should begin by using the minimum aperture setting, say f16 at 1/30 of a second; then increase the aperture and shutter speed for succeeding frames. If the film transport mechanism is working on a 35mm camera, the rewind knob should turn every time the film is wound on. The film counter should also be in working order. A contact sheet should be adequate to check that all the pictures look correct. One frame should be blown up large to test the sharpness of the lens. Results of this test can be distorted by any dust or fingermarks on the camera lens. Look for any ominous scratches running along the film, caused by a fault in the winding mechanism.

Most private sellers are happy to wait a day or two for the results of a film test to turn up, but there is always the risk of a less cautious buyer jumping in. Some verdict on the camera's condition can be given on the spot without taking a single photograph, although cheap cameras cannot really be judged with any confidence.

Set the shutter speed to 1 second, as the slowest shutter speed is the one most likely to stick. Set the aperture to its minimum—probably f22; if it will stop down this far the other settings are probably in working order. Open the back of the camera as if to load a film. With the back open, press the shutter re-lease button and it will be obvious whether the shutter opens and closes correctly.

Jamming of the wind-on mechanism is a common fault. Place your thumb over the transport spool and wind the "film" on—the resistance of your thumb should not prevent the spool winding on. A reliable light meter can be taken to the test to check the performance of an inbuilt meter.

A camera case is a useful extra. Not only can it protect the camera from dust and impact damage, it can also stop a pinhole being burned through a cloth focal plane shutter in a camera which has been left uncovered with the lens facing the sun. The focused sun would not damage a metal shutter, but cloth is very vulnerable.

Make sure the lens being offered with the camera is the one you want. It may not be the most versatile (normally 50mm for a 35mm camera). It may not even be the manufacturer's own lens, but a cheap substitute.

The instruction booklet can be an invaluable guide to complex modern cameras with their plethora of controls, although many are in a strange

Japano-British dialect. An explanation by the seller is no substitute.

The risk of buying a stolen camera is an added hazard. A buyer needs only to suspect that an article might be stolen property to fall foul of the Theft Act. London's police used to circulate West End camera dealers with a list of stolen cameras, but the list was scrapped when it grew too long. Honest shops now rely on thieves to give themselves away when they bring in a stolen camera. The nervous thief will often pitch his asking price too low, and few will haggle for long over the price. Not many thieves accept payment by cheque.

New cameras are ludicrously cheap in Far Eastern cities, and they are real bargains for tourists as long as customs duty is evaded. Many otherwise upright citizens therefore smuggle a camera into the country. If you buy a used camera on which no duty has been paid, you become liable to pay it. If the evasion was deliberate, Customs and Excise can seize the camera if they ever find out. The surest way to avoid any problems is to ask the seller for the original receipt proving that the camera was honestly acquired and all duty paid.

Photographic dealers often take old cameras in part exchange and resell them. The photographic shop has much to recommend it as a source of secondhand cameras. If things go wrong, repairs may be easy to arrange, and consumer protection is relatively strong. In 1980 the Office of Fair Trading and the main photographic trade associations introduced a code of practice known as the Photocode. Photocode dealers should give secondhand equipment a thorough presale inspection and offer good guarantees. Manufacturers have also agreed to keep stocks of spare parts for five years after withdrawing a camera from the market.

The photographic magazines are a useful source of small ads and information. Back issues may contain test reports on cameras now obsolete but available secondhand. Features on individual models which appeared in the *Amateur Photographer* are quickly traced through Oldtimer Cameras Ltd, 14 Gables Avenue, Boreham Wood, Hertfordshire. They have catalogued almost a century of *Amateur Photographer,* put the results on microfilm and made them available to the public.

EXPOSURE METERS

Relying on readings from a faulty exposure meter can ruin your finest shots, and bad meters cost a lot to put right. Nevertheless, second-hand meters from a reliable manufacturer should be a bargain, as their average life is long. Buying from a dealer, although more expensive on the whole than private sales, has a double advantage: you will be able to check the meter's accuracy over its whole range against the performance of a brand new and expensive meter from the dealer's showroom, and the guarantee gives a couple of months to unearth the dark secrets of a dud meter. When comparing two meters, both should be pointed at a shadow-free area of even tone such as a large sheet of white paper, and each meter brought up close enough to maximise the reading. Agreement to within a stop is sufficient. Some fine adjustment may be possible to compensate for a consistent degree of error. It is important to check an old meter's response to very intense light. In a private sale, a camera with an inbuilt meter is an adequate substitute for a reliable meter for the comparative test.

FLASH ATTACHMENTS

You can often smell out a bad flash gun. There is a pungent odour lurking around the battery compartment when an old battery has been left to leak into the working parts and ruin the whole attachment. A leaking battery could also have eaten away the battery contacts, rendering the thing unworkable. On other intact but obsolete attachments, replacement batteries may be impossible to find. The theoretical life of a flash tube is some 50,000 separate flashes, considerably more than most amateurs need to light up a lifetime's work. However, a collapsed capacitor is a more common problem, and one which breaks the flash, so the attachment should be seen in operation before it is bought. It is advisable to carry out the test with your own camera to ensure compatibility. Even this test may not reveal the intermittent faults which first put the flash on the secondhand market. Alternatively, the flash can be bought on guarantee from a dealer, who will have checked its output on a flash meter.

CINE CAMERAS

You can save money by buying a cine camera secondhand, but you could save even more by not buying one at all. The running costs are very high, and photographic prophets are forecasting that cheaper video will soon destroy the market for cine cameras. A major move to video could put a lot of good cine equipment on the secondhand market, but processing costs are unlikely to go down.

Professional cine cameras just go on for ever. Ancient clockwork cameras are still brought out of retirement to shoot where sparks from electrically-powered equipment could prove disastrous, such as in a coal mine or on an oil rig.

Optical systems have improved dramatically in the past ten years, and it is common practice in the professional film world to take the precision-made mechanical innards of an old camera and surround them with sophisticated new optics. When the film business in the UK or the USA finally tires of equipment and declares it redundant, it is often given a further lease of active life in the Third World. Indian film companies are usually in the market for secondhand movie equipment.

Cine cameras for the amateur market are less durable, but they too take advantage of recent improvements in lenses. They are noticeably lighter than their primitive predecessors. Automatic light metering systems normally control the aperture in today's home movie cameras.

Before testing a used camera by putting a film through it, examine the body for signs of impact—cine cameras take badly to violent vibrations, which destroy lens alignment. Look also for corrosion caused either by leaky batteries or by the bracing salt air on seaside holidays. Sand can grind away a camera's insides, so if the owner's home movies feature the family hurling sand, avoid the camera. A camera case offers worthwhile protection against damage and should be included in the kit. An instruction book is also worth asking about, especially for an obsolete camera where the manufacturer may no longer be able to supply a replacement.

If the camera is loaded with batteries and primed to shoot, run a film through it to check the noise level and, more importantly, that the motor works and the claw mechanism is hauling the film through. The claw is the most likely part to wear out, and repair to the claw mechanism will be expensive. Even if spare parts are available for a repair, the cost will usually be too high to make a broken camera worth buying. Diy repair is not recommended, as special tools and specialised skills are needed for almost all camera repairs. Even a camera in good working order would probably benefit from a thorough cleaning, and this is worth paying for.

CAN OPENERS

The working end of a wall-mounted can opener consists of a serrated drive wheel and a knife to slice through tin lids. In time the drive wheel accumulates a greasy cocktail built up of traces from every tin in its past, and the teeth disappear under the gunge. When the wheel is clogged up, cans start to slip.

A dirty can opener cannot normally be cleaned throughly without removing the knife and wheel. This is a simple job, but some owners prefer complete replacement to dismantling. As dirt-induced slipping is the major cause of can opener failures, a cheap secondhand can opener could be a bargain. If you dismantle a can opener, note the sequence of operations carefully, as parts are sometimes confused during reassembly. It may be possible to sharpen the cutter when the machine is in pieces; replacements are usually available.

An electrically-powered can opener should never be bought without plugging it in and switching it on, unless the price is ludicrously low. A failure to start may merely be caused by a faulty flex or switch. Both of these faults are easily remedied, but worn-out gears and motor bearings will probably make an expensive repair necessary. The usual symptom of a worn gear is a hum from the motor but no action from the wheel.

CANOES

The most basic choice facing the buyer of a canoe is between folding and rigid models. Racing canoeists find that the folding canoe's lack of rigidity slows them down, but others think this slowness is more than outweighed by the folding canoe's far greater ease of transportation. When dismantled and packed into carrying bags, the folding canoe can easily be fitted on a car's roof rack and can save the rail traveller considerable sums of money as it is accepted free of charge for transport by British Rail.

Rot and cracks are easier to spot in the frame of a folding canoe, as the frame and skin can—and should—be separated for inspection. Reassembly can also be instructive, as a frame damaged by constant or severe impact against rocks or beaches will be so warped that assembly could prove difficult. If the frame of a secondhand canoe needs revarnishing or repair, this is obviously simpler on a folding canoe. A torch and some contortions will be needed to look for rot and damage in the inner depths of a rigid canoe. Rigid canoes have the edge when a hull needs recovering, as this is a simpler and cheaper diy job than tackling any repair more ambitious than a patch on a folding canoe with anything but a rubberised fabric hull. A large number of patches could indicate general rotting of the skin.

Look out for little bumps showing on the material where it hugs the frame on canoes with skin-over-frame construction. These could be caused by tiny trapped pebbles which will eventually lead to holes.

The currently dominant fibre glass construction is almost maintenance-free, although imperfect manufacture is all too common. This can show as crazing of the smooth gel coat or in fibres penetrating the resin inside the boat. Manufacturing faults are more likely among the many home-built canoes built following the popular diy plans.

The canoe's spray cover is normally made of canvas, which can be repaired quite successfully. Rubber, on the other hand, can be perished irrevocably just by sunlight.

It is unwise to buy a canoe

without at least sitting inside it. Rough patches or sharp edges on the seat can quickly grow very uncomfortable. Ideally, an experienced person should try the canoe out on the water, which may not be convenient. A folding canoe will be carried to the water in its two carrying bags, which should be checked over for holes and signs of wear, especially at the seams. Bags are essential, and if they are missing, their absence should be reflected in a lower price.

Replacement bags can be made by anyone with access to a sewing machine and a rough idea of the shape to achieve.

Almost as essential as the bags is a two-wheeled trolley. This too should be tried out before purchase. The canoe should also be equipped with two painters at least one and a half times the length of the canoe and, of course, paddles.

However confident a buyer is in the wisdom of his or her judgment, it is not sensible to go on the water without a life jacket. Whether new or secondhand, a jacket with the British Standard Kitemark is a useful and reassuring ally.

Clubs affiliated to the British Canoe Union (BCU) may be able to help buyers locate canoes for sale. Their quarterly magazine *Canoe Focus,* which is free to members, has a small classified advertisement section. They also publish a very handy booklet on *Choosing a Canoe,* which contains information useful to buyers of both new and secondhand boats. The BCU is found at 45–47 High Street, Addlestone, Weybridge, Surrey. Canoes for sale are also advertised in the monthly magazine *Canoeing.*

CARS

Used cars cause more headaches for local Trading Standards Officers than any other single item. The villain of the story is usually that old archetype of corruption, the Used Car Salesman. In 1979 the Office of Fair Trading (OFT) handled over 50,000 complaints about used cars.

Against a background of rising consumer discontent the big four associations of car dealers have produced noble but voluntary Codes of Practice for the sale of used cars. These say that any price quoted must include VAT, and that member dealers should inspect cars before trying to sell them. Although the customer cannot see the results of a particular inspection, a copy of the type of checklist used should, says the Code of Practice, be available. Dealers should also take reasonable steps to verify the mileage reading. This is an attempt to limit the epidemic practice of "clocking", or turning back the mileage reading. Average annual mileage hovers around 10,000 miles, but everyday use by travelling reps pushes the mileage on many company cars grossly over this figure, and high mileage depresses prices. An OFT survey found that the mileage reading had been turned back significantly on over half the company cars sold secondhand. The death of the old log book stimulated clocking, as this made it impossible to contact previous owners before buying a used car.

A free leaflet in the OFT's *For Your Protection* series outlines the Codes and the customer's options if things go wrong. It is available locally from libraries, the surviving Consumer Advice Centres, and Citizens' Advice Bureaux, who will also advise distressed buyers when things go wrong with used cars.

Connoisseurs of the used car lot seem to dismiss the small dealer as a parasite, offering neither the lower prices of the private sale nor the workshop facilities and trained mechanics of the large, well-equipped garage. They usually just add polish and a profit margin to the cars they buy. They know that clean cars attract buyers — shiny paint, an empty ashtray and a filth-free carpet encourage the customer to sit behind the wheel, and that is half the battle. Buyers in some areas can contact data banks of used cars for sale. Like computer dating operations they try to match a customer's requirements from their files of what the dealers have. Like computer dates, the cars don't necessarily work.

Dealers large and small base their prices on *Glass's Guide,* which is available only to the trade. If you can sneak a glance at *Glass's,* use it to gain a thorough advance knowledge of the dealer's current pricing policy. Alternative price guides are on open sale in any newsagent's shop and are certainly worth consulting. The annual *Motoring Which?* report on used car prices is useful.

Prices are consistently lower in private sales, but so is the buyer's protection. The Trade Descriptions Act does not apply, and the power of the Sale of Goods Act is diluted. The law—widely ignored by bad dealers—says that even the most decrepit of old bangers sold by a dealer must be "of merchantable quality", bearing in mind the price paid and the dealer's description. This law does not apply to defects pointed out by the dealer before purchase or which the buyer ought "reasonably" to have spotted.

An interesting halfway house between the dealer and the private bargain appeared in 1980 in the car park of Walthamstow Greyhound Stadium in London. Following a successful continental lead, an entrepreneur hired the car park every Sunday and charged private individuals £5 to drive their cars inside and sell them direct to the public without any middleman. The public paid no entry fee. The scheme arrived in the Greyhound Stad-

ium after meeting extraordinary hostility in three London boroughs and several local newspapers.

A less desirable halfway house between private and professional used car sellers is the dealer's own home. In 1977 it was made illegal for a dealer to put ads in the local newspaper which hid his identity as a professional dealer. The practice continues.

Prices at specialist car auctions are unpredictable, although these are almost exclusively the haunt of dealers, who need to buy cheap and increase the price for resale. Car auctions are dominated by the British Car Auction Group, who averaged over 50 auctions a month in 1980; some 3500 cars came under the hammer each week as dealers with cash flow problems turned to the auctioneers for quick cash. Prices often drop towards the end of the day's bidding. The biggest auction bargains are often the uncommon foreign cars and the obsolete models, which dealers don't like. Bear in mind with imported cars that the date of first registration in this country, given by the last letter of the registration number, is not necessarily the same as the year of manufacture.

Cars are sold through auctioneers by government departments and private individuals. Others may be part of a company's fleet or unsold cars from a dealer's courtyard. These may be complete lemons, and caution is therefore vital. Unfortunately the law allows you to return a bad car to an auctioneer only if you discover within 24 hours that the auctioneer's description of the vehicle's age or condition was false.

The main problem with buying at auction is the impossibility of driving the car before you bid. Examination of the stationary vehicle is possible before the sale, but the only clue to its mobility comes when it is driven into the ring during the sale. Dealers sometimes mark the cars they want by bending the blade of the fan so the car makes a nasty noise when the engine is started up, making rival bidders back off. Other pre-sale tampering is common.

Buyers are in an unenviable position if they buy the wrong car, as the cost of repairs can be vast, and getting money back from motor traders is notoriously hard. Nevertheless, buying secondhand is often a good economic proposition, as the second owner benefits from the huge depreciation in the value of a car during its first year on the road.

Most buyers feel daunted by cars. An expert examination is probably worth paying for. The AA and RAC arrange inspections of used cars, but these can take days to arrange. Some garages even offer cars complete with an AA/RAC test certificate. A mechanic from your local garage will probably come with you to check a car over. Even if no expert is available, taking an ignorant friend is better than going alone into the dealer's world. The reason is mainly legal. If the dealer's glowing description of the car's high quality turns out to be over-optimistic, it is useful to have a witness.

Absolute ignorance of the internal combustion engine leaves you far from defenceless. A set of simple tests involving no mechanical skills at all will reveal many of the

106

problems a used car could hide. Too many buyers are distracted by the colour of the car and the quality of the in-car entertainment. They notice the stereo cassette deck but not the rust. They admire the new paint without realising that a respray probably follows a recent accident and could hide acres of rusty metal.

Faults are harder to spot at night, even with the help of an inspection lamp, yet many private deals are done on dark evenings. It is usually worth waiting for the weekend to examine the car, even at the risk of missing a bargain.

Rust is the motor car's mortal enemy, the biggest single cause of MOT failure and the best reason to reject any used car. If the rust is bubbling through the paintwork, ask the owner to prod it to see if the metal is still solid. Bodywork repairs, where still possible, are astonishingly expensive.

Useful information on rust-prone parts of particular models is given by the Cunsumers' Association magazine Which? in their annual car reliability survey. For example, they forewarn prospective buyers about the rusty floors of old Renault 4s, the doors of older Ford Granadas and the back wings of old Rovers. Volvos, Mercedes and VWs survive outstandingly well. On most cars rust will attack under the wings, where stones and mud are fired upwards from the road. Doors and door sills are also very vulnerable. Other likely spots are under the carpet and around the headlights, body trim and chrome brightwork. A leaky boot lid lets in water which can cause rust. A magnet will reveal the presence of body filler where rust has been cut out of bodywork.

The most serious damage occurs when rust corrodes the points where the suspension meets the body, and the box sections which normally run underneath the car along each side. The only way to check these is to jack the car up, but be extremely cautious, as rust may have rotted the jacking points. Reject any car if this has happened, or if the doors stick when the car is jacked up. Undesirable signs of welding may also show up under the car.

While the car is securely jacked up, grab the top of each front wheel with both hands and make a vigorous effort to wobble the wheel. Any movement indicates bad bearings. Look at the wheel rims for signs of distortion and damage.

Tyres are easy to replace but they are very expensive. All should be of the same type, including the spare, with a tread depth well above the legal minimum of 1 millimetre.

With the car back on the ground, bounce it at each corner. When it bounces back up, rocking should stop immediately. If the car keeps bouncing, it needs new shock absorbers.

Turn the steering wheel; it should not move more than two inches without turning the wheels.

The state of the springs and upholstery on the driver's seat, signs of heel marks on the carpet under his feet and wear on the rubber cover over the accelerator pedal can all be used to judge the use the car has had. It is easy to ignore all doors except the driver's: they should all open and close easily. Any problems could be due to accidents reshaping the car. Windows, lights, wipers, heater and horn must also work, and the battery should be powerful enough to keep the lights shining. Look out for cracked batteries.

Under the bonnet the engine should be clean, but spotlessness may mean a reconditioned engine. Start up the engine and wait a few minutes. Dealers have been known to load up the gearbox and sump with heavy-duty sludge to cover unwanted noises. As the oil warms, the noises will come through, and oil may begin to drip from damaged engines. During the wait, ask the seller whether he has the owner's handbook, a workshop manual or any other literature. Receipts for servicing and repairs are also handy indicators of the car's past history. An MOT certificate is vital on a car over three years old.

Engines are hard for the uninitiated to judge, but a bad engine bears some obvious signs. The first place to look is inside the radiator. Rising bubbles or traces of oil on the surface could mean the engine is about to die. Traces of water or scum on the end of the oil dipstick are similarly offputting signs of a cracked block.

Worn engines produce smoke. Extensive work will probably be needed on cars with smoke rising in billows when the oil filler cap is removed. When the car has idled for a while, rev up hard—blue smoke from the exhaust means the engine is worn. The handbrake can be checked by trying to push the car with the brake on, but only a road test will put the footbrake to a thorough test, and the prospective buyer must insist on taking the wheel himself or herself for the drive. Make sure you are insured. You are entitled to drive on a dealer's trade plates even if the car's tax disc has expired. There could be insurance problems in a private sale.

Brakes are obviously crucial: check them early on. They need immediate attention if your foot sinks slowly to the floor as you apply foot pressure, if you have to press hard to get any response from them, if the car pulls over to one side or emits a grinding noise when you brake. Long-term problems could be on the way if the brakes scream, as this could be metal being worn away in the drums.

Steering problems are usually expensive to rectify. Tyre-screech during low-speed cornering could be a symptom of steering difficulties, as could a thud when the wheel is turned. Drive "no hands" at normal speed on a straight piece of road with no camber: if there's any trembling from the steering wheel, you've got serious steering problems.

A juddering clutch is equally undesirable. The engine speed should not increase when you touch the clutch. With the car stationary, the handbrake on and the engine running, put the car in gear and let the clutch out slowly—the engine should stall at once. If it takes time to slow down and stop, the clutch is probably barely there. The gear lever should not jump into neutral when you pump the accelerator up and down, but put it deliberately in neutral during the test run and listen for the grinding sound which indicates worn wheel bearings.

Back in gear, take your foot off the accelerator and listen for whining noises from the gearbox. Listen too for an ominous "clonk" when you press the accelerator again—this is a sign of worn transmission and the end of the car's active life.

An irregular knocking noise from the engine is the dreaded big end knock; repair is usually very expensive.

The test drive will leave you with a general impression of the car's appeal. If you have found too many faults, don't buy it at all. If you still like it, start haggling over the price.

Don't allow the seller to apply pressure. If you decide to pay a deposit to keep open an option on the car while you try to fix insurance cover, raise the cash or arrange an inspection, get it in writing that the deposit is returnable if you decide against buying. It is best to pay no deposit at all. Remember that you cannot drive the car away without tax, insurance and a valid MOT certificate if one is needed

Beware of guarantees on secondhand cars. The late 1970s saw a spate of insurance-linked used-car guarantee schemes, typically covering the car for twelve months or 12,000 miles and typically transferring respon-

sibility from the dealer to the insurance company after one month. Some of these policies demand that the buyer fulfils outrageous servicing conditions before any claims will be considered. Check whether any warranty covers labour as well as parts; with the hourly cost of mechanics rising so dramatically, this is crucial.

Some motor manufacturers offer used-car guarantees through their franchised dealers. Cover can rarely be arranged for cars over seven years old, and no guarantee is a substitute for pre-purchase caution; getting money back from a garage can be a lifetime's work, often with no reward at the end.

A car becomes more liable to breakdown as it grows older. Broadly speaking, a seven-year-old car can be expected to need four times as many major repairs as a yearling. Besides the horrible cost of even the most incompetent mechanic's time, repairs mean spares.

Spares for recent models —particularly large cars— can be expensive, and they can be both expensive and hard to find for obsolete cars. Although stylish 1950s hubcaps of the American chrome age have become collectors' items, bought to be hung on fashionable walls, second-hand spares from the car breaker's yard can usually provide a cheap solution for the spares problem.

Large stocks of classified spares are often laid out by the breakers on racks for over-the-counter purchase, but if the part you need is unusual or still fixed inside a wrecked car lying in the mud, you may have to drag it off the wreck yourself. Tools will be needed. Locate breakers through "Car and Commercial Vehicle Breakers and Dismantlers" in the *Yellow Pages*. Parts are also advertised in the magazine *Car Mechanics* and *Exchange and Mart*.

Mechanical failure can mean a major outlay on an antique car, but most classic makes have owners' clubs which know the sources of parts.

Wrecked cars worldwide provide incomparable raw material for the creative entrepreneur. In Morocco old tyres are cut into strips and made into high-mileage sandals or water bottles to be carried by donkey-power. In Western Europe motoring enthusiasts and metal workers use the steering columns of desirable but deceased cars as standard lamps in the sitting room. In Tanzania the blades and shafts of the carpenter's tool kit are fashioned from the hard steel of old car springs. Throughout the Third World oxcarts roll on salvaged car or lorry wheels rather than the traditional solid or spoked wooden wheels. Windows, seats, hoods and lights can all be put to use when the car's driving days are done.

CARAVANS

The major faults of a touring caravan should all be revealed by a layman's careful inspection, and to that extent secondhand caravans are a safer buy than used cars.

Before you leap at some super bargain caravan quite unsuited to your needs, consider such basic matters as your car's towing limits, the number of people the caravan must accommodate and the type of accessories you want. In the restricted space of a caravan it is better to have fixtures such as fridge and cooker already built in rather than having to juggle with awkward spaces and equally awkward furniture later. Professional fitting services can prove very costly.

A purposeful stroll around the major dealers' very expensive show sites will provide some idea of current prices. Dealers can be found in the *Yellow Pages* under "Caravan Agents and Dealers", and many advertise in the caravanning magazines.

The salesmen at caravan showrooms can be awesomely persuasive, but bear in mind that buying in the private market usually proves cheaper than the dealer's showroom. However, this method does restrict the buyer's protection under the Sale of Goods Act. A rotten chassis makes a caravan almost worthless, but as with any form of housing the major enemy of a caravan is damp, which rapidly rots timber structures. Obvious sources of wet patches will include the water tank, water pump and toilet; other visible signs may be rippling surfaces on plywood panelling, lifting veneers and bulging boards on the ceiling. Water may have penetrated around rotten window seals or guttering, and you may find the tell-tale musty smell lurking in cupboards and lockers, all of which should be opened.

Rusty brake rods can be troublesome, but the rust which condemns so many cars to the scrap heap is less of a threat to caravans. The almost inevitable sight of a rusty chassis and A-frame under the caravan need not cause despair.

The standard of fittings and insulation should be far higher in recent vans than in the primitive boxes which first carried holidaymakers to equally primitive sites. No examination of a caravan should omit a try-out of every last piece of equipment to see that it works and that hinges are secure, with doors fitting snugly in their frames. Caravans are easily dented by impact, and any difficulty in opening or closing doors may be a symptom of harsh treatment. Beds should be opened into position, and if there is any doubt about the adequacy of their size for long members of the family, it's wise to measure them.

A caravan which rocks and bounces alarmingly as you climb in and move around with the legs up probably has ruined suspension dampers.

Tyres are rarely worn, as a caravan's annual mileage tends to be low. However, over-winter parking may have flattened them, sunlight can harm them, and stones can be embedded in them. By law, tread depth must be at least 1 millimetre.

Repairs to the braking system are unlikely to involve major expense. It is sensible to overhaul the brakes of any machine as soon as you buy it.

After looking the caravan over for obvious faults, hitch it up, check that the lights work and take it for a test run. As you accelerate and brake there should be no clunking sound or on-off shunting from the caravan's brakes; both these faults indicate a poor coupling damper.

Older caravans often lack the convenience of auto-reverse. This means jumping out of the car to override the brake mechanism at the coupling each time you want to go backwards. Marwood overrides can be fitted quite easily. Check the condition of the coupling.

Shabby caravans can be bargains. Although cleanliness puts up prices, dealers often sell traded-in models untouched. A car polish such as T-Cut can quickly work wonders on dull paintwork, as any used car showroom bears witness. Look out for acrylic windows scratched opaque by abrasive cleaners. The remedy for this problem is found in motorcycle shops, which sell suitable scratch removers for visors. Drab and worn carpet need not be offputting. This is easily replaced by cheap offcuts from carpet shops. Offcuts can also be used to recover any ruined plastic laminate worktops at little cost, while a coat of polyurethane varnish will often resurrect tatty cupboards. Curtains are small enough to be replaced cheaply, but threadbare furnishings can be troublesome to those without upholstery skills. Upholstery can be removed and dry cleaned.

Bear in mind that every car's pulling power is limited, and hauling over-heavy caravans can give a car a mechanical heart attack. The car's handbook or manufacturer can give the hauling limit. Otherwise consult the annual *Caravan Fact Finder* published by *Caravan* magazine in Spring.

Prices fall after the summer holidays, as few buyers want a caravan to spend a whole winter on the front garden before it can be used. However, a lengthy period off the road is a fine opportunity to repair and refurbish a shabby caravan.

The major caravanning magazines, from *Caravan* and *Practical Caravan* to *Mobile Home and Caravan,* carry extensive classified advertisement sections of caravans for sale, and also provide information about prices and features of new models, but the main national medium for secondhand caravans is the incomparable *Exchange and Mart*. Caravan hire companies may sell off older models at the end of the season.

Motor caravans face the buyer with far greater problems, adding the familiar hassles of used car purchase to the difficulties of choosing a touring caravan. Advancing age and mileage cut value, but motor caravans tend to hold their price well, far better than cars. Guides to prices can be found in *Parker's Car Price Guide* and the *Motorists' Guide to New and Used Car Prices*, both available from newsagents. As with custom cars, home caravan conversions can be problematic unless there is absolute certainty that the conversion follows the vehicle maker's specifications strictly. Otherwise reselling may not be easy, and the vehicle is quite possibly unsafe on the road, a fact the insurance premium may well reflect.

No motor caravan should be bought without a trial lasting at least half an hour. If possible, the best guide to the suitability and condition of a caravan may be to hire it for the weekend. Motor caravan hire companies renew their fleet every couple of years and sell off the old vehicles secondhand.

The buyer's main concern should be the mechanical state of the motor van. If you feel incapable of testing the vehicle yourself, both the AA and RAC can arrange examinations of motor caravans.

CARPETS

Oriental carpets are investments and art works rather than floor coverings.

Expert judgement is needed to buy well and to maintain the woven wonders of the east. Details of specialist carpet cleaners in any area can be supplied by The Drycleaning Information Bureau or the specialist Carpet Cleaners Association, 97 Knighton Fields Road West, Leicester. Cleaning costs can be high, currently running at over £2 per square yard, so estimates are an important prelude to going ahead. Members of the same association will also concern themselves with the more mundane cleaning problems facing the buyer of less exotic secondhand carpets.

A good introduction to both carpet care and carpet selection is the booklet *The Care of Carpets,* published by the British Carpet Manufacturers Association Technical Centre, Aykroyd House, Hoo Road, Kidderminster, DY10 1NB. It costs 20 pence. This booklet was designed to help staff in carpet shops but is just as useful to the customer. It includes an excellent guide to diy stain removal, covering methods of attacking such undesirables as alcohol, coffee, fruit, ink, oil, paint, polish and pee.

Carpet users are divided about whether the lingering smell of pets' pee can ever be cleaned out of carpet, opinions varying with the sensitivity of the individual's sense of smell and their attitude to cats. All agree that the smell can be terrible, and careful buyers will scrutinise the back of any secondhand carpet, where suspicious traces are more likely to be visible than on the surface.

It is usually safe to assume that stains showing on the face of the carpet are permanent. Some can of course be removed but treatment is complicated by ignorance of what caused the stain. Identification problems may not be limited to the nature of stains—the carpet fibres themselves may be hard to identify, and fibre can affect value enormously. Secondhand and junk shops are unlikely to offer reliable diagnosis, but in specialist auctions the chances are higher. This is important, as the life of a poor quality carpet in a heavy-traffic area of the house can be as short as a year, and that's what the unwary may be buying. While almost any carpet will be fit enough for the easy life in a spare bedroom, few can stand the dirt, damp and suffering of life on the stairs.

The type of fibre dictates

how badly dirt will show. On the whole wool absorbs more filth than the synthetics before the surface looks dirty. On the other hand synthetics resist staining better and are easier to clean. The method of attaching the fibres to the backing will influence wear. Bend the carpet back to spread the pile—the denser it is and the closer the rows, the better. It can be useful to examine some new carpets before buying secondhand to get an idea of pile density and price: take samples for comparison if possible. No carpet should be bought without examining every square inch of both sides, preferably in good natural light. If a carpet has been damaged by damp it will crack and rip when it is flexed—as you turn the carpet over, try the flex test with some force and reject any carpet which fails. It would certainly rip during fitting.

Moths can devastate carpets made of wool or other natural fibres. Their presence is usually betrayed by white cocoons near the carpet edge. If the fluff comes away too easily in your hand, moths have probably been active. Loose or missing tufts on tufted carpet are more likely to indicate poor manufacture.

First signs of general wear and tear normally appear on parts fitted near the doorway and next to the seams: narrow-loom carpets with sewn seams are particularly vulnerable. Damage could occur anywhere on badly-laid carpet. An electric flex running underneath the carpet will cause wear, hot coals from a nearby fire could have scorched it, and uneven floorboards will soon show through. Draught-carried dirt blowing between floorboards and around skirting boards will mark carpet with grey lines.

If only part of a carpet is damaged, it may be possible to disguise the damage with a rug (the seller may already be trying this theory out). If a torn carpet is too large for your purposes, the damaged section can be lopped off; certain designs can be cut down to make a fringed rug. An enterprising Suffolk company has for years been buying up damaged carpets, odd scraps and ex-ministry rejects, washing them and turning them into very attractive bags. Called, appropriately, Carpet Bags, the company is linked to Green Deserts, a charity dedicated to planting trees in the desert to halt the advance of sand.

Proper fitting can lengthen the life of a carpet, and it can be quite expensive. Underlay is another major cost of carpeting with anything other than foam-backed carpet. These costs must be calculated before buying second-hand; freelance carpet layers will give an estimate for laying, usually based on the cost per square yard plus underlay. Diy laying will save money.

Do-it-yourself cleaning can be tackled at home to some extent. The vacuum cleaner is the best first phase of cleaning any carpet. It can be followed by a carpet shampooer, which can easily be hired by the day or for the weekend. "Deep clean" machines get at the badly-ingrained dirt. It is unwise to cover an Indian carpet with shampoo—the colours may run. The only reliable home method is powder cleaning with for example a spray of Goddard's Dry Clean, left to dry and vacuumed off.

A more traditional method is to sprinkle the surface with fresh and slightly damp tea leaves, then brush them off. This will at least clean the carpet of tea leaves, but it might make the colours fade. Sunshine and salt water may, incidentally, have a similar fading power. An even more bizarre cleaning recommendation from the Victorian domestic guides is ox-gall—"it must be fresh"—to clean whitewash from carpets.

CASSETTE DECKS *see* Audio equipment

CASSETTE TAPES

Britain was introduced to the cassette tape in the early 1960s. Since then competition has grown and standards have improved. The introduction in the mid-70s of super-ferric cassette tapes and new formulations such as chromium dioxide (CrO_2) have led to several marked improvements in quality: today's tapes offer better frequency response with a more faithful reproduction of both high and low notes; the overall signal-to-noise ratio has improved and distortion has decreased. In short, the sound is clearer and there's less hiss. Even the box itself has undergone positive modifications, and modern tapes are less likely to jam or snap than old ones.

All this means that old tapes are bad buys. However, pre-recorded tapes are another matter, as they may contain a special piece of music which is no longer available. Sound purists often insist that cassette tapes are less sturdy than records, and that the sound deteriorates with playing. This may be true within earshot of the careful enthusiast's expensive sound system, but the rough and tumble of a normal life is likely to leave a secondhand tape in a fair state.

After being played on machines with worn heads, the tape may be crinkled at the edges, and dirty rollers can cause erratic movement, even breakages. Filth is a problem—a dirty tape can be lifted off the record or playback head, causing loss of signal. Handling the tape can impair quality. A sunny day baking on the back seat of a car can warp the cassette housing and cause "print through", when a minute magnetisation passes from one layer of tape to the next and prints an echo on it. Storing the tape for a long time

after a fast rewind can cause the same "print through" problem.

On good machines, the working life of a high quality tape is almost limitless. Moving straight from "fast forward" to "fast rewind" can stretch dud tape, but a good brand will not stretch noticeably. After years of playing it will take an electron microscope to detect the amount of stretch. Nevertheless, it remains important to choose the best brands, and reputation is the best guide when buying secondhand. Cheap cassettes will often bind and jump, causing wow and flutter. Be prepared to hear too much treble on a Dolby tape played without the Dolby noise-reduction system.

Prerecorded tapes can often be wiped clean if you don't like the music. However, the manufacturer will have removed the tabs covering the holes in the back of the cassette to prevent accidental erasure, and these will have to be replaced by crossing the gap with a piece of masking tape before the sounds can be wiped out. If erasure is not a complete success, it could be that the masking tape has been pushed in or broken by the cassette deck's wheels. Try a thicker piece in this case. The failure to erase may be due to a difference in head alignment between your machine and the machine used for the original recording. There is a risk that the recording has already been accidentally erased after storage in a powerful magnetic field.

The ease of duplicating prerecorded tapes and the potentially high profits in an operation avoiding all royalty payments have combined to attract tape pirates. They offer superficially convincing low quality duplicates of popular tapes, and these turn up quite regularly in secondhand shops. They can sometimes be spotted by the inferior colour printing on the inlay card, but good knowledge of the genuine article is usually needed to sort them out. It is of course wise to check that the tape inside any box is in fact what the label claims it to be.

Old prerecorded tapes are usually on sale wherever used records are found. Prices are comparable, and since quality does not deteriorate noticeably with age, they are often good value.

CATS *see* Pets

CHICKENS

Hens lay heavily in their first season in the battery, but then their output quickly drops below the tolerance threshold of profit-conscious chicken farmers. A typical 20 per cent fall-off in the second year of laying can mean the end of the road for the "spent layer". Soft-hearted backyard poultry farmers may like to offer a retirement home for these secondhand hens, who can still keep a family in eggs. They have the advantage of needing no feeding up to develop from a fluffy yellow ball of chicken to productive layers. However, it is usually difficult to buy live chickens from a battery farm when their working days are done. They tend to become boiling fowl or pet food after eighteen exhausting months dropping eggs.

CHILDREN'S COTS

A secondhand cot could place a baby's life at risk every night. Deaths have occurred when a child's clothes have caught in the guide rods of a sub-standard cot; the projecting rod holding the dropside on old cots can work loose, catch the baby's clothes and lead to strangulation; babies have died when they have slipped between the mattress and the cot.

A mattress must fit the cot quite closely, with a gap no larger than two inches (50mm). This can rule out cots of unusual shape such as the bow-ended style which was fashionable for a time. If a secondhand cot needs a new mattress because the original is badly stained, sags or fits too loosely, there may be a problem if it is not a standard size. British Standard BS1877 covers mattresses for children's cots and prams.

In 1977 a voluntary British Standard for cots was introduced. It condemned the use of transfers inside the cot. These are a common and often very attractive feature in old secondhand cots. They are particularly hazardous once they begin to flake and should be sanded off completely. On older cots toxic paint presents a very real health hazard.

A cot sold before the introduction of the standard may of course be perfectly safe and sound, but there is no way of being certain that it complies, and the risks are really too great. It is therefore sensible to limit the choice to those bearing the British Standard number BS 1753:1977 and the British Standard Kitemark. Foreign-made cots are not covered by the BS, and there are reports from the USA of buttons and fastenings on children's night clothes becoming entangled in the mesh fabric sides of certain modern cots: death resulted.

The sides of any cot should rise at least two feet (595mm) above the mattress base. The new British Standard stipulates gaps between vertical slats or dowels in the sides of between one inch (25mm) and two and a half inches (60mm), but slightly larger gaps are not a major hazard. There must be no splinters on wooden parts of the cot. Obviously a prime consideration is the overall stability of the cot. Once assembled, the cot should be rigid enough to rule out the possibility of collapse. This check is especially important with collapsible carry cots, which should be easy to fix in position, but quite rigid once secured. The handles of carry cots should also be carefully examined for signs of weakness. Shaky legs will rule out any cot unless the fault is clearly due to missing screws or nuts which will be simple to replace.

CHIMNEY POTS *see* Building materials

CHISELS *see* Tools

CIGARETTE LIGHTERS

Smokers run a high risk of receiving lighters every Christmas and birthday, which means large numbers of quite serviceable lighters come onto the secondhand market. Paying more than a few pence for an undistinguished lighter that doesn't work rarely makes sense. The cost of repair is usually enough to make secondhand buying a bad investment.

Some types of lighter are widely considered worth repairing. These include stylish table lighters of the 1930s, which were often made with a perfectly useless lighter in the middle. Old Zippo lighters are gaining in antique appeal, and their classic simplicity makes repair a straightforward matter.

Dunhill's will mend old Dunhill lighters, but they cannot guarantee a continued supply of parts. At present they have components going back to the 1930s, especially for the popular models. Chances are lower for models which had limited production runs, and parts cannot be manufactured for obsolete lighters. Some of these lighters are lovely machines, and it may well be worth buying a broken one in the hope of cannibalising spare parts from another to mend it. Dunhill operate a postal service, and estimates are free. Ronson also have spares for certain obsolete models.

Caution is required when buying more modern lighters. An almost-empty throwaway lighter is not much better than a box of matches, as these are not refillable. Oddly enough the Afghans and Czechoslovakians are eager to buy empty stick lighters, finding it worthwhile to dismantle, refill and rebuild them, but that's a long way to go for a lighter repair.

Check that there is a facility to refill any lighter, whether gas or petrol, and access to wicks, flints and wheels on traditional lighters. Wheels will probably need cleaning out with a stiff brush or glass paper, and if too worn they are usually an easy d y replacement job on both gas and petrol lighters. Wheel sizes vary, and some are no longer produced. On moderr lighters—apart from reissues of popular old models—the wheel has usually been replaced by a crystal or e ectronic ignition. As a new battery may be needed to get a spark out of these, the action can't properly be tested.

If the packing is missing from a petrol lighter, use rayon wool rather than cotton wool. A missing screw on the bottom can mean trouble on an old lighter. Even if the flint is worn down, the spring pressing against it should be there. Other parts can also be worn down, especially the link between plunger and pinion. The Lighter and Shaver Repair Centre in Oxford Street, London claim to be able to repair 95 per cent of all broken lighters that arrive in their shop.

CINE CAMERAS *see* Cameras

CIRCULAR SAWS *see* Power Tools

CLAMPS *see* Tools

CLOCKS

Time is running out for the clock menders of Britain. Along with the independent chemists and fishmongers, they are disappearing fast from the High Street. The arrival of the cheap and accurate quartz clock makes many of the mender's traditional skills redundant. It can be cheaper to replace a broken clock than repair it, and some of the surviving repairers simply refuse to mend the standard, old-fashioned alarm clock, relying exclusively on broken wrist watches for their income. At the same time, traditional clocks have become expensive antiques. Grandfather clocks are beyond the financial scope of this book, and the postman's clock and railway station clock are following the trend. Mantel clocks are a better buy.

Buyers without horological ability who are tempted by a lovely but broken clock should be warned: clocks may have fewer delicate parts than watches, but trouble is usually serious. Gamblers can buy pretty clocks which refuse to tick, hoping to buy new innards to match. This method is often successful, but clock parts tend to be in very short supply.

The fact that a clock works is no proof of its quality as a timekeeper. A poor clock which gains or loses time excessively may be beyond the limits of regulation. Without some knowledge of what makes clocks tick, there are no tell-tale signs indicating a bad buy. Movements can't be opened up and would in any case have little to tell the uninformed. The best approach in such circumstances is to buy on approval, for say a fortnight, making sure you have a receipt. Use the fortnight to obtain an estimate for repair and an opinion from a knowledgeable person. Such transactions are legally binding even in markets, though they rely absolutely on the seller sticking around long enough to make a refund possible.

Home maintenance of cheap clocks is possible with limited knowledge. Rust can be removed by rubbing parts carefully with fine steel wool soaked in rust remover. Movements can be cleaned by immersion for fifteen minutes in petrol, followed by an oiling with the special clock oil; oil should not be allowed to touch the cog teeth of timepieces, as it quickly clogs them up. Clockwork is not a difficult system to understand, and certain spare parts can be improvised by the inventive. A missing pendulum for a small wall clock, for example, can be replaced by hooking up a chain and weight, then adding a movable button which slides up and down the chain for fine tuning. A pendulum length of 39½ inches should give exactly one second between ticks.

Missing keys can often be duplicated by repair shops or model shops; even a radiator key may work. It could be simpler to make your own basic key from a piece of copper or brass tubing. The internal diameter of the tubing should be no greater than the diagonal measurement of the clock's winding spigot (the part the key will turn). Flatten one end of the tube with a hammer until it is square. To improve grip, cut a slot in the other end with a hacksaw and glue in a cross piece. Keys for old clocks are sold by specialists, many of whom advertise in trade and enthusiast magazines, such as the "clock mart" section of *Clocks*, which appears regular as clockwork each month. There you will find the addresses of experts to restore dials, supply parts, repair clocks and sell the tools for diy.

Specialist dealers' catalogues should alert buyers of secondhand clocks to some possible pitfalls; they may note for example that very convincing "old" makers' labels can be bought to stick inside a clock. Easily-fixed dry transfer dials are also on sale: "white, antique-stained or yellow-age" are typical shades on offer.

Electric clocks As with other electrical equipment, the flex of an electric clock should be examined for signs of fraying or looseness. Since 1975 clocks have been covered by the Electrical Equipment Safety Regulations. Among other sensible edicts, the regulations state that there must be no possibility of any tension on the cord being transmitted to the terminals on the clock. Pull the cord to check that it is held securely. Old electric clocks are often in a dangerous state, despite the regulations, and give easy access to live parts.

CLOTH AND HOUSEHOLD LINEN

Neatly-folded fabric can hide problems. A sheet, for example, is far more likely to be worn and dirty in the centre, where people sleep, and a tablecloth will normally sustain stains in the middle. Checking a secondhand sheet or tablecloth for stains, rips and wear is straightforward, but the chance of examining the entire length of a whole bale of cloth is slight.

Sale-by-sample rules apply in bale sales. The law says that any sample—and that would include the visible part of a secondhand bale—must correspond to the whole. Even this limited legal protection is missing at auction, where bale-buyers are on their own. An auction is unfortunately where most secondhand bales are bought, when clothing manufacturers go broke or sell off old lines. If the auction catalogue says that every lot is "sold with all faults and errors of description" or uses similar disclaimers, buyers must beware. The average buyer is more likely to be tempted by smaller quantities of fabric, a sheet for example, or a tablecloth.

If you buy a lovely tablecloth at auction which later turns out to be torn, it could be rescued—at a price—by an invisible mender. These worthy people appear as "Invisible Menders" in the *Yellow Pages*. The British Invisible Mending Service, 1 Hind Street, London W1, will use their skills on almost any woven or knitted fabric except chiffon, printed silk, velvet and corduroy, which are the hard ones. An alternative is to put the cloth to charitable use. Charities sell old cloth to the rag industry for recycling.

Old fabric may need washing, and an hour in the launderette could destroy it. Check for colour fastness first on a small, hidden area. A previous owner could have dyed the cloth badly, and it should not therefore be washed for the first time with anything else. Weak or fragile cloth can be protected in the wash by sewing it up in muslin bags. Old material shouldn't be washed in anything stronger than lukewarm water and liquid detergent or mild soap. Do not count on being able to remove stains from cloth. Stains can become permanent if they are allowed to dry out, and it is difficult to choose the right treatment when you can't be sure what caused the stain.

The colour may be uneven on old textiles, as they fade when left folded for years in the light. It is unwise to rely on being able to dye old textiles to a suitable colour. Man-made fibres are notoriously resistant to even dyeing. Only the natural fibres are suitable subjects for treatment, with wool and cotton best of all, though old cotton fibres are often too weak to take the strain of change. Results are normally happier if you dye to a darker colour. Few dry cleaners will take on dyeing jobs, but the Drycleaning Information Bureau will supply the names of some who do.

Sheets Sheets exist in a bewildering range of sizes, and a fitted sheet in the wrong size can be unusable. The only way to be sure of an old sheet's size is to measure it up. A sheet should be the size of the bed plus the thickness of the mattress plus about a foot all round for tucking. There should be no more shrinkage problems with old used sheets.

Genuine linen sheets are genuinely expensive, but they feel so luxuriously cool on hot nights that it is well worth hunting them out secondhand. They turn up regularly in auctions of house contents. Age need not spoil linen; its durability is proved by finds such as the quality linen in Tutankhamun's tomb. The pharaohs would no doubt have been less happy in old flannelette, which "pills" into little balls. The pyramid of old sheets in today's secondhand shop will probably contain the cotton/polyester easy-care mix which now dominates the market. Pure cotton is hard to find.

New sheets must be marked with the fibre content, but this useful piece of information is often missing from secondhand sheets. A visual examination of an unmarked sheet should quickly reveal whether it is made from spun yarn or a filament yarn. This is some clue to its content, as silk is the only non-synthetic filament yarn. However, confusion between silk and mercerised cotton or rayon is easy. Blends of different fibres are common,

and these can be extremely hard to identify.

If a sheet has no label, its content cannot really be judged by the feel. The wetting test can help identify linen, whose high flax content makes it absorb large quantities of water almost instantly. It is this quality which makes it so suitable for tea towels.

Mildew is a common problem with secondhand sheets. The entire surface should be examined for mildew marks, which can resist cleaning with anything milder than bleach, which is little use on coloured sheets. Strong bleach can weaken sheets, especially if time has already worn them thin. The old-fashioned cure for mildew is a dab of sour milk followed by a day in the sun.

An alternative to harsh bleach for dealing with light stains on white sheets is to dye them cream/beige by immersion in a bath of cold, strong tea. The very rich can use coffee. Stir the mix around to get an even colour. When the sheets look a shade darker than the colour you want, rinse them and dry. Keep them out of the white wash for months.

126

CLOTHES

Hand-me-downs and cast-off clothing cast off their undesirable image years ago. Now a fashion for old fabrics and styles boosts business for some very stylish secondhand dealers, just as quality-conscious as the best that Bond Street can offer.

Cast-off couture is sold by "dress agencies", who buy discreetly from the rich, then repair and clean their clothes carefully before reselling at prices beyond the pocket of the people. *Vogue* itself carries classified ads for the dress agencies, and the *Yellow Pages* list them.

At the other end of the *Yellow Pages* and the social scale are the "Wardrobe Dealers" and "Surplus Stores", and then come the unclassified jumble sales with their trestle tables piled high every weekend with cheap clothing, much of which needs the attention of a good tailor, some of which might be cut up and converted to patchwork or appliqué, furry cushion covers or jolly tea cosies. Old coats are chopped down by the gifted to make new waistcoats. Drab jackets are quickly enlivened by new buttons.

In between dress agencies and jumble sales are the less exclusive secondhand clothes shops, where buyers must often judge the suitability of clothes in low light levels and shops without changing facilities. Orderly racks of ironed clothes are sold by Oxfam's chain of excellent shops and Flip's fashionable London shops selling American clothes of yesteryear.

Clothes often feature at auctions, whether from the stockrooms of bankrupt rag traders or lost property offices. For obvious reasons lost property tends to be outer garments such as raincoats.

Clothes hire firms such as Moss Bros sell off formal wear whose hiring days are over. Such clothes will have received regular and expert attention throughout their social life. Similar guarantees apply to the theatrical costumiers who sell old and exotic costumes in which the famous may have perspired.

The fashion possibilities of secondhand clothing were promoted through the military surplus stores during the 1960s, in the peaceful days when khaki became just another colour. Now that the Ministry of Defence has cleared away the vast stocks of clothing left over from WW2, the surplus suppliers find stocks harder to replenish. However, the military are well treated all over the world, and good quality surplus is now on offer from Italy, Scandinavia and America.

The brief fashion for bright uniforms in the "flower power" age of the 1960s led to some unfortunate trend-followers being prosecuted for their secondhand clothes, since the Ministry of Defence frowns on the unauthorised wearing of buttons, flashes, regimental badges and insignia. It was not for this, old soldiers argued, that we fought in etc. The legal ban on military buttons remains.

Cleanliness is a major problem facing the buyer. On the positive side, the price will often be low because of an ugly stain which is easily removed. A knowledgeable buyer could therefore snap up a series of easy bargains, by knowing the secrets of stains and cleaning science. On the other hand, the most successful method of cleaning up spills and stains is to strike while the spill's still wet, before it even becomes a fully-fledged stain. This avenue is closed to the secondhand buyer. Indeed the stain problems are usually insuperable, as the buyer will not even know what caused the stain, and treatment for grease, wine and make-up is very different.

The secondhand buyer needs a working knowledge of the possibilities and limitations of the thousands of available cleaning products, services and methods. Dry cleaning can be costly, and it can destroy old and feeble fabric; the wrong solvent can damage any fabric. Fabric damage may have been inflicted by a previous owner's botched cleaning efforts. Incorrect cleaning may have shrunk the lining more than the rest, pulling the garment permanently out of shape. Other visible traces of past owners may fade from washable fabrics after a few hours soaking with an enzyme detergent. No woollen garment should be soaked; 'matted woollen jumpers are beyond rescue and can't even be unpicked to salvage the wool. A good dry cleaner can, if asked, deal with "white ring" perspiration marks.

Special fabrics and garments need special attention. Suede cleaners are scattered all over the country. One of the best known is Suede Services of London NW11; they operate a postal service for dirty skins and clean nothing but animal skin garments, though even they won't accept gloves, shoes and bags. However, they will tackle dirty pigskin, which few others will handle. The London Pigskin Company of 144a Royal College Street, London NW1 0TA are a famous exception. If dirt and grease have been left untouched on leather for years, they can penetrate the skin and be very tough to remove.

Moss Bros offer a tie cleaning service through their many branches. An alternative to the brothers is to wash the tie gently in warm water without squeezing, hang it to dry and insert a cardboard template inside the tie before pressing with an iron over a pressing cloth.

Information about specialist cleaning services will be supplied by the Association of British Launderers and Cleaners (ABLC), 319 Pinner Road, Harrow, Middlesex, HA1 4HX (tel: 01–863 7755). ABLC members give compensation if goods are damaged. The ABLC set up the Drycleaning Information Bureau (DIB) specifically to provide consumer information and advice on dry cleaning and dyeing services. They will supply the name of the nearest member cleaner capable of tackling any problem. Specialist services include cleaning silk, leather and ties, reglazing curtains and de-shining trousers. (It might be worth having a go on glassy trousers yourself, using very fine glasspaper.) The DIB's address is 178–202 Great Portland Street, London W1N 6AQ (Tel: 01–637 7481).

Cleaning can be complicated by the common lack of labels. The Home Laundering Consultative Council, 41/2 Dover Street, London W1X 4DS, has a free leaflet explaining the mysterious care labelling symbols used increasingly on garments. It is all but impossible to identify unmarked fabrics. Problems are less severe with clothes sold in Britain since January 1976, when new regulations obliged manufacturers to mark all textiles with the fibre content. The percentage of the main fibre is given, together with a list of others down to ten per cent, below which they qualify as "other fibres".

Lack of precise information about fabric make-up can close the dyeing option. The problem is that various fibres take dye differently, giving a speckled effect to mixed cloth which is probably unwanted. Stains are rarely removed by dye, and the stained section will take dye differently from the rest. Though diy dyeing of nylon is often very successful, acrylics and other man-mades are notoriously hard to dye. These problems can be a positive advantage during an examination of secondhand clothing, as uneven colour at the seam threads will betray a dyed garment. A sticking zip is another common result of dye. A garment whose colour-fastness is in doubt can be tested by washing just the belt, if there is one. Advice on dye comes free from the Consumer Advice Bureau at Dylon International Ltd, of Worsley Bridge Road, London SE26.

Women's clothes The smartest secondhand clothes will bear no size label, only the name of a famous designer, for these are the couture dresses made with a special client in mind. More information comes for less money lower down the market, until you reach the unlabelled home-made items.

Every square inch of secondhand clothing should be scrutinised. The clothes moth can leave holes in the most unlikely and embarrassing spots. Fabric under any lapels or pocket flaps should be lifted to check for colour-fading of the exposed cloth. The strength left in the fabric—especially the lining—can be tested by pulling gently, perhaps coughing to cover any ripping sounds; if it tears, make your excuses and leave. Should you buy a torn garment, invisible mending may be possible with iron-on interfacing fixed to the "wrong" side of the garment.

Perspiration may have marked or even rotted the fabric under the arms, a spot where broken stitching is also common. Other stress points for stitching are side seams and slits, but such minor faults need not deter buyers who can handle a needle, and they can lower the price. The same applies to broken, missing or unmatched buttons. More worrying is a mark where hems have been lowered and darts altered. Many signs of wear are obvious, for instance on collars and cuffs, but it is easier to miss marks where bags have rubbed consistently against coats and trousers.

Secondhand gloves may be put to odd uses. If too horrid for normal use, sturdy old gloves can be put to work in the garden or cleaning box. Haters of waste can also marry odd gloves or imitate the old practice of cutting off the tips of white kid gloves to cover wounded fingers—the rest was used to cover chapped hands in winter.

Fur is notoriously difficult to identify. If the price is high, only the expert should back his or her judgement. Even the catalogues of the regular fur auctions cannot guarantee infallibility, and there's no Sale of Goods Act protection in the saleroom. The uninitiated can make certain intelligent guesses about any fur. Natural furs will tend to be paler near the root, and of course the size of the pelt will depend on the animal who once wore it: foxes for example are long and wide compared to the mink, the mole or the rabbit.

Men's clothes Men traditionally change clothes less

WASHING	BLEACHING	DRYING	IRONING	DRY CLEANING
ᨈ	△	□	⟁	◯
DO NOT WASH	DO NOT BLEACH	DO NOT TUMBLE DRY	DO NOT IRON	DO NOT DRY CLEAN
HAND WASH ONLY	HOUSEHOLD BLEACH CAN BE USED	CAN BE TUMBLE DRIED	USE WARM IRON	CAN BE DRY CLEANED
2 60°	NOTE: the symbol on the left is for programme 2, one of the 9 washing processes explained on washing powder packets		NOTE: an iron with one dot means cool; 3 dots mean hot	NOTE: the circle may contain a letter A, P or F, depending on the solvent to be used

the international textile care labelling code

often than women, developing love over the years for an increasingly squalid jacket, keeping trousers till the backside wears to the smooth shine of a bald head, the knees bulge absurdly, and the pockets, if anything remains other than the holes, are badly stretched and frayed. Trousers may also develop what one dealer described colourfully as "crotch rot".

This male tendency to preserve clothes longer than the body that goes inside them puts the fastenings under great strain. Zips must be tested, hooks examined for stretched backing, buttonholes checked for strain and elastic tried for stretch. Zips can of course be replaced and elastic can be renewed—sew the new elastic, measured against the old in the garment plus join allowance, to the end of the exhausted piece to pull it through. Machine-stitched elastic cannot easily be replaced.

Secondhand shirts can be more satisfactory than new ones. If they are wearing thin, there are collar and cuff replacement services advertised in the national newspapers. Steven King of Lythgoes Lane, Warrington, for example, will bring new life to old shirts with a gleaming white collar and cuffs. Why, as Mr King's advertisement asks, bother with an "ordinary" new shirt at up to five times the price?

But the great advantage of the used shirt is the lack of packaging. New shirts come defended behind paper, plastic and an almost military array of hidden pins. Once released, the shirt may turn out to be quite wrong, with the sleeves too short, the cuffs too tight, and the body too bulky. The stated sizes of any new clothes can be very misleading, and are at best only a rough guide to which clothes might be worth trying on. With the secondhand you have the chance to try them all on.

Children's clothes Kids grow faster than clothes wear out, and at the same time kids are demanding and getting expensive fashions rather than cheap and practical tradition. This expensive combination of events has encouraged the development and use of "nearly new" shops selling high quality clean clothes on behalf of parents whose kids keep on outgrowing their clothes. Such shops normally hold stock for two months. If a garment is sold during that time the shop keeps a third to a half of the price as commission, the rest going to the parent.

A slightly different operation — hand-me-down clothes clubs—involves a group of parents in regular meetings to swap and sell their children's clothes. Good organisation and advance pricing seem to be crucial to avoid squabbling over relative values.

Activities often centre on school uniforms, which are both horrifically expensive to buy new and grossly underused before the child grows out of them. Some schools help hard-pressed parents by selling well-pressed uniforms at hand-me-down stalls set up at school bazaars and parents' evenings. The school normally pockets a small commission, and the parent saves about 50 per cent of the new price.

Although old name tapes are cut out of the clothes, some parents still feel there is an unacceptable stigma about secondhand clothes for their kids. Oddly enough, this feeling is commonest among the parents least able to afford shop prices.

Beware of old nightdresses, bought before the laws covering flame-resistance of girls' nightdresses were introduced in 1967. Nothing prevents a parent buying an unprotected garment abroad and selling it secondhand later. Home-made nightdresses may also be nonresistant. To prevent strangling, cord-fastenings have been outlawed since 1976 on all garments under 44cms across the chest.

Shoes Children's shoes are so expensive that they are a great secondhand temptation. The temptation is best resisted, although wellington boots may be all right if they are still watertight. Sports shoes are worn for so short a time that they present little danger of deforming little feet.

Secondhand shoes have a reputation for deforming even adult feet, leaving them scarred with athlete's foot and corns. Only if shoes show no sign of wear should purchase be considered, for both health and financial reasons, as shoe repairs have become very expensive. Before road testing any shoes, they can be flexed to test for (or cause) split soles. Look also for high heels leaning to one side or inwards, as repair may be impossible.

Rags Beyond the limits of the acceptable, clothes become rags, but a brand-new suit may in a real sense be "secondhand clothes". Wool merchants buy bales of old clothing from specialist rag dealers who buy rags by the hundredweight from the shrinking army of rag and bone men, tatters and totters whose horse-drawn or hand-pushed carts patrol the inner suburban streets. Mixed with new wool, and re-spun, an old sweater is transformed into a new garment. The totters' cotton rags are washed and cut into squares to be used in industry, appropriately enough as cotton rags. Synthetic garments are little loved by the rag dealers.

COFFEE GRINDERS

A coffee grinder's only purpose is to grind coffee beans into a powder of the desired degree of coarseness. The only valid test of a secondhand grinder therefore requires a pocketful of beans.

If the grinder is electric, check before grabbing it that there are no potentially lethal chips and cracks in the plastic base holding the motor. The stability of the flex can also be checked over, bearing in mind that flexes are often dragged quite violently from the wall socket outlet.

The blades of an electric grinder can work loose, rendering the machine useless. This condition may only be temporary if there is a nut holding the blades which can be tightened, but once blades held by a rivet work loose, the grinder is not worth buying. Other parts can easily be replaced if the model is still manufactured.

Mechanical grinders are adjusted by a screw with slotted edge: this may be seized up. Look inside wooden or metal drawers for signs of decay.

COFFEE MACHINES

Coffee percolators are reliable and long-lived. However, it is advisable wherever possible to put a secondhand percolator through its paces, even if no beans are on hand, to make sure it is capable of heating water, circulating it and then storing it at a high enough temperature.

Failure to heat could simply indicate a blown fuse in the plug or a faulty flex connexion. Both these faults are put right easily and cheaply, but the problems would be more serious if the heating element had blown, to be suspected if the pilot light comes on while the plate fails to heat up. A continuity test is necessary to diagnose the fault, and a new element may be needed.

If the coffee/water is not warm enough, there is probably thermostat trouble. A simple adjustment may rectify the problem, and broken thermostats are rarely hard to replace completely, unlike the more inaccessible element. An inability to pump the water around the percolator is normally explained by a sediment blockage in the basket or the tube carrying water from the pot to the coffee grounds. These are easily cleared out and need not put off a bold buyer.

Alternatively, a clogged or worn washer may need replacing. The entire inside of a secondhand machine may be encrusted with old coffee grounds, and in hard water areas there could be furring inside the percolator. This is cleared by a proprietary descaler available from hardware stores. Old grounds should be cleaned out to stop the coffee tasting bad.

An alternative to the percolator is the electric filter machine, in which water is heated by an electric element and then passed along a tube to drop through the ground coffee waiting in a filter paper and funnel poised over a jug. The jug stands on a hotplate (make sure this heats up) to keep the coffee warm once it is made.

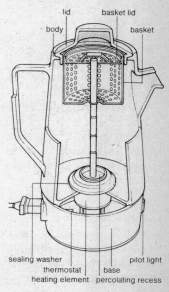

lid   basket lid
body   basket

sealing washer   pilot light
  thermostat   base
heating element   percolating recess

The most dramatic flaw in a filter machine is a missing jug. Replacements are normally available, and an exact fit is not absolutely crucial. More irritating is a cracked hinge on a plastic jug lid, which makes operation fiddly.

The jug may be clouded up with furring, which may also have clogged the element and by making the appliance inefficient may have prompted the sale. Furring is not hard to clear away. Before buying a proprietary descaler, it is worth trying to clear the problem by running the machine with a mixture of white vinegar and water, following it up with two clear runs of water to get rid of the vinegary smell. At all events, scale needn't tip the scales against purchase of a secondhand filter machine.

A secondhand appliance would be a better bargain if filter papers and a measuring spoon were included in the price. These are worth asking about.

COMPANIES

Banks and suppliers are often happier giving credit to a company—however unstable, insolvent or dishonest—rather than to the most industrious and sensible of individuals. Large cheques from a limited company's bank account are happily accepted by suppliers, who will offer discounts on demand and even offer time to pay. All this tempts many people into forming their own limited company.

Setting up a company yourself is a tedious and rather unnerving experience, especially with limited knowledge of company law. Buying or selling a secondhand company which has been involved in active trading for years is not a complex affair, but caution is needed. Basically the transaction just involves the shares being sold to the purchaser. Legal advice is advisable, as lawyers can avert the danger of buying a company with bad debts.

Any would-be director with a history of bad debts may himself be barred from directorship, as undischarged bankrupts cannot buy a company without special permission from the court.

Perhaps the best compromise, costing only a few pounds more than a diy job and taking only half an hour once a few simple documents are completed, is to buy a company someone else has set up but which is guaranteed never to have traded. These "instant" companies are much loved by international banks and similar enterprises who suddenly need a limited company for a particular transaction. They are sold by operators listed in the *Yellow Pages* under "Company Promoters". *Exchange and Mart* also features a few. They carry stocks of names suitable for most trades, and availability is immediate. All the prospective company director needs is one other person to be either co-director or secretary, and about £100 in cash. Two shareholders are demanded by law, but the individual retains absolute control by keeping all the shares but one.

You can't choose the company's name if you use this avenue of ownership, but the name chosen by an individual founding a new limited company could be rejected by Companies House as being identical or too similar to an existing company. The name may just be on the "disapproved" list, which includes Royal, King, Queen, British, National, International, Commonwealth and Co-operative. It is unwise to have the company stationery printed before the name is registered.

Always read the print—it's all small—on any information or forms you are sent, to make sure you understand what is being bought, what your obligations are and whether there will be any extra charges for services such as searches. Never allow a sentence to pass by undigested. They are all there for a reason.

COMPUTERS

The price of new computers keeps on tumbling far faster than depreciation can reduce the value of old ones. In this way the micro-electronics industry defies the logic of a secondhand market. Each new model represents a genuine improvement on the last—for once the classic claims of any manufacturer about new products' virtues are true.

This should have condemned the secondhand market to a desperate position somewhere between depression and non-existence. However, the market in outmoded computers remains lively, and buyers are not limited to obsessed enthusiasts and far-sighted scientific museums. The secondhand computers are put to work in their old age. Even the government, through its advisers at the Central Computer Agency, is a major buyer and user. Underlying government interest is the familiar problem of spare parts and servicing. Vast numbers of ageing government computers can only be kept working by cannibalising others less fortunate. Buying secondhand can save money. After only four years' use a machine may be sold at half the price of a comparable new model. However, there are problems.

It is absolutely crucial to contact the manufacturers before buying any computer, to drag some definite servicing and maintenance undertaking out of them. Machines are normally maintained by the original manufacturer, but old secondhand equipment tends to be given a very low priority on the servicing schedule. Such problems may intensify in the mid-1980s when ICL stop servicing many older models.

Alternative arrangements can be made with one of the independent computer maintenance companies, but their charges can be horribly high, pushed even higher if you can offer work on only one small and inconvenient computer. So important is the maintenance question that it has become a major influence on price, as influential as the arrival of a new and improved model to replace an older one.

Dealers in secondhand computers rarely provide maintenance, nor do they deal in software, so buyers must know their needs precisely before entering the market. This is not a market for the ill-informed. To be reasonably sure of finding a reliable "box" to fill with software, cautious buyers use dealers who have their own engineers and workshops, where equipment can be tested, repaired and generally revitalised, despite the manufacturers who often prove obstructive about access to manuals and spare parts. A typical workover may involve renewing the plastic case, taking advantage of the strip down to wash the mechanics and bake the lot in a dehumidifying oven.

Besides the stock of specialist dealers in secondhand

computers, mainframe computers are often sold through the computer magazines, when a company updates its computers to cope with newer data processing needs. Such advertisements usually invite the interested buyer to join in an auction and are of interest only to the enthusiast. The primitive monster computers are often extraordinarily cheap, but their demands on the power supply can push up an electricity bill to dizzy heights. Hobbyists often buy these ancient machines to rip out a few useful parts, selling off the heavy remainder as scrap.

On the rapidly expanding home computer front, classified advertisements are placed by amateurs in specialist magazines such as the monthly *Personal Computer World*. However, by the time the ad appears, cheaper new models may be in the shops.

Pocket calculators There is no established market for secondhand pocket calculators, although desk models frequently appear in the catalogues at auctions of office equipment. Pocket calculators have become thinner and smaller than they were. Both these desirable features make the calculators more likely to be squashed in a pocket, and only a flat calculator is likely to work.

Early calculators—and today's cheap ones—usually have a red LED display visible in the dark. This type eats batteries too fast to be a bargain. Modern low-power LCD displays are a better buy, with batteries lasting perhaps a year. Non-standard batteries can be hard to find.

The manufacturers' instruction booklets are usually so mystifying that their absence is not a serious drawback. Test all the features, which may include memory, clock, calendar, stopwatch and alarm.

CONTINENTAL QUILTS

Continental quilts are still enjoying a boom in the British bedroom. Few have reached the secondhand market yet, where the buyer of bedding is more likely to find the blankets which were thrown out when the new quilt arrived.

The most fundamental information about any secondhand quilt is the type of filling used. This is the major influence on price. The lightest, warmest and most expensive filling is pure down; a mixture in which down is dominant is labelled "down/feather" and should be more expensive than the so-called "feather/down" filling.

Man-made fibres are cheapest of all, and have a further advantage in that they can be washed. Natural fillings cannot.

If the label is missing, the most reliable method of identifying the filling is to open up a corner of the duvet and have a look inside. The colour of the filling is no real help in identifying it, but the shape is. Down has no quills and looks like dandelion seeds or snow flakes. It is also very light. Fluffy feathers with springy quills are much to be preferred to coarser kinds.

It is often not possible to carve holes in someone else's quilt, but some information can be gleaned from giving any duvet a firm squeeze: the absence of quills on down gives it a very soft feel, whereas the undesirable curled poultry feathers feel uncomfortably sharp and lumpy.

A further guide to quilt quality is the method of construction. The most popular

type for all-round warmth has a cover with walled channels rather than seams joining top and bottom, as these lead to cold strips. If the label is still there—and if it's the right one!—it may give the British Standard "tog" warmth rating. The coolest rating is 7.5, moving up to 10.5.

A torn and filthy duvet is best rejected. Replacements for stained and soiled cambric cases can be bought and fitted but they add considerably to the overall cost of the venture.

All secondhand duvets benefit from a lengthy airing before use, but complete cleaning is seldom vital. Synthetic fillings can be put in the washing machine—if they fit—but cleaning the contents of a feather or down quilt calls for an expert. No quilt should be put in a coin-op dry cleaning machine, as the potentially lethal fumes tend to linger, and down may be harmed. The Drycleaning Information Bureau knows companies who will tackle the work.

The same organisation can locate companies converting old eiderdowns into new duvets. Old eiderdowns often look decidedly tawdry and may be very cheap second-hand. Advance Laundry charged some £20 for a 1980 conversion job, the price including, within reason, the cost of extra filling.

A specialist cleaning and renovation service is provided by the German Bedding Centre at 138 Marylebone Road, London NW1. Their method involves sterilising the filling by an attack of ultraviolet light. They claim that a duvet conversion represents a saving of up to 50 per cent on the price of a new quilt. In other words it is a very false economy to pay half the price of a new duvet or more for a secondhand eiderdown.

Pre-war eiderdowns almost certainly contain nothing but down, and post-war ones are equally surely filled with coarse-quilled, rigid, curled poultry feathers or a feather-and-down mix. Buying duck down to replace discarded feathers may make a conversion uneconomic. Feather cushions are useless for duvet making as they are usually made of poultry feathers.

CONVECTOR HEATERS *see* Electric fires

COOKERS

Electric cookers are large but simple appliances, problems are generally few, and repairs are cheap. The largest expense the buyer is risking is normally the cost of installation: a cooker needs its own circuit going through a cooker panel to its own fuse, and home wiring costs can be very high. Failure to install a separate circuit will almost always lead to a series of blown fuses or worse. Dramatic faults inside the cooker are uncommon, but it is wise to have any newly-bought secondhand cooker serviced and reconditioned by a good electrician.

Reconditioning cookers is easy work for a smart electrician. Buying a reconditioned cooker from an established dealer in electrical appliances should therefore guarantee satisfaction. Dealers selling secondhand appliances can offer as wide a selection of cookers as many shops selling new equipment. The buyer could choose among the double ovens, eye-level grills, self-cleaning facilities, automatic timers and drawers for keeping the plates warm.

Buying a split-level cooker

may mean redesigning the kitchen, and both the cost and availability of oven housings for a particular model should be taken into account by anyone unprepared for diy carpentry, especially if the cooker is obsolete.

Wherever possible it is reassuring to have a limited life guarantee, lasting perhaps six months. This is long enough for any serious faults to show up. Non-specialist dealers seldom give guarantees. Private sales are particularly dubious, as few familes sell the family cooker before it is utterly worn out. Moreover, buying from a private individual leaves you with minimal legal protection.

Most cookers have a hard and dirty life, so they are usually well-etched with signs of wear and tear. Things you can easily check include chipped enamel surfaces, rusty metal on shelves and trimmings, loose or squeaky door hinges, scratched glass on doors, even a missing glass door inside the oven.

Other parts liable to be missing are grill pans and shelves. Replacement shelves may be tricky to find for old cookers of odd sizes. None of the miracle oven cleaners is quite as good as an advertiser might hope, so greasy grills are common and hard to clean.

The oven may be tired after slaving away as a hot stove. As ovens grow older, so they grow colder, and it takes them longer to heat up to a normal cooking temperature, although that doesn't prevent them burning up electricity all the time. If you can test the cooker in action, heat it to its minimum temperature and then see how long it takes to reach cooking temperature. Really accurate temperature checks can be made by "baking" a reliable oven thermometer and seeing whether the chosen temperature is reached. Some expensive oven heat may be felt escaping around an ill-fitting door, a problem not unknown with new cookers. Door hinges are often strained on drop-down doors after years under heavy weights. The springs are easily replaced on many models.

Overheating usually indicates a fault in the thermostat or switch, both of which are simpler to have replaced than repaired, although certain oven thermostats have an accessible adjusting screw.

If the oven won't heat at all, the element or thermostat probably needs replacing. If parts are available it is often easy to disconnect an element from its leads and earth cable and replace it. Make sure no washers and nuts are left off during reassembly. The oven thermostat sensor tube should be seen inside the oven near the top of the back panel. If it is cracked or fallen from its clip, it won't work.

Cooking rings grow slow in old age and should all be tested out, not only for their ability to heat but also for their ability to cut out when the desired temperature is reached. If a ring fails to heat at all, the problem could be the element itself—which is usually a simple diy replacement job once an identical replacement element has been bought from a repair shop or the electricity showroom. Try a continuity test on the old element before wasting money on an unnecessary replacement. The main difficulty in

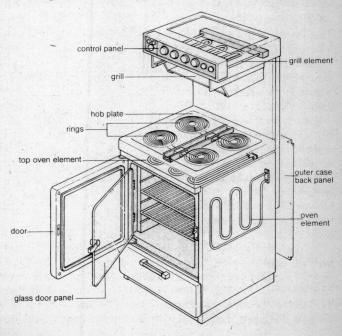

control panel

grill element

grill

hob plate

rings

top oven element

outer case
back panel

oven
element

door

glass door panel

removing an element is often hacking a way through years of congealed grease covering the terminals. Remember to disconnect first.

Defective wiring is not a likely explanation for ring failures, although connections occasionally work loose at the element. Often the top cover of the cooker will lift off to give a look at the wiring: look for corrosion and loose wires.

The switch may also be at fault. This is by no means a tough repair job but is one usually requiring the manufacturer's manual. During disconnection of the old switch, be sure all wires are wrapped with marked masking tape to make reconnection possible.

Check that any hob lights and oven lights work. Problems can probably be traced to an easily-replaced, burned-out bulb. Watch an automatic timer going through its paces, as the clock and switches may have gone utterly haywire.

Very modern electric cooking appliances are harder for the non-expert to examine. Microwaves, for example, cannot be seen escaping from a damaged microwave

oven. However, it is simple enough to test the cooking power of such a machine, as they plug into a normal power socket and cook food so fast that a practical in-store demonstration is perfectly possible. Nevertheless, buying secondhand is widely considered to be risky.

Ceramic hobs are less menacing than microwaves. It is important that the surface should be clean and absolutely smooth to the touch. If too abrasive a cleaner has been used, the surface may be damaged.

Cooker hoods The family defences against smelly cookers have been reinforced recently by the cooker hood, not yet a common secondhand article. Some are merely extractor fans leading outside, while others hover over the cooker and recycle the smell-laden air. A new filter or batch of charcoal is all most used hoods need to restore their strength.

Gas cookers There are real dangers in careless buying of secondhand gas cookers. British Gas figures show that over half the accidents caused by faulty appliances can be traced to secondhand equipment. The chance of a safe buy is higher from a specialist dealer who will offer guarantees covering safety and efficiency. Safest of all are the reconditioned appliances sold by gas showrooms.

Don't use a lighted match to test a suspect secondhand gas cooker for leaks. In doubt, turn off the gas supply at the main tap near the meter, open the window and have the appliance checked over, either by the gas board or by a gas installer displaying the CORGI sign of competence. A CORGI-registered installer will check the appliance out at the time of installation. If leaks don't stop when the main tap is closed, call in the gas service centre immediately. Competent consumers can locate leaky pipes and joints with a little washing-up liquid put over a suspect spot: if bubbles come through the froth, there's a leak.

It is not only dangerous to use a faulty appliance, it may also be illegal under the Gas Safety Regulations 1972, which cover secondhand appliances and installations. Compliance with the law can be guaranteed by having any newly-bought used appliances serviced by a gas service centre or a CORGI-registered installer. Old or disabled people living alone can have a free safety check of gas appliances arranged by the social services department.

Proper installation is important, and it can add noticeably to the cost of an appliance. A cooker may seem cheap, but if it has a rigid pipe connected to the back, the installation costs will be several pounds higher than for a self-sealing, plug-in flexible connection, and it is illegal to make the connection yourself. Diy installation is both allowed and easy with a flexible connection. Use no installer who will not give a guarantee.

At installation time it is wise to check old domestic gas pipes. Rats find tasty gas pipes handy for teeth sharpening. The high lead content makes pipes softer on the rodent dentures, though it might lead to brain damage. This gnawing is a fairly common cause of gas leaks.

Satisfactory examination of secondhand gas appliances is normally impossible, as they are not connected up. For this reason a warranty is crucial. Only when the cooker is connected up can the operation of grill, burners, oven and thermostat be properly tested. Many cookers converted to natural gas during the dark days of the early 1970s just go out irritatingly often. Many of these are understandably sold off second-hand, so be careful of buying one of the sturdy pre-war cast-iron models.

Several points can be checked before connection. Damage to the casing is easy to see. Small chips can be covered by heat-resistant enamel paint or the entire cooker can be sent to the local garage for a respray. Look at enamel surfaces inside the oven—damaged or rough surfaces are hard to clean and are no longer properly protected against heat. Pay particular attention to the surface just above the back burner in the oven, feeling for roughness on the metal. Close the oven door on a piece of paper and try to pull the paper out—the seal should be strong enough to hold it firmly.

Operate every control to make sure it moves. Dirty burners are usually simple to clean out, but if the cooker's burners or the stands on which pans sit are missing, check with the manufacturer or the local gas showroom that replacement parts are available. The manufacturer is also the source for the instruction booklet, which may be unavailable for obsolete appliances. Gas showrooms can supply manufacturers' addresses. The showroom can also tell you whether a BSI Safety Mark was attached to the cooker when it was new. British Gas recommend buying only appliances with this label.

The most common problem is a faulty pilot light. Pilot jets are often clogged up with the grease of spilt dinners. Any gas showroom should have supplies of simple probes—"primus prickers"—to clean out dirty jets. Jets can be damaged by clumsily handled needles and pins. A stiff brush or a matchstick are standard and effective tools for cleaning out burner holes.

(*See also* Microwave ovens.)

CRICKET BATS

Despite such recent developments as a polyurethane coating designed to extend the life of the blade, cricket bats are made in the time-honoured way, of willow with a cane handle. But balls have changed. All except the most expensive balls are harder than those assaulted by W. G. Grace, and impact force is now quite capable of smashing through an immature modern bat. Old bats, when well cared for and regularly oiled, grow more resistant to damage, toughened by the combination of linseed oil and many seasons of use. Such bats are very desirable objects, but they are also uncommon. Old cricketers keep their bats.

Visual examination can reveal a lot about a used bat. A good, strong bat will still be smooth-faced, with a close, straight grain running up the face. Only bad bats have knots. Butterfly marks are not considered important.

Poor players make heavy use of the bat's edges, which are the weakest points, and this abuse can lead to cracks down the grain. Splits can develop if a bat is stored away for years and allowed to dry up. On old bats the rubber grip may have perished or split or become hard and smooth. Grips are very easily replaced. Handles can come apart or grow weak at the rubber splicing. If the handle is in good condition and the blade bears no signs of dryness or excessive blemishes, the bat has probably had a good life. Rough, cracked and dry bats are bad buys. When bats break up, the process normally involves odd bits of wood falling from the surface rather than complete disintegration. Bats can be effectively repaired by experts, who can fit a replacement blade or handle.

A bat must have the right balance and "feel" for the individual player. The correct size of bat should reach the bottom of your hip when held vertically against your leg. The correct weight and width are matters of personal strength and preference.

CROCKERY

Some couples are loaded up with a complete dinner service at wedding present time. Other people can indulge in a delightful lifelong hunt for secondhand plates, building up their own esoteric and unmatched cupboardful of appealing oddments. These will be found piece by piece in weekend jumble sales, or in the boxes full of ordinary saucers and unmatched eggcups lying outside most junk shops. Cheap and jolly items can be bought and brought back from foreign holidays. Auction rooms too are rich hunting grounds, where boxes of unclassified crockery are a common lot. Buyers with a little knowledge can readily find cheap, unnoticed antique plates in junk shops and on market stalls, but the uninitiated should never rely on the information given by the marks under a plate. These are notoriously hard to interpret accurately, and also notoriously misleading.

The market is rarely the place to buy cheap new reject crockery. Seconds from unknown manufacturers are a bad gamble, as the glaze is often very faulty. Market stalls are usually the last clearing house for "The Lump", the true garbage crockery on the reject side of seconds.

Sets of old plates, indeed whole dinner services, are simple to find and remain much cheaper than new articles. They are often identical to new ones, for the pro-duction life of a crockery design can be very long, making it possible to replace any missing items which bring down the secondhand price.

Standard items in the junk shop now date from the 1960s. Many of these designs are very dated, though not necessarily undesirable. Many 1960s designs are still current. For example, Wedgwood's parade of best sellers in 1960 was led by Gold Florentine, with Edme at number 2, Turquoise Florentine at 3, Summer Sky 4, Hathaway Rose 5 and Lichfield 6. Only Summer Sky and Lichfield were discontinued by 1980.

At Johnson Brothers, the 1960 Top 4 were Friendly Village, Coaching Scenes, Old Britain Castles and Indian Tree, all under-glaze prints, and all selling just as strongly twenty years later. Other 1960s favourites are now around in vast numbers—Doulton's classic design Tumbling Leaves was wildly popular, and their Burgundy pattern sold 643,975 pieces. By the time Doulton's bone china Coronet was made obsolete in 1979, 250,000 pieces had been sold. Royal Worcester's Roanoke, introduced in the

1940s austerity period, was still selling well as Britain entered a new depression.

Complete services can be built up piece by piece. The very enterprising China Matching Service exists to help owners of incomplete and obsolete china services find the missing parts, whether it is just one cup, a lid for a vegetable dish or a few saucers. For a fee (£3 in 1981) your name and requirements are put on the register for six months. The service is definitely not limited to the costlier and antique items. Indeed, chances of success are highest with post-war services and well-known names such as Royal Doulton and Wedgwood. Most enquiries come from people who bought sets in the 1950s and 1960s, smashed part of them and found the manufacturers unable to supply replacements. The China Matching Service is run by Margaret A. Janes from Tamarisk, Warren Road, Kingsbridge, S. Devon.

It is difficult to know precisely what makes up a complete service in any particular design without consulting the manufacturer's original catalogues, and old catalogues can be very elusive. Six place settings is commonly quoted as a standard set, but the contents of the place setting vary from pattern to pattern. Most secondhand buyers rightly consider such matters unimportant.

The fundamental principle of buying any set is to examine *every* item for damage, allowing no lapse of concentration. Only a very foolish dealer would put the most cracked, chipped and faded plate on top of the pile—the most obviously damaged articles are usually hidden on the bottom.

Repairs can be hard to spot before the plate falls apart in warm water. An instant check for cracks is to tap the piece lightly with a coin: a dead sound means a crack. Discoloured cracks can be broken apart, cleaned up and reglued but this, like other repairs, is only worth undertaking if you enjoy the job, as it is long and delicate. Old glued cracks can be opened up by a soak in warm water or a dose of acetone (nail varnish remover), meths or white spirit. When the edges are cleaned, put a thin film of epoxy resin (Araldite) on the surfaces to be joined and hold them together with gummed paper laid in strips across the join—the strips will shrink tighter as they dry.

Badly crazed crockery is unhygienic, as bacteria lurk in the cracks and cleaning is ineffective. A glaze is glass, and cleaning cracked glaze is as fruitless as cleaning cracked windows. The only permanent solution, and an extremely impractical one, is to refire the piece. However badly the glaze is crazed, it should never lead to a plate going soggy in the washing-up bowl. Bone china has an almost gloss-like impenetrability, and water should never get inside, but porous earthenware can develop stains under the glaze which are impossible to clean out.

Bleach can be used to clean up crockery which won't carry food, but before assaulting a plate with the bleach bottle, try washing it in liquid detergent and hand-hot water, which will do the crockery no harm and may clear the grime. Grease will come off with meths or white spirit, but this treatment can leave brown stains behind. Bleach, on the other and fiercer hand, can even remove an old and faded pattern painted over the glaze. Tea leaves leave tea stains on cups, mugs and tea-pots—this brown tannin can be shifted by a soak with a special stain remover such as Chempro T, which works on glass and melamine as well as crockery and metal. If there are any false teeth in the house, try the denture cleaning tablets before buying new cleaners. If there's a toothless baby in the house, try sterilising fluid (but not on metal).

It can be difficult to tell whether a pattern is under or over the glaze. If it is hand-painted, an over-glaze can be felt, but if applied by modern lithographic techniques the layer will be too thin to feel. Colour then becomes the only guide: delicate colours, feathery strokes and gold are typical of over-glaze painting. This type of old crockery is particularly likely to be damaged by the very hot water used in dishwashers, and the harsh dishwasher detergent.

Dubious china can be made safe for food and drink by a dose of the solution used to sterilise babies' bottles, but such treatment won't neutralise a heavy metal. The Glazed Ceramic Ware (Safety) Regulations 1975 lay down the limits of lead and cadmium in articles used for food, but even these do not apply to "artistic" pieces or anything over 100 years old. If there is any doubt, a plate can be wired up and hung on the wall as a decorative object hiding a damp patch.

CURTAINS

Curtains spend their time hanging around windows, where the full force of sunlight can fade the fabric. This can be a hard fault to spot while the curtain is still up, but it should become obvious when the entire curtain is laid out flat in good natural light.

Fading and wear are most likely to occur near the edges where greasy hands pull them, and at the hems, where they rub against window frames, walls and floors. These are very convenient positions to have any stains, as it opens the possibility of buying cheap, damaged curtains too large for your windows and cutting off the damaged edges. This method should also cope with the common problem of water damage along the lower edge of a sill-length curtain, where condensation has dripped down the window and soaked into the fabric.

Draping may be improved by weighing down the curtains with weights hung in lead-weight tape inserted along the bottom of the hem.

If a curtain has been stored for some time in a junk shop or left in an attic for years before finally being unloaded onto the secondhand market the exposed surface may have faded, it will probably have noticeable creases and stains along folds and will certainly need cleaning. Cleaning can be pricey, and the likely cost should be known before buying secondhand.

Dyeing is possible as long as the curtains have not deteriorated through over-exposure to the sun. The strength left in the fabric can be tested by flexing the material. A good lining will have minimised damage from light as well as increasing the curtain's insulating properties. A good lining is a considerable advantage in secondhand curtains. Detachable linings can be fitted at home.

Dye should not be relied on to restore whiteness and brightness to grey net curtains made from synthetic fibre. There are proprietary remedies such as Glowhite and white nylon dye, but success is far from guaranteed.

A different treatment which may be worth considering for any curtain is fireproofing, though this may affect the colour of the curtains. Any local fire protection department should supply enquirers with approved recipes for home-made flame-retardant treatments.

A final cheap alternative for desperate privacy-seekers in old houses with vast windows is to abandon curtains completely in favour of shutters. Many old houses still have their shutters, hidden away behind the plaster and wallpaper. They exclude draughts, keep in heat and don't look as genteel as even the greyest of net curtains.

CUTLERY

Bent forks and blunt knives are rarely worth buying, however lovely, but ordinary secondhand cutlery can be a very good bargain. All junk shops seem to have a box of unassorted and very cheap cutlery, much of it solid and sharp, even if undistinguished. The high price of ugly new cutlery should convince the cynical that secondhand articles are good value. A rapid rummage through the box usually provides a matching set for only a few pence per item.

Without a little knowledge of hallmarking, it is easy to pay too much for secondhand cutlery as makers' marks can be deliberately deceptive. The manufacturers' marks on much plated cutlery look convincingly like silver marks. If an item doesn't have the *Lion Passant* symbol on it, it is not sterling silver. The definite guide to silver is the two-volume *Jackson's Silver,* which covers the subject exhaustively into the 1960s. A guide for quick reference is Judith Bannister's *English Silver Hall-Marks*. The guides make it possible to pinpoint maker, year and town of assay.

Discoloured blades can be too pricey a problem to overcome. Any cutlery marked "EPNS" (for electro-plated nickel silver) should be checked for signs of tarnish on parts of the base metal—usually nickel—where the silver plating has worn away. The only satisfactory remedy is replating, and this can be a very costly process. The price of replating varies with the price of silver. If just one piece is replated it will look dazzlingly shiny in the service, and show all the other pieces up.

There are many qualities of EPNS, but there is no universally recognised standard. The "A1" mark just means that this is the best grade produced by that particular manufacturer: "A1" has no official status as a grade. Quality of plating varies dramatically, and the durability of silver plating could be anything from five to thirty years.

Damaged chromium-plated cutlery is a bad secondhand buy unless you consider the cutlery has some unrecognised antique value. It will cost more to have it replated than to buy a brand-new set of stainless steel cutlery. "Stainless" is a slightly misleading name. Stainless steel won't rust, but it will certainly stain. Stains can normally be removed by Goddard's Stainless Steel Care, available from hardware stores. Silver polish can spoil the stainless quality.

Dull steel can be cleaned up with washing-up liquid applied with very fine steel wool (Grade XXX or XX) in a circular movement; Brillo pads are quite acceptable.

Rust spots can be rubbed off non-stainless steel by fine emery paper. It is unwise to try to avoid future cleaning by an application of rust preventative—these are toxic and best reserved for use on bicycles and the like. Ivory handles can work loose when hot water melts the old glue holding them in place. Refixing is simple. Discoloured ivory may be bleached clean with lemon.

Blunt knives can be sharpened. This is an easy diy job using any of the standard knife sharpening tools, but serrated knives present a problem. The "Cutlery Merchants" category in the *Yellow Pages* is the one to check out for sharpeners—many merchants will tell you it is impossible to find people to do the job, others will just quote a price for the job and get on with it. £1 or less is the 1980 price for a bread knife. The franker sharpeners will confess that sharpening slowly destroys the serrations. Diy sharpening is possible: sharpen one side only, the side away from you when the knife is held in the right hand. Using a good steel, draw the knife firmly but carefully across the steel at an angle of 45° or less. This should prolong the life of a stainless steel knife by a few years.

It is hardly worth buying bent knives, twisted forks and dented spoons — they are really too hard to straighten convincingly despite the confident assertions of the diy manuals.

D

DECKCHAIRS
see
Garden furniture

DISHWASHERS

Secondhand dishwashers are tricky machines to judge. Like televisions, they have most of the important mechanism shut away inside the case. Unlike televisions, they can't just be switched on to see if they work. There are several distinct operations in the washing cycle, as the machine starts, fills, heats the water, washes and dries the dishes and finally stops. This full cycle can last 90 minutes, and few sellers can reasonably be expected to put the dishwasher through its paces every time a prospective buyer shows up.

Dishwashers are not noted for reliability, very few do-it-yourself dishwasher repairs are easy, and major parts are very expensive. A replacement motor, for example, may cost £50 before labour costs and VAT are added. Broken elements, thermostats, pumps and timers can all be costly. Buying blind, without seeing the machine work, is therefore risky. Risk can be minimised by buying from a reputable specialist dealer selling reconditioned machines with a guarantee. Sale of Goods Act rights are valid in such transactions, and a dealer should have complied with the relevant safety regulations, which cover all secondhand appliances sold in the course of business. The regulations do not apply to deals between friends or through private advertisements in local newspapers or the newsagent's window.

Many machines will not be plumbed in for the viewing, making leaks hard to spot. Perished pipes may be visible at the back of the machine, and it is safe to assume that the hoses inside are no better than those on view, though they may well be worse. Leaks are likeliest at joints and points where hoses are kinked. Traces of dried-up trickles may be seen on dusty hoses.

The door seal should not be flattened, torn, loose or rotten. The hinge on a front-loading machine should keep the door tight shut. Hinges are often ruined by the weight of plates placed on them. Rust will also attack them.

A rusty case is a bad sign, for the case holds the machine together. Signs of rust and chipped paint could show inside or out. A look behind the machine should provide an opportunity to test that a floor-standing machine rolls around easily on its casters. Inside the dishwasher, the rollers and guide tracks for the trays should be in smooth working order. All the trays should be there—any doubts about the correct number should be resolved by a look in a similar new machine or the manufacturer's handbook. This is a useful booklet, explaining for example how to load the machine with dirty dishes and which type of detergent to use.

There could be unwelcome traces of hardened detergent clogging up the detergent dispenser, which may indicate a negligent owner. The level of filth in filters can give a clue to the treatment a dishwasher has enjoyed. If there is a waste trap inside the machine it can be lifted out and inspected for traces of old dinners. The waste filter at the back of the machine can also be checked. Blockages are not hard to clear. The holes in the rotor spray arm may be blocked with food, but these can often be cleared with a pin.

Secondhand plates should not be put in a secondhand dishwasher, as old hand-painted porcelain was not designed to cope with harsh detergents and high water temperatures. Some plates won't even fit in a dishwasher, so take your largest plate to the viewing and try it for size. Painted or lead-crystal glassware should also be kept out of the dishwasher.

DOGS *see* Pets

DRESSMAKING AND KNITTING PATTERNS

Fashion regularly turns to the past for new ideas. Home dressmakers and knitters can go direct to the designers' source of inspiration by digging out the original old patterns which often stand in dusty piles in charity shops and junk shops.

The first paper pattern to be marketed was cut out and sold by Ebenezer Butterick over 100 years ago. Vogue Patterns, which began as part of the magazine, have been run as a separate enterprise since the 1930s. The earliest Vogue patterns you might find therefore date from this period. The Vogue Patterns operation was sold together with the rest of the Condé Nast organisation in the 1950s, and the new American owner resold it to the American company Butterick, who kept the name unchanged. Other American patterns of the period are Simplicity, McCalls and, of course, Butterick themselves.

Pre-war patterns tended to assume a lot of dressmaking skill, and they can be tough for the ordinary person to use successfully. In the 1960s there were dramatic improvements. Secondhand patterns made since then should be quite straightforward to work from, but remember that tolerance of fit changes with fashion and accompanies changes in styles of underwear. The general emphasis in recent years has been on loose and comfortable clothes, whereas twenty-five years ago people wore their clothes tighter, and dresses featured lots of figure-hugging darts. The secret lay underneath, where women wore corsets. The dress was fitted to the corset rather than the body squeezed inside. Secondhand corsets may be on sale.

The switch from imperial measurements to metric is no cause for worry, as modern dressmaking patterns have not really changed unrecognisably. The sizes of new patterns remain as they were (10,12,14 etc.) rather than using continental sizing systems. It is unwise to attempt to mix imperial and metric measurements in the same pattern. Imperial conversion charts appear in the back of the Vogue pattern books.

Secondhand knitting patterns should present no great problem. Indeed, many of the most popular knitting patterns today are only slight adaptations of 40-year-old originals. Emu claim their patterns improve over the years: as users point out sources of confusion, so the phraseology is made clearer.

Metrication has made the knitter's life slightly more awkward. Wool is now sold by the gram, whereas weights are given in ounces in old patterns. Conversion is not difficult, and any local wool shop should be able to advise. The shop can also supply exact metric equivalents for imperial knitting needles.

Older patterns nearly always use woollen yarn, either 3-ply, 4-ply or "double knitting" wool. The 3-ply is hard to trace nowadays, but the other two are readily available. About ten years ago the manufacture of fashion yarns, sold by name only, began. As these are often phased out after as little as two years on the market, there may be severe problems in finding the correct yarn for a comparatively recent pattern. It is important to use the type of yarn the pattern recommends. Most of today's knitting yarns have a recommended needle size on the label. Choose a yarn made for the same needle size as that given in the old pattern. Patterns give a tension guide: knit a sample square to check that the yarn is suitable. Changing needle size will adjust tension.

If you manage to find a batch of secondhand wool, be sure to buy enough, as you can't always go back for more!

DRILL BITS *see* Tools

E

ELECTRICAL APPLIANCES

Secondhand electrical appliances are potentially lethal. Nine times out of ten a broken appliance will be suffering from mechanical rather than electrical problems, but just switching the tenth one on could give you a nasty shock.

Electrical faults are among the commonest causes of domestic fires. It is therefore not surprising that the Electricity Council and the Royal Society for the Prevention of Accidents advise the public to "steer clear of buying appliances secondhand". Their advice seems unnecessarily cautious, but it is certainly risky to buy an untested secondhand appliance from a dubious dealer.

The safest dealers in secondhand appliances should be the Electricity Boards. Policy on secondhand sales varies from region to region, but any used appliance sold by the board will have been thoroughly checked, cleaned, reconditioned and tested before being offered for sale with a solid guarantee. Specialist electrical retailers may offer guarantees on little-used appliances, but buyers are usually unprotected from broken or dangerous appliances at auctions, where there is rarely a chance to see the appliance working before the bidding begins. Although legal protection is minimal in private sales, at least the appliance is likely to be wired up, plugged in and ready to test.

Faced with the problem of examining a used modern appliance of unknown origin, the buyer will find the task grows tougher year by year. It grows with both electronic sophistication and the number of working parts hidden from view. When electronic controls replace traditional switches on new appliances, do-it-yourself fault diagnosis and repair become harder. However, growing sophistication has steadily improved the performance of electrical appliances. The transistor, for example, is more durable than the old-fashioned valve.

Even obsolete electrical appliances are now covered by safety regulations.

These govern the sale of secondhand appliances, including those made before the regulations became law. However, buyers would be unwise to believe that safety regulations have put an end to the sale of unsafe appliances. The regulations do not even try to regulate private sales, and many secondhand dealers know nothing about regulations; others just ignore them. A Salisbury dealer, cautioned in 1979 for selling an allegedly unsafe fire, could only grumble about being set up by "a pretty girl from the Trading Standards Department". Antique dealers often try to sidestep the regulations when they sell objects such as unearthed metal art deco light fittings, by claiming that the lethal fittings are just decorative antiques which are not meant to be used. Junk shops keep Trading Standards Officers busy looking for dangerous electric fires and other old appliances which fall short of modern safety standards.

Secondhand dealers will hesitate to volunteer false information about their goods. It is therefore worth asking if an interesting item complies with the safety regulations. A test by a qualified electrician is a better guide in a private sale, but this is rarely practical.

Dangerous appliances flooded into Britain after World War 2, and many of these are still sold secondhand. The safety standards for new appliances have been consistently improved since 1960, when the British Electrotechnical Approvals Board (BEAB) approval scheme began, with the first safety accolade going to the Russell Hobbs kettle. Tests on sound and vision equipment started in 1971. Samples of any approved equipment have been tested for design, construction and durability of safety features. The scheme is voluntary. All BEAB approved appliances conform to British Standard BS3456 for electrical safety of household appliances (or BS415 for tv sets and sound equipment). Unfortunately the BEAB mark, like the safety regulations, can't guarantee that secondhand appliances are still safe. Bad maintenance or incorrect use can sabotage any safety system.

The safety regulations are useful in that they have outlawed some specific danger points. These points are worth checking out on any secondhand appliance. For example, the 1976 safety regulations say that when a lead (flexible cord) is pulled, this should not put any tension on the terminals connecting the flex to the appliance. Look for loose connections where the lead joins the appliance. The flexes on vacuum cleaners and floor polishers are often damaged by tugging. The flexes on irons are more likely to be frayed by years of rubbing on an ironing board edge or by being wrapped around the iron while it is still hot. Look out for broken insulation and signs of crushing and always replace a damaged flex.

The Consumer Protection Act 1961 makes it an offence to sell electrical appliances— including secondhand ones— with three-core flexes in any colour combination except brown (live), blue (neutral) and yellow/green (earth). The old standard was red, black and green. Two-core flexes should be used only with double-insulated equipment.

The Electrical Research Association believes there are about 70 million dangerous plugs in the UK. There is no point in bringing home one more. Chipped or cracked plugs must be changed. Before plugging an old appliance in, check that the wires inside the plug are securely connected to the right terminals, and held by a cable grip. Old round-pin 2amp, 5amp and 15amp plugs will not fit modern sockets.

The appliance should be protected by the right fuse, which will be 3amp for appliances with a rating below 720 watts, and 13amp for ratings between 720 and 3,000 watts. The rating should be marked on a plate fixed to the back of big machines or underneath small ones. Don't buy an appliance if the rating plate has gone. It tells you the frequency of the supply in cycles per second, which varies from country to country (the British standard is 50c/s). The plate also gives the voltage and tells you whether the appliance is AC/DC or AC only. The local electricity board showroom can give the details of the local supply.

If an appliance doesn't work, the trouble may be a broken fuse. A simple test for fuses involves a metal torch. Remove the torch base and touch one end of the fuse on the metal torch body, the other on the battery base. Now switch the torch on—if the torch and fuse are working, the bulb should light up.

A circuit tester will be needed to check for broken wires. An inexpensive multimeter can be bought for the purpose, but a basic tester can be improvised using a 4½-volt or 6-volt battery with screw terminals. Connect a length of insulated two-core lighting flex to each terminal, and fix a crocodile clip on each free end. A torch bulb mounted in a bulb holder should be cut into one of the flexes. To test the continuity of a wire, connect one of the clips to the end of the wire near the plug; when you touch the other clip on the same wire at the appliance end, the bulb should light up.

The circuit tester will check the all-important earth continuity. Attach one clip to the plug's earth pin, and touch metal on the appliance body with the other clip: if continuity is correct, the bulb will light up. If the casing of an appliance is cracked or broken, avoid it, as metal could get inside the appliance and cause shocks.

On certain appliances, you can also test a switch with the circuit tester. Unplug the appliance, attach the clips to the live and neutral pins of the plug and switch the appliance on and off: if the circuit is all right, the switch will control the light, unless resistance in the appliance is too high.

To check a heating element, touch both ends of the element with the clips: if the element is burned out, the light will not work.

Even such safe and basic tests on an unplugged appliance deter most people. Confidence can be found in experience. Besides the local authority evening classes introducing the public to the mysteries of electricity, there are several useful publications from the unique and admirable Electrical Association for Women, 25 Foubert's Place, London W1V 2AL (tel: 01–437 5212). They produce a leaflet called *Common Sense and Electrical DIY*, run a course in "Electricity for everyday living" and publish a cheap and highly informative book of the same title; this gives a comprehensive explanation of the way most domestic electrical appliances work.

The Mutual Aid Centre (MAC), set up in Hackney in 1977, has pioneered community workshops for maintaining and repairing household appliances and furniture. The first Domestic Appliance Repair Workshop opened in Shrewsbury in 1979, providing members with the right tools and equipment for the job, plus expert tuition and advice from three skilled instructor/technicians on the premises. The instructors work at recycling discarded domestic appliances and furniture. This is the main activity in "Brass Tacks", opened by MAC in April 1980 in Hackney. Renovated appliances are sold in a shop on the Brass Tacks premises.

It is sensible to examine old electrical goods before buying. Heavyweight and bulky appliances can't easily be carried back to a repair shop, and call-out charges have grown very large. Some repairmen have stopped repairing small appliances altogether, claiming that it is cheaper to buy a new appliance than pay for a repair to a broken one.

Disappointed buyers of

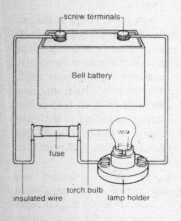

simple improvised circuit tester

faulty appliances should not aggravate their problem by calling in an incompetent repair service as an alternative to diy. Only qualified repairers such as the electricity board, recognised electrical retailers, manufacturers or their agents should be allowed anywhere near broken appliances.

Independent repairers tend to get appliances working faster than the manufacturers or the even slower electricity boards. The average repair takes a week if spare parts are readily available. A shortage of spares can put a good but incomplete appliance on the scrap heap. Before attempting any diy repair, ask the manufacturer if spares are still available. The only information the manufacturer should need in order to give you a verdict is the serial number marked on the rating plate fixed to the back or base of the appliance.

The Association of Manufacturers of Domestic Electrical Appliances (AMDEA), to which most British manufacturers belong, has responded to the public discontent about lack of spares by recommending minimum times for maintaining stocks of spares after an appliance goes out of production. Their recommendations cover "the reasonable life of the product". The electrical and mechanical parts without which the thing won't work safely are called "functional parts": these are to be kept as follows:

Cleaners
Direct acting heaters   8 years
Refrigerators and freezers
Spin and tumble driers

Cookers
Dishwashers
Washing machines   10 years
Water heaters

Small appliances 5–8 years

Non-functional parts, which are decorative and inessential, should be kept for not less than four years. Once these times have lapsed, all is not lost. There are firms specialising in spares for obsolete appliances. They normally supply trade only, so you may need a cooperative retailer.

The AMDEA code also says that no new appliance should be sold without explanatory literature about installation, use, spares availability and

163

guarantee terms. This literature may be available from the manufacturer. The most useful information for the diy repairer is hidden in the manufacturer's manual. Many companies refuse to supply manuals to the public, despite a call from the Price Commission for an increase in diy repairs.

The basic toolkit for diy electrical repairs contains a soldering iron, cutting knife, adjustable spanner, hacksaw, long-nosed pliers, wire strippers and continuity tester. Without an ability to handle these tools and a bit of mechanical aptitude, repairs are best left alone. Any job requiring special tools is usually uneconomical for the handyman, and television repairs are best entrusted to the professionals.

Rule number one of electrical diy is to unplug before you do anything. Before plugging back in again at the end of the repair, make a habit of checking earth continuity. Put one clip of the continuity tester on the plug's earth pin, and the other on any metal part of the appliance. The light should come on.

Merely opening up an appliance can be a long and frustrating job. There are so many ways of fixing panels in place, and it is often impossible to identify the method used before you make an awkward mistake.

The usual range of diy work goes from checking the electrical connections to replacing elements, switches, brushes and flexes. If a new flex has to be fitted, make sure it is the correct rating for the appliance.

Enamelled panels are often chipped when you buy goods secondhand or when you attempt repairs. Chipped or rusty panels can be resprayed by garages, where several coats of paint will be baked on. The choice of colours is vast. Home resprays usually leave the panel with the orange peel look.

A separate entry covers each of the various types of electrical appliance.

ELECTRIC BLANKETS

Electric blankets start fires and kill people. It is safer to fall asleep at the wheel in the fast lane of the motorway than to take your chance on a secondhand electric blanket. Problems come with age, when insulation starts to wear thin and heating wires inside the blanket are bent. This often occurs when the blankets are folded up for summer storage and creases become set in the wires. When the blanket is unfolded, the bent wire snaps. Any secondhand blanket which has been left folded under a pile of heavy bedding is a definite hazard. Feel for bends and breaks along the whole length of the heating element. A new element is too expensive to contemplate.

The manufacturers insist on the crucial importance of servicing every couple of years to check the condition of the blanket and prevent accidents. Almost nobody bothers to take their advice. Since half the beds in Britain are warmed up in winter by an electric blanket, there must be millions of unsafe nightspots in the land. Some of these lethal blankets will be on sale secondhand.

A basic overhaul by the manufacturer is a good investment costing only a few pounds, but this may still be enough to make a secondhand blanket a bad buy. When the life expectancy of even a well-serviced blanket is only about seven years, poorly-maintained secondhand blankets are obviously a foolish purchase.

There are certain signs of a particularly bad blanket. One worrying signal is the old British Standard number 2612, which became obsolete in 1963. Any blanket bearing this number should be destroyed or completely rebuilt. The material will have been chemically fireproofed, but the design is obsolete. This is unfortunate, as the material used in the 1960s was often superior to today's. The latest British Standard is BS3456.

Among other visible signs of decay, scorch marks are only marginally better than bare wires; frayed edges and worn fabric also mean a service is overdue. By holding the blanket up to the light, it may be possible to spot wires which are out of alignment.

The blanket is kept from creasing dangerously during use by tapes fixing it to the bed. No blanket with missing tapes is worth considering.

Like other used bedclothes, secondhand electric blankets are likely to look squalid, and cleaning is both difficult and potentially dangerous. Dry cleaning can be lethal, as the cleaning fluids may attack the insulation. The manufacturer can usually clean used blankets, and should also be able to supply home laundering instructions. Overblankets may be safe in the washing machine, but they have to be stretched back to their original size before they dry to prevent wires becoming dangerously twisted. This could easily have happened with old blankets.

Manufacturers can be traced through AMDEA, 593 Hitchin Road, Stopsley, Luton, Bedfordshire. Old blankets can be posted off complete with controls for examination and overhaul. Two companies handle most makes: CEBRA, 261 Queen's Road, Halifax, W. Yorkshire (tel: Halifax 67544); Johnson and Calverly, Brook Street, Elland, W. Yorkshire (tel: Elland 76320). They can bring some ancient blankets up to present standards. For example, a blanket with an element stitched unacceptably to the inside of one of the panels can be modernised by machining tunnels into the fabric. If the material is not fireproof, the blanket is best destroyed before you are. If a repair would be expensive, both companies will ask for approval before going ahead. Postage can be expensive, and there may be handling charges to pay even on a condemned blanket.

ELECTRIC CASSEROLES

Slow-cooking electric casseroles give little trouble, but an inefficient casserole could just be cultivating salmonella in your lunch. The casserole cooks at low temperatures over long periods, so a practical cooking demonstration is not possible. Furthermore, some do not have indicator lights to prove they are switched on, so it can be hard to tell if an old one works.

The commonest fault is a burnt-out heating element, which cannot easily be replaced at home. The element can be looked over for signs of a break by removing the centre screw holding the appliance base. A simple circuit tester will diagnose element damage. Before plugging a casserole into the mains, make sure it is safe by checking the earth continuity. This is done by attaching the terminals of the circuit tester to the plug's earth pin and the screw on the casserole's base. A breakdown could be caused by a faulty connection at one of the plug terminals or at the casserole end of the flex. Casseroles should never be plunged in water, and clumsy owners who have dropped them in the sink could have caused a short circuit.

A casserole's ceramic lid or bowl could be cracked or chipped, making it a bad buy. Lids are particularly easy to break, so check spares availability with the manufacturer. If food is stuck inside the bowl, don't buy the casserole, as cleaning can be tough if the bowl is scratched by abrasives.

Frying pan An electric frying pan should be simpler to check out than a casserole, as indicator lights are standard and cooking temperatures are higher. A family would have to fry themselves to the verge of heart disease before a new electric frying pan could pay for itself in fuel saved, but a cheap secondhand appliance could be a bargain. If there is a non-stick surface, feel it for roughness. A BEAB safety mark is reassuring.

Give the pan time to overheat—if it gets too hot, the thermostat or control unit are damaged and the pan is not worth paying for. Look for signs of overheating or meltdown on feet and handles. If there is no heat, the heating element could be broken.

ELECTRIC FIRES

Old electric fires don't necessarily die, they may just fade away. Fires will burn up the same amount of expensive electricity for ever, but the amount of heat produced can be cut dramatically just by a poor reflector. Cleaning a reflector is usually straightforward, but a previous owner's bungled efforts with an abrasive cleaner will have destroyed the reflecting surface. Non-abrasive cleaners such as Duraglit are the right kind to use.

It is easy to buy a dangerous secondhand bar fire, as even a lethal fire will probably work well enough to convince the naive buyer. Safety regulations have been introduced to protect the consumer, and these regulations will cover secondhand fires sold by dealers. Nevertheless the Institute of Trading Standards Administration still finds a need for periodic statements warning against the purchase of used bar fires.

The law says that the regulations apply to all goods, even those made and sold before the regulations came into force. Experience, on the other hand, says that many secondhand fires are sold by dealers blissfully unaware of their obligations, ignorant of the law which makes the sale of unsafe fires a criminal offence. Many secondhand fires are older than the regulations and were made in the days of more lenient legislation. Unless they have been reconditioned, such fires are potentially unsafe.

Further problems arise with fires sold privately, as these are outside the scope of the safety regulations and may quite legally be lethal.

The combination of professional ignorance of the law and private unconcern puts lives at risk. Despite being a grossly expensive form of heating, electric fires tend paradoxically to be used by the poorest, oldest and most vulnerable people, who haven't either the capital or the long leases needed to make the installation of a more efficient heating system worthwhile.

The clearest indication of a primitive fire is a fabric-covered old flex. These fray easily, and the rubber insulation inside is often truly rotten. The flex on any fire should be examined, bearing

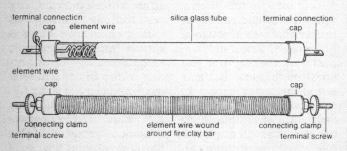

a modern glass tube element (*top*) and the older fire clay and spring element

in mind that fitting a new one or having a dubious one examined by a competent expert will add noticeably to the cost. It is not sensible to buy and fit a flex yourself unless you are certain you know the right type to buy.

Chances of a bad buy can be cut by checking that the guard conforms with the Heating Appliances (Fireguards) Regulations 1973. Fires which predate these regulations may not have been adapted to prevent any possibility of contact with the red-hot element. A nursery guard is a good companion for a secondhand fire.

If a bar fire doesn't work because of a broken element, you can take a chance of being able to find an exact replacement. All elements can be taken out by the competent and checked with a multimeter. Elements can be found to fit most old fires if you shop around.

The type of element will give some clue to the fire's age. Modern elements are enclosed in a glass tube, and these are easily replaced. It can be harder to find the older type which consists of a cylinder of fire clay with a long spring wound around it. Even more difficult to replace are the oldest type, made of moulded fire clay with long springs wound *inside*. With this kind, check that the element is firmly in place: cracked or broken clay will not give enough support to the element. New supports can be hard to find for any old fire. Sparks or signs of charring around the ends of the elements suggest that a replacement part is needed.

Convector heaters—a class which embraces fan heaters—do not have red-hot elements, but the heat is nevertheless provided by elements, and these may blow. A convector could contain several elements, so a partially broken fire will not necessarily run stone-cold.

Replacement elements for convector heaters are not very easy to find. In most cases a faulty convector heater will need a professional repair, and that can be very expensive. If there is a thermostat or switch, these must be fiddled with to make sure they still control the fire. A thermostat's efficiency can be checked by switching on a radio next to the fire and turning the thermostat control until it cuts in or out: a neat click should be audible on the radio. If the noise is a lengthy buzz, the thermostat is probably about to fail.

Because of their very heavy fuel consumption, electric fires tend to be very cheap secondhand buys, especially if they lack the guarantee of a specialist electrical dealer. Bargains are found, for example a convector heater with no greater problem than a broken fuel effect lamp, but the possible dangers built into secondhand fires should never be ignored. Nor should the bills to follow.

ELECTRIC FLOOR POLISHERS *see* Floor polishers

ELECTRIC FOOD MIXERS *see* Food mixers

ELECTRIC FRYING PANS *see* Electric casseroles

ELECTRIC SHAVERS

Never buy an electric shaver —or any other electrial appliance—sold as "flood damaged", as the Electrical Safety Regulations exempt goods damaged by flood or fire. Shavers are swallowed up by floods surprisingly often, as this catastrophe includes such accidents as a fall into the wash basin or the loo on a numbingly cold and tired morning. The subsequent damage is virtually the only fault which can put a shaver beyond repair, as water penetration can lead to rusting in parts which don't normally get wet. Other faults can usually be put right unless the shaver is an obsolete model for which spare parts are unobtainable. When a particular model is withdrawn, the manufacturers undertake to provide spares for ten more years. This could make a 15-year-old shaver irreparable, although specialist repair shops, found under "Electric Shavers" in the *Yellow Pages*, may have the necessary parts in their store. The Electric Razor Hospital at 491 Commercial Road, London E1, for example, is forced to turn down only one broken shaver in every three or four hundred. Repair will include a service and carry a six month guarantee.

A service every couple of years is a sound idea: current cost is about £4. No normal repair to a secondhand razor will push the cost above that of a comparable new one. Shavers are not suitable for diy repair work, mainly because of the problem of getting spares from the manufacturer. However, the owner can keep his shaver clean to prevent accumulated dust from accelerating wear.

Only a limited examination may be possible before buying the shaver. In such cases try to buy the appliance with a guarantee giving any faults enough time to show. Otherwise come to an agreement with the seller that you can return the razor within a fixed period—two weeks should be enough—which gives you a chance to take it in for an estimate for any repairs.

It is not sensible to buy a shaver with certain obvious faults such as a cracked case indicating a hard landing at some time, or corrosion eating away around the batteries in cordless shavers.

Shavers are often pulled rather harshly from the shaver socket during the morning rush in the bathroom. This may loosen or split the cord—test it by plugging in, waggling it around near a switched-on radio and listening for the crackling noise which indicates intermittent connection.

The shaver will be protected from damage in the future by its case; this should be included in the package. Certain cordless shavers have rechargeable batteries, and the mains charging unit should not be missing. The head assembly may have its own cover. Without any cover a foil head can easily be dented, making replacement necessary. New replacement covers and cleaning brushes for routine maintenance can easily be bought.

The cutters on almost any secondhand shaver are almost certain to be blunt. Cutters shouldn't be changed in isolation, as they are ground to match an individual grille. Damage to a grille will normally show up as a high-pitched whine which stops when the grille is taken off.

EXPOSURE METERS *see* Cameras

EXTRACTOR FANS

An electric extractor fan is an electric motor driving a set of blades which are housed between two grilles. The fan is usually operated by a pull-cord switch, which may also operate shutters over the inner grille: these close to prevent draughts when the fan is not in use. The switch should control the shutters on a secondhand fan even if the appliance cannot be plugged in.

Fans are usually employed to clear the kitchen air, and even the cleanest kitchen can generate ounces of greasy filth over the years. Much of this hits the fan, and sticks. In time it can glue up the shutters; besides looking and feeling very unsavoury, the filth impairs the fan's efficiency by preventing the motor cooling properly. Eventually a clogged motor may burn out. No fan is worth buying once the motor is dead, as this is almost the only component.

A bent or broken blade presents a noisy problem on old fans by throwing the mechanism out of balance. Broken blades condemn the fan to the scrapheap, but an attempt at straightening bent ones is worthwhile if the fan is very cheap indeed. Test for bends by placing a point lightly against the back edge of one blade and rotating the blades: each one should just. stroke the point as it passes. Realignment should be attempted by hand pressure, and not by using a hammer.

Home maintenance will be limited to an annual dose of heavyweight oil. More extensive diy repair is a waste of time for all but electrically competent enthusiasts.

F

FIREPLACES *see* Building materials

FISHING TACKLE

The construction of a fishing rod is simple: a cork handle and rod rings are attached to a length of split cane, fibre glass or carbon fibre. A modern angler would pick up a greenheart split-cane rod with the same nostalgic reverence as a photographer handling a pinhole camera; both represent the roots of their art, before technological advances improved user control and end results. Cane rods may turn up on the second-hand market when the original owner is converted to fibre glass, but most old anglers will treasure their split cane rod even when its fishing days are over. An intimate understanding can build up between an angler and a well-used cane rod. You have to play the fish according to the strengths and flexibility in the wood grain, which varies from rod to rod with the way the wood is lashed.

A "set" (kink) in a split-cane rod is supposed to be a bad sign, and should certainly bring the secondhand price down. However, rods are made to catch fish, and the set proves that the rod has caught more than a few. As the set should not impair performance, a split-cane rod with a set could be a bargain.

Only a historian of river-craft would prefer split cane to fibre glass, which is undoubtedly a better material for the purpose. Before fibre glass appeared, anglers experimented quite successfully with tank aerials instead of split cane. Since solid fibre glass rods first swept the market, there have been two worthwhile developments—hollow fibre glass, which is an excellent all-round material, and the very expensive carbon fibre, which is virtually indestructible, with very high tensile strength. Carbon fibre rods are the best for tackling the heavy fish such as carp and pike.

Rods rarely break in use, as the line will break first, but hollow fibre glass rods need to be examined carefully for cracks, as they can easily be damaged in transit. Cracks may not be evident until the rod is flexed. The bend in a secondhand rod could be tested by pressing it against the wall in the corner of a room.

The rod rings which hold the line must be examined on every used rod; if the whipping on the rod rings is worn, a repair will be needed. An agate inner lining on the rings is a desirable feature, as long as it is not cracked.

The old-fashioned centre-pin reel has been almost completely replaced by the fixed spool. The crucial element in a fixed spool reel is the slipping clutch, which must be checked for smooth running on a secondhand reel. Beware of any reel showing signs of corrosion due to salt water attack. The famous names such as Intrepid, Mitchell and Abu all offer a good back-up repairs service. Spare parts may be unavailable for foreign makes.

FILES *see* Tools

FLASH ATTACHMENTS *see* Cameras

FLOOR POLISHERS

Even secondhand, an electric floor polisher is a luxury, genuinely of use only to those with acres of polished floors. Secondhand polishers share the problems of other electrical appliances—the plug fuses blow, the flexes work loose, switches stop functioning, motor windings burn out and motor brushes wear away. A faulty motor can cause poor polishing, but a more likely cause of poor performance on the floor is a worn set of polishing brushes. These are easy to see underneath the machine and easy to replace as long as spares are still available. A polishing machine uses two types of brush—a scrubber and a buffer—and both

should be supplied with a secondhand appliance. If the brushes are damaged and distorted, the polisher will be very noisy.

A broken drive belt can be hard to replace if you don't know exactly how it fits in the machine.

A secondhand appliance would probably benefit from a little lubrication before being put to work. The cover can be removed to clean out accumulated dust and lint. Washing usually improves the brushes.

FOOD MIXERS

An electric food mixer is basically a traditional egg beater with an electric motor replacing wrist-power. A fan is added to keep the hot spots cool. Some mixers are handheld, but others are sold complete with stand and mixing bowl. With free-standing mixers check that the bowl is free of chips and cracks. Bear in mind that an accident could leave it smashed before it reaches its new kitchen and the manufacturer may no longer supply replacement bowls.

The beaters themselves are easily bent by high-speed im-

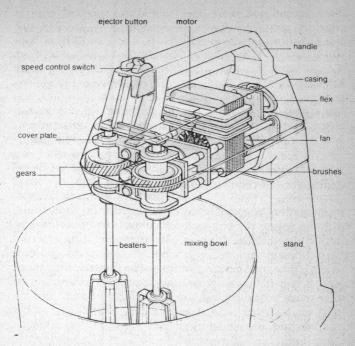

ejector button   motor

handle

speed control switch

casing

flex

cover plate

fan

gears

brushes

beaters   mixing bowl   stand

pact against the side of the bowl or stones in the cake-mix. This problem takes approximately two seconds to put right as long as spare parts are obtainable, but as beaters can't be straightened, a lack of spares means the machine is useless.

Distortion of the beaters is often apparent only with the machine plugged in and switched on. The on-off switch normally gives a choice of three speeds, though infi-nitely variable switches are fitted on some models. All three speeds should be tried, preferably with something in the mixing bowl to give the machine a fair working trial under load. A machine with a broken switch is not worth buying, as professional repair will be necessary and costly.

Mixers are tough machines, but they are widely abused. For example, if the power cord is dragged from the wall socket by hauling on the mixer rather than the plug, the connections may be pulled loose. Unfortunately, it may be necessary to remove screws and lift the case off in order to check over the connections at the mixer end. Loose connections can be "heard" by waggling the flex near a radio with both machines switched on and listening for tell-tale crackling on the radio.

Those confident enough to lift the casing off can look inside the machine; a neglected mixer may contain enough food for a family dinner. It is particularly important to keep the fan clean. Kitchen debris can also clog the bearing on which the bowl turns; this is easy to clean out and lubricate.

Cooks in a hurry often send the machine whizzing at maximum speed through everything. Others force the beaters to do battle with food too heavy even for a motorway cafe, and this can strip the gears or damage the motor. Once gears are worn, the beaters will stop turning under load, even though the motor still works. Damaged nylon or plastic gears are cheap and easy to replace, but once the motor goes, the machine goes with it.

Before a broken machine is discarded, it may be worth examining the carbon brushes. If they are worn down to less than about half an inch, this could explain the breakdown. Exact replacements are just dropped into place.

The owner's manual is a useful guide to a secondhand mixer, as it gives the correct speed for different kinds of operation. If it is available, the buyer can follow its step-by-step operating instructions to test the mixer out. It will also illustrate the various accessories which should be part of the sale. If any are missing, the mixer may not be such good value compared to the price of a new one.

FREEZERS

Freezers don't often go wrong, but they sometimes make too much noise if they are kept in the kitchen. Noise can be cured by tightening loose compressor mountings or merely by adjusting the position of the freezer so it is level on the floor.

Freezers are kept cool by a thermostatically controlled electric motor driving a compressor, as in most refrigerators. Although the freezer is a more powerful machine than the fridge, potential problems are identical. The commonest problem is a leak in the sealed system causing a loss of refrigerant, a problem beyond the scope of the handyman.

Perhaps the best precaution against a faulty freezer is to insure the contents! (*See* Refrigerator.)

FURNITURE

Secondhand furniture has been a very good idea for a very long time. In 1894 *Spon's Household Manual* informed its Victorian readers that "Secondhand furniture is often preferable to new.... The price, in comparison with that of new, is often much less than the amount of wear and tear would indicate." A certain amount of wear and tear is usually evident on the faces of people buying new furniture before the goods are delivered. Months can drag by between ordering a brand-new sofa and taking final delivery. A recent Code of Practice for the furniture industry could only suggest morosely that "the retailer should check the delivery position with the manufacturer from time to time." When at last the new furniture comes, it is often depressingly dented and scratched. Secondhand furniture presents no such problems. It is there to see, at a price decided on the spot, and delivery is immediate if you can arrange transport. Nor does the secondhand buyer face the exhaustion and frustration involved in assembling "knock-down" furniture, which never seems to fit together as simply or neatly as it does in the display model.

Avoid bad buys by choosing pieces of secondhand furniture with care. A cheap chair could have a short leg or be a leg short, and it may harbour an army of woodworm waiting to occupy your entire house. If woodworm worries you, look closely before you buy. Woodworm loves soft sapwood and thrives in plywood or wicker. It hates tough teak, which has been widely used in furniture since the 1930s, and it can't stomach the resin in chipboard which is the basis of cheap modern furniture. Look for worm flight holes in drawers and in the rough unvarnished timber behind chests and mirrors and under chairs. You can't spot worm until the larvae chew their way out leaving the typical hole. If there's fresh sawdust around the holes, the attack is active. Woodworm is easy to treat with a heavy dose of proprietary killer. Don't get the filthy stuff in your eyes or down your lungs. After treatment, fill holes with a wood filler to strengthen the wood and to make any further invasion more noticeable.

Do-it-yourself enthusiasts deliberately choose broken old bargains. The real bargains are often damaged, but structurally-damaged furniture is only for the skilled. If you don't enjoy repair work, don't buy damaged furniture. Professional repairs are too expensive to contemplate on an averagely shabby piece of no special merit. Normal buyers should remember the basic rules of diy: all jobs take longer than you expect; jobs normally call for expensive tools which you don't own; jobs create dust, blood, noise and mess; jobs occupy enormous space; jobs usually hang around the house for a year before they are tackled.

Missing parts can mean real trouble for the unwilling restorer, but some faults look far more serious than they are. These can depress the price and can be rapidly repaired by the average person. A loose or missing hinge which causes a door to dangle is easy to fix, as long as the door is not warped. Hinges need a secure fixing point; if the base wood is too torn for screws to bite, glue in a new piece of wood or plug the holes with dowel. To make new steel hinges look old, heat them in an oven in a bed of sand. Bent, damaged or missing handles can be replaced to good effect: the *Yellow Pages'* "Architectural Ironmongers" sell handles and catches. Scratches may vanish under a proprietary scratch remover or oil; others are part of the patina. Sand shallow scratches away with fine sandpaper lubricated with linseed oil. Deep ones will need wood filler. Dents will sometimes swell up under a damp cloth pressed with a warm iron. Furniture covered with varnish or clumsily applied and flaking paint is often cheap, though the fashion for stripped pine has pushed up prices of anything strippable. Paint can be scraped off at home after a dose of proprietary stripper. Follow up with fine steel wool, sandpaper and wax. Always work with the direction of the grain, and don't use a power drill with a sanding disc—it scratches wood horribly. A useful free leaflet on stripping and finishing old furniture comes from Stirling Roncraft Information Service, Chapeltown, Sheffield S30 4JP.

Professional antique and junk dealers often put their fierce caustic tanks at the service of the public. Costs are not high, but damage can be. Joints may need reglueing afterwards, and wood can buckle after a long dip. Before deciding to strip furniture, try cleaning it with linseed oil and white spirit. Domestic bleach may shift stains, and meths moves grease. French polish can be tackled with meths, but it is hard work.

A soak in caustic will lift veneer off. Of course the wood undereath may turn out to be appealing to modern taste. If a small section of veneer has bubbled up, it can be cut open, reglued with PVA adhesive and pressed back in place. New veneer can be bought to replace a damaged piece, but an odd section salvaged from another piece of furniture may be a better match. Renovators always keep odd bits of unusual wood for future use.

Veneered furniture can be spotted by looking at the unseen surfaces of the furniture, where a different grain pattern from the top will betray veneer. Look closely for cracks in the veneer showing that the base wood has buckled and shrunk.

Split wood panels can be troublesome to repair well. Repair involves cutting a strip of wood to fill the split, glueing it in position and flattening with a chisel. But worse than doing your own repairs is making good someone else's botches. Steer clear of furniture covered in nails and metal bracing brackets.

Warped wood is usually beyond repair. A warped door can tear hinges clear of their screws. Try all drawers to check they fit well. A sticking problem is often cured simply by swapping the drawers around. Runners can be lubricated with a wax candle. Solid wooden table tops are often warped, and warp can ruin a table. Table leaves should always be tried for fit before buying. Loose joints are the other common problems with tables; test for looseness by shaking the table. Joints can be knocked apart, cleaned up and reglued firmly.

Chairs are seldom stable. Wobbly chairs can be improved by tightening the screws holding the corner blocks in the frame. The blocks can also be reglued if they have worked loose, and new ones are easy to cut from an odd bit of wood. Stretcher rails and rungs add stability; broken ones are simple to mend or reglue, if they are all there. Chair frames also suffer from loose joints. Sit in the chair and rock it around to check the solidity of arms, legs and back.

It is not worth buying a chair that needs recaning unless you like doing it yourself. Recaning is straightforward and, unlike most furniture repairs, a clean job, but it can easily take an entire day to do a kitchen chair. Recaning is a suitable job for blind people, and your local branch of the Royal National Institute for the Blind may know of local craftsmen able to help. Prices are normally calculated per hole.

Upholstered chairs in need of repair are even worse bargains unless you love doing it yourself, though hessian hanging down under a chair need not put anyone off. It may just provide the chance to look inside at the state of the webbing and springs, and hessian is easily replaced. Springs should be unbroken, and be fixed to the webbing where two pieces cross.

Attempts to patch up damaged upholstery are rarely successful. Professional upholsterers are extraordinarily expensive and may have waiting lists of months.

If an armchair seems sound apart from ripped, worn or faded fabric, it may be worth hiding the damage under a new loose cover. Some tears can be repaired by tidying up the edges and sticking a patch underneath. A leather patch can cover torn leather. A torn surface in vinyl furniture can be mended by modern adhesive, though not always as neatly as demonstrators claim. Worn or snapped springs, torn webbing, a sagging front edge and lumpy or sagging seats are serious—the chair will need reupholstering. Reupholstering a sprung chair is possible, but can prove depressingly difficult for the newcomer to stuffing. An upholstery manual or a course of evening classes is probably the best approach. Teachers at the local college will know the local sources of elusive materials needed for upholstery and furniture renovation.

It is unwise to take on such a major job before trying your skills and patience on an easier job such as a drop-in chair seat. Foam upholstery is simpler for the novice than traditional springs and horsehair, but true diy scavengers will buy a discarded mattress, wash the horsehair filling and reuse it. You could find a miser's fortune stashed away inside the stuffing. Horsehair can be stitched inside a pillow case for the washing and rinsing.

Beware of secondhand furniture with polyurethane foam upholstery. Modern living room furniture is the main cause of casualties in domestic fires. Hot poisonous gases rise from the foam and kill. Traditional furnishings burn more slowly and produce piles of warning smoke. The most fire-resistant coverings are heavy wool or leather.

Dirty covers can be cleaned, but burn marks will not come off. Vinyl covers come clean with car upholstery cleaner from car accessory shops. Leather is cleaned with a damp cloth and an occasional dose of hide food. Dralon velvet needs a dry foam shampoo—too much wetting distorts the backing. First step in cleaning covers is the vacuum cleaner or soft brush. Diy dry cleaning is the next stage.

Jumble sales are cheap, but many jumble organisers find furniture too much trouble to be worth handling. The PDSA's jumble departments have impressive supplies of cheap furniture, and the Salvation Army is worth sounding out. Auctions remain the best source of secondhand furniture, if you can overcome the transport problems. Suitable transport can add considerably to the price of a successful bid. Large pieces of furniture often offer best value at auctions; dealers don't like them as they take up too much room in the van and shop. Demand for big furniture is slack, partly because it will not fit in the typical modern house. Pushing bulky items through doors and up stairs is painful. Renovated furniture will normally cost more than battered pieces, but it is worth paying the extra if you value your time and don't enjoy renovation.

Auctions of government surplus furniture are particularly interesting. Such auctions are dominated by dealers, who buy tables by the dozen, but many lots are single pieces or standard four- or six-piece sets of chairs. The military look doesn't dominate. There are nests of coffee tables, fireside chairs, children's cots and patterned carpets alongside the predictable military lines.

Office furniture can be a bargain, especially when demand falls during a recession. In the specialist shops and auction rooms dealing with office furniture, you may find a secretary's chair and an executive desk, a drawing board, a stationery cabinet and a cash box. Keys are regularly missing. A cheap and ugly filing cabinet with chips and scratches on the paintwork can quickly be painted or covered with wall-paper for use at home. Test all drawers, as the runners are often gouged and twisted.

Antique shops seldom give bargains in secondhand furniture, but the secondhand section of a major store is normally even worse, due largely to high overheads. Back-street general junk shops are a more fruitful source, especially for the post-war furniture which turns up in most house clearances. Bedroom suites and dining room and kitchen furniture of the 1950s and 1960s are still unfashionable and cheap in most areas. It is often worth buying if its negative associations with mean landlords of bedsits and seedy guest houses are not too strong. If a piece has survived the '70s, it should last well. Heavily-varnished Edwardian and Victorian furniture of undistinguished design but sturdy construction can be bought more cheaply than new equivalents, and can be stripped down to lighter wood. Bentwood chairs remain good value, and sets are easily built up.

Older kitchen furniture is often less convenient than today's. Exotic fittings can be bought by mail order from Woodfit to update old kitchen cupboards. Take careful measurements before buying any kitchen furniture to match existing fittings, as metrication may have altered sizes.

Modern furniture is often built from laminated chipboard. It has the advantage of deterring woodworm and avoiding the problems of wood identification. Softwood (normally pine) is eas-ily recognised, but hardwoods can confuse the experts. Furniture manufacturers have for centuries been expert at disguising bad wood. Staining cheaper wood to make it look like mahogany is one of the basic professional tricks. This can of course also be practised by the clever buyer, who can use woodstain to improve the looks of a dull piece or disguise a repair.

G

GARDENS

Secondhand items proliferate in gardens, which provide a handy graveyard for many bad buys on the secondhand market. A leaky kitchen sink or a cracked loo, a split wellington boot, a punctured car tyre or a broken chimney pot can all enjoy a glorious resurrection as plant containers. The only practical limitation on garden containers is the gardener's imagination, though suburban owners of supremely tidy plots may find painted empty paint pots or upturned sawn-off plastic washing-up liquid bottles quite unacceptable intrusions in Eden.

The recycling enthusiast can revel in gardening, where every successful cutting from a friend's garden represents a further triumph. The entire garden may in a sense be secondhand, taken over from an unenthusiastic or incapacitated owner.

In the early 1970s, Friends of the Earth (FOE) realised that a lot of urban gardens were lying idle, exploited only by weeds and snails, while green-fingered flat-dwellers moped on the top floor without gardens and longing for a plot to dig. In 1975, as food prices rose and the waiting lists for allotments grew longer, a garden-sharing scheme began, matching unused gardens to unemployed gardeners. It sounded perfect, but it fizzled out.

The problems varied from area to area. A very practical obstacle in many cases was the need to go through the house to reach the garden behind, an inconvenience to both parties. Other projects ended in acrimony, often over the question of stolen produce. Most surprisingly, there was a shortage of volunteer gardeners, while large numbers of garden owners—especially the old—were eager to have their gardens cultivated. Even where the scheme was well publicised, as in Stevenage, where details were sent to everyone on the allotment waiting lists, few stepped forward.

In many towns all the large gardens are concentrated in one district, remote from areas dominated by concrete. A garden owner unable to cultivate his/her own garden would therefore have problems in attracting anyone local, as everyone has a similarly large plot, while volunteers would find travelling too inconvenient.

Some schemes continue, and others would be resurrected if interest grew. To find if there are any second-hand gardens on offer in your area, contact either the local FOE branch or the local volunteer bureau. The Town Hall or Citizens' Advice Bureau may be able to put you in touch.

A grander scale of second-hand gardening is seen in the City Farms which have taken temporary root on unwanted inner-city waste land.

Gardening was the first activity on the rubble-covered land in Kentish Town, London, where the pioneer City Farm began in 1972. The idea behind the farms is to give city communities (both children and adults) an experience of country activities. In October 1980, with over fifty city farms alive and growing, the Federation of

City Farms was launched to help newcomers. A directory—*Where to find City Farms in Britain*—is available from the Federation at 15 Wilkin Street, London NW5 3NC (tel: 01–267 9421), price £1.

GARDEN FURNITURE

A lazy summer day in the garden can be ruined by a chair collapsing or printing a rusty mark on your whitest sports wear. Cast-iron seats can never be rust proof, yet hundreds of pounds change hands for traditional cast-iron garden seats of no particular merit. Any such seats clogged with paint must be sand-blasted clean, sprayed with zinc oxide and painted again to keep the rust down and the pattern up. New paint may be hiding rust on seats bought from sly dealers.

Aluminium does not rust, nor is it heavy to hump around. For these reasons, reproductions of Victorian seats are now cast in aluminium: attractive as they are, their price should be lower than the originals'.

Those nostalgic for memories of a first kiss on an old park bench will probably meet disappointment, again. Only theft or luck can secure a secondhand London park bench, as the GLC, like other financially pressed councils, just restores old benches and puts them out again for a new generation of young lovers to carve or spray. If you are lucky enough to spot a park bench in a junk shop or scrap metal yard, look out for chips or cracks in the casting, as these are extremely hard to repair satisfactorily. The only practical repair method is welding, but this leaves vicious scars which would be hard to disguise.

Seaside memories are a more practical evocation in the garden, stimulated by secondhand deckchairs. However, the seaside, with its corrosive air, is not the best place to buy them. A wet winter in a garden shed anywhere can rot away the fabric. Look out for mildew, rips or frays, especially at tension points around the rails. New lengths of rotproof deckchair fabric can be bought from hardware or department stores and upholsterers to recover a deckchair, but this may put the total price beyond the limits of sense. Signs of rust may have appeared on the tacks holding the canvas or at pivots and rivets. Loose rivets can be tightened simply by hammering the head when the other side is supported. Wooden sections may be loose at the joints, rotten or even broken. If the chair seems safe after careful visual examination, sit gingerly in it. It should feel supportive, comfortable and wobble-free. Lean back as far as you can. If you are buying several chairs, give every one a rigorous examination: the seller is unlikely to show the worst first.

A similar examination should show up the faults in canvas directors' chairs and metal-framed chairs, where extra attention should be given to missing screws and worn screw threads.

A full-length sun lounger must be tried out in every position, as many old ones can't hold them all. The fabric is often torn along the stitching at the edge where it takes the strain of sitting sun-soakers. Check underneath for broken support cords, torn cover flaps and missing hooks. Cord repair kits are on sale.

The garden magazines are not the place for advertisements for secondhand garden furniture. Look in the newsagent's window, local newspapers and auction sales.

GARDEN TOOLS

The traditional design of garden tools with no cutting edge has changed little since Saxon times. Damage should be obvious and is usually limited to the wooden handle. Beware of "whipping"— string wound tightly around the handle—which may hide splits. New wooden handles are sold by most tool shops. The mail order catalogue of Self-Sufficiency and Smallholding Supplies of Wells, Somerset offers wooden shafts in five designs at the bottom end of the handle and four different grips at the top. The same company will also post replacement scythe handholds and handles in wood or aluminium, together with five sizes of scythe blades. Their choice of four carborundum stones should cope with most sharpening chores. Handles for hay forks and pick axes are also listed as well as the rivets to hold them in place. Reshafting a spade, fork, rake or hoe with a broken handle is a straightforward job, and damaged tools can often be bought for absurdly low prices. A rivet may have to be punched out to release the remains of the handle from traditional tools, but a screw is more common on modern tools. If the handle has snapped off in or near the socket, it may be impossible to grip: a long screw driven into the broken end may provide a grip to help withdraw the old handle. Most new handles will need cutting to length and shaving to fit the socket exactly.

Replacement handles may be hard to find for garden shears, but loose handles are often made secure by cleaning up the surrounding area and sticking the handle in place with epoxy resin adhesive.

Cutting tools are best judged in use. Secateurs are graded for British Standard purposes according to their ability to chop through different thicknesses of green wood. Light-duty secateurs comfortably cut stems up to 10mm in diameter, general-purpose models cope with 16mm and heavy-duty ones handle 20mm. Try out secondhand secateurs with this test. Neglect by past owners can involve secondhand buyers in extra expense. It is not worth paying much for a spade with a bent, rusty or cement-encrusted blade, as renovation may be impossible. Rusty secateur blades cannot always be cleaned up by diy rust removal treatment: they may need professional regrinding. Wilkinson tools should be returned to a specialist dealer. Age is no clue to condition, as a dedicated rose grower could blunt the finest pair in a season.

The sharpness of shears can be tested out at any time of year: a good pair should cut cleanly through a piece of linen, or even better a sheet of newspaper, along the whole length of the blade. The tips of the blades should overlap very slightly but the blades should not touch in the middle. Rusty, chipped and dented blades can be ground sharp, but buckled blades are potentially more troublesome—a tempered steel blade cannot be straightened without reheating it. The less expensive untempered steel can be straightened out. Unfortunately there's no easy way of telling the two steels apart.

The expert test is to score the steel with a dart—the cut will go deeper on untempered steel, but this will be no consolation to the seller left with a scratched tool.

No less a guru of gardening than Percy Thrower recommends going for stainless steel tools because they are so easy to keep clean and they don't rust if left out in the garden. The absence of rust will provide a clue to the identity of secondhand tools. Percy adds that "stainless steel tools these days are very expensive but they will last almost a lifetime." "A good pair of shears or a good pair of secateurs", he believes, "should keep themselves sharp as they are used and should be made so that they suffer from the minimum amount of rust."

A loose or missing bolt or rivet at the pivot of shears can normally be replaced. Those in Wilkinson shears need a special service agent as they are more complex than the ordinary nut and bolt. The rivet or bolt should allow the blades to swing open without being loose when one handle of the shears is held pointed downwards.

Old men in allotments remember the days when any ironmonger would sharpen shears for a few pence. Now few will take on the job. One central London shop offering this rare service is House Bros of 85 Brewer Street, W1. The cost is approximately £3. The "Grinders and Sharpeners" in the *Yellow Pages* may oblige.

Hoses Garden hoses spring leaks, and these usually show up only in use. If you buy a bad one, cut up the broken section and fit a proper compression connector, or join the two lengths by jamming a piece of tubing inside, held by jubilee clips. Unroll the hose to spot permanent kinks at bends. Wire hose reels are often snapped at the joints.

Sprays Absence of spray is the problem with these appliances. Bits of dirt often block up spray nozzles. A bicycle pump may blow the blockage back inside the pump, but don't rely on this when buying a secondhand spray, as bungled attempts to clean out dirt with wire or pins may have damaged the valve or jet. The possibility of insecticide traces on the spray makes the use of lung power unwise.

Garden poisons often perish the spray's pair of leather washers, leading to liquid leaks into the barrel which may seep out through the bleed hole in the spray body. This pair of washers, fitted back to back, is easy to replace as long as the retaining nuts and metal washers are intact.

Watering cans Never buy a watering can without filling it up and giving water a chance to ooze through cracks. Any signs of repair should warn you off. Replacement roses can be bought.

Wheelbarrows Barrow bodies are often caked in concrete, or crushed and cracked by heavy loads. Spare bodies are available, from Self-Sufficiency and Smallholding Supplies for example, who can also supply wheels to replace those damaged by impact against stones and kerbs. Check the tyre carefully to see if replacement will be needed, and spin the wheel to listen for any grit damage to nylon wheel bearings. Old pram wheels can be used as makeshift wheels but these don't stand up to much travelling over rough ground. Look also for rust eating away the frame.

(*See also* Hedge trimmers, Lawnmowers.)

GAS APPLIANCES

Secondhand gas appliances are quite justifiably frightening. Very real danger lurks in leaks and blockages. Unsafe appliances are not only a threat to life and home; insult can be added to your injuries in the form of a £400 fine under the Gas Safety Regulations. The regulations make it illegal to use any gas appliance which you suspect is dangerous. Fortunately, most gas appliances are very simple, and safe bargains can be bought.

The safest source of secondhand gas appliances is your local gas showroom, where properly reconditioned goods are often on sale. New appliances sold by British Gas bear the BSI Safety Mark label, guaranteeing their quality. The label will almost certainly be missing from secondhand appliances, but the model can be checked out with the showroom. British Gas will provide comprehensive service facilities for all such approved appliances. Any appliance sold by British Gas has good spare parts availability. Certain reliable specialist gas appliance retailers are "British Gas Authorised Dealers". It is a very bad idea to buy gas appliances from a general junk shop or in a private sale without a guarantee. The possibility of buying an old appliance which has not been converted to burn natural gas cannot be ruled out.

A crazy installation can turn a safe appliance into a bomb. Do-it-yourself installation is undesirable and illegal, as the Tyneside man discovered when hauled before magistrates after causing an explosion by plugging a gas pipe with a carrot. His home blew up and he was fined. Under the Gas Safety Regulations, only a "competent" person can install or repair gas appliances, and that includes secondhand equipment. "Competence" comes only with adequate experience and technical knowledge. The Gas Board's own fitters should fit the description, and they can carry out installation and repair work.

Otherwise, choose a fitter from the CORGI list of registered installers — you can consult the list in any showroom. The fitter will check out any secondhand appliance before he connects it up.

If the house gas pipes are old and disused, they should be examined at installation time, as rats and mice sharpen their teeth on old lead-rich pipes; this causes both brain damage and gas leaks.

An appliance could be up for sale because the previous owner is tired of the smell of leaking gas. Never test for gas leaks with a lighted flame — your suspicions could be dramatically confirmed. If you suspect leaks, don't risk so much as a small spark from using an electric switch. Put out all cigarettes, throw open the doors and windows and then check to see if a gas tap has been left open or a pilot light has blown out. If the smell of gas remains a mystery, call the Gas Board, listed under "Gas" in the 'phone book. Repairs of leaks are normally free, but if new parts are needed there could be a charge.

Gas appliances may be difficult to operate without the user's handbook, which has normally vanished before an appliance is sold second-hand. The manufacturer can be contacted for a replacement copy. Gas showrooms have the makers' names and addresses. If possible, leave the showroom alone on Monday mornings, when they usually appear harassed and the switchboards are jammed.

GAS COOKERS *see* Cookers

GAS FIRES

Approaching an unguaranteed secondhand gas fire with a lighted match is a foolish and inglorious form of Russian roulette. The risk of explosion is too high for the mentally normal to contemplate.

Secondhand gas fires are most unlikely to be connected up and ready to fire when you examine them, and damaged fires are very dangerous. It is therefore absolutely essential to buy only a reconditioned and guaranteed appliance from the gas board's own showrooms or a guaranteed appliance from an authorised dealer who has carried out a thorough safety check before selling the fire.

Fires from any other source are suspect and must be checked professionally before they are installed. Dealers and installers displaying the CORGI symbol are generally reliable, and some form of advice is available from any gas showroom.

It may be illegal under the 1972 Gas Safety Regulations to have a dodgy secondhand appliance, and it is theoretically impossible to buy an unconverted gas fire from the dark days before natural gas lit our lives. However, rogue appliances have survived all purges and are difficult for the layman to spot before an accident. The British Gas Corporation recommend an annual service to keep any fire working efficiently and to prevent you burning away the money you saved by buying a secondhand appliance.

GERBILS *see* Pets

GLASS

Delicate drinking glasses stand up badly to the rough and tumble of junk shops, auctions, markets and jumble sales. Buyers should therefore be very cautious. Glasses with cracks running right through can't be repaired, and these are usually quite obvious, but visual examination of secondhand glasses is not enough to test for faults. Remember that glasses will touch your very sensitive lips, and the slightest chip can cut. Run your finger around the rim of every glass to check for minute rough spots.

A few specialist firms will grind chips out of rims. Price goes up with the size of the chip and its distance from the rim. Grinding out a deep chip can alter the look of a glass dramatically. Grinding out even the smallest chips from cheap glasses is normally costlier than a new glass, but it may be worthwhile on crystal, especially if only one glass in a set needs repair.

Eradicating a large chip from a wide bowl or a decanter can put the price up considerably. Diy grinding is possible with carborundum paste and jewellers' rouge but it is very, very tedious.

The Information Office at the Glass Manufacturers' Federation, 19 Portland Place, London W1 (tel: 01–580 6952) keep a list of firms prepared to tackle this type of work. Perhaps the best alternative is the "Glassware Manufacturers and Suppliers" category in the *Yellow Pages*—they can't usually do the job, but they may tell cheerful callers who can help.

The few firms operating in the field are all busy. Indeed, work is flown in from all parts of the world to R. Wilkinson and Son of 43 Wastdale Road, London SE23, known internationally for putting new glass feet on broken glasses. If you need the service, it costs about £5 if a suitable foot is in stock, more for a custom job. New bowls cost even more.

If a rare item has snapped in two, Wilkinson's will grind each stump flat, polish them, stick them together and cut over the joint, making a link nearly always as strong as the original. On cheap glasses the trusty epoxy-resin Araldite will make a serviceable repair, but probably a very visible one. An astonishing new adhesive from Loctite, called "Glass Bond", uses the power of sunlight to dry to a glass-like clarity in seconds, making scarcely-visible diy repair possible.

Glued glass—and any crystal—will be damaged by dishwashers. Glued glasses come out broken, crystal turns cloudy all over and can't easily be cleaned. Exotic and unlikely recipes for cleaning glass abound. A mixture of tea leaves and vinegar is traditionally advised to clear lime scale. Chempro SDP and denture cleaners are also recommended to remove sediment and stains. Clinically clean glass is essential to home winemakers, and home-brew shops sell products such as Silana pf crystals to attack filth and germs on glass.

A mild abrasive such as silver sand or other non-soluble grains, even crushed egg shell, can be swished around the dirty glass in a little water, but the professionals don't like diy efforts with such substances, or with leadshot and Vim, which often make future expert cleaning ineffective. An unharmed but stained decanter will be professionally cleaned up for about £3.

Chances of a decanter being sold cheap increase if the stopper is missing, broken or just jammed inside. Wilkinson and Son will make new stoppers or withdraw old ones which have broken off. They also have a large stock of stoppers for antique perfume bottles. F. W. Aldridge of 2 Ivy Road, London E17, who specialise in crystal wine glasses and Bristol blue glass linings, will grind unmatched stoppers to fit a decanter. The same firm will grind chips out of glass plates, vases, decanters etc.

Broken windows—part of the trade's "Flat Glass" category—are almost proverbially useless, but the information office at the Glass and Glazing Federation, 6 Mount Row, London W1 (tel: 01–629 8334) has a list of members who will repair stained or leaded glass, make new glass tops for tables and other furniture, or resilver mirrors.

Replacement parts for hand-painted leaded glass are expensive. Ordinary Victorian decorative windows are simply leaded coloured glass rather than glass which has been painted and then fired. Nevertheless, replacement glass for these often has to be imported from Germany at great expense.

Glass Distinction of Bethnal Green Road, London work in traditional stained glass and leaded lights. Prices fluctuate with the price of lead.

If you want to cut down a large piece of glass for reuse, don't buy a cheap cutter for the one-off job. A good cutter makes the work a lot easier. Lines should be scored from edge to edge.

GOATKEEPING EQUIPMENT

Most smallholders share their life with at least one family goat, but newcomers to the goat life can rarely afford all the equipment they need. Good quality, purpose-made equipment is highly priced, which is normal in such restricted markets, where one or two small manufacturers make limited numbers of specialised articles. Buying everything brand-new—from stainless steel buckets to milking machines and separators—can gobble up the smallholder's capital faster than hungry goats in the vegetable patch.

The exhausting realities of the self-sufficient life soon sap the enthusiasm of the half-hearted, who sell up the trappings of their rural life and drift back to town. This regular pattern of disillusionment following initial zeal brings a regular supply of good secondhand equipment to the market, but locating it can be troublesome.

The undercapitalised goatkeeper should head for Hereford, and seek out the Harvester shop in Maylord Street, heralded as the only goat shop in Britain. Remote goatkeepers can write for their mail-order catalogue, enclosing a stamped addressed envelope and 10 pence. Visitors to the shop can consult the free buy/sell advertising noticeboard and examine the ever-changing range of secondhand goatkeeping equipment. They will sell anything that can be used again in the goat world, believing it right to pass on well-made items at prices which will encourage the poor goatkeeper to use the best equipment rather than a brand-new but inferior substitute.

Most items goats need are simple, and secondhand equipment can be put to use as soon as it is sterilised. Few articles are complex enough to need spare parts, but spares can normally be bought to keep a secondhand separator working.

Secondhand goats bought to use the secondhand equipment will need a thorough cleaning and worming before they are unleashed on the farm. Examining goats calls for a competent person.

GOLF CLUBS

You can buy golf clubs from golf clubs, where the club professional will normally deal in new and used clubs, bags and trolleys. Secondhand equipment makes a significant contribution to the average professional's income, as it does to the customer's bank balance. Its popularity has grown with the sport itself and the rising price of new clubs.

The club professional can normally be trusted not to deal in dubious articles, but a professional may not repair or recondition used clubs before sale. Indeed, traditional golfing repairmen often mutter scornfully about the modern professional's inability to reshaft a club.

Shops selling new equipment are an alternative source of secondhand equipment when old clubs are taken in part exchange, and there are some rare specialist dealers in secondhand golfing equipment. One such dealer is Tom Lester, who runs the Golf Shop in Leominster, where clubs are sold both singly and in sets, and repairs are carried out.

Wherever you buy, try to negotiate a fortnight's approval, to give you a real chance to test the clubs out. Many players freeze under the eye of a forceful salesman and can't swing a club properly until they are alone on the course. Even the fact that the set of clubs is for a left-handed player can go unnoticed until you take a swing. Clubs are classified as "woods" or "irons". Woods are designed for distance and are therefore swung at the ball with maximum force. The face can quite easily sustain damage in unskilled hands, and in time the head may work loose from the shaft. Check both points on secondhand clubs.

Old woods are likely to have solid wooden heads shaped by hand from seasoned oak, but the newer laminated blocks are commoner finds in the secondhand market. These are reinforced at the point of impact by a facing, which can be damaged or missing. A repairer can replace it without difficulty. Wooden shafts have become antique rarities, of more interest to the collector than the player.

Modern golfers find better balance and strength in steel shafts, although early steel shafts were in fact disguised as wood. Wooden shafts warp, but steel is unlikely to distort—it just snaps. All British shafts are true tempered.

Check that the binding of head to shaft is secure. The head quite commonly drops off certain early Japanese steel-shafted models. This is not necessarily an irreparable fault, but it is unwise to buy snapped clubs as it may be impossible to remove the broken shaft from the head socket.

The head of an iron can stand a lot of punishment, but iron heads can be chipped. Avoid clubs where the grooves on the face have worn down—these serrations give the club its ability to spin the ball and are therefore vital. Gouge the dirt out of the grooves of a secondhand club.

Rust is a possible problem with secondhand irons—it usually begins to attack on the back of the face where the manufacturer's name is worked into the metal. Rebuffing the surface of irons, like revarnishing woods, adds value to a secondhand club without really improving the performance.

On both woods and irons, the perspiring hands of a nervous player can rot away a rubber handgrip in time. A shiny grip will be hard to hold steady and should be replaced. This presents little problem.

Clubs can be bought individually or in sets. Different manufacturers have very different ideas about how they want clubs to stand. Players' preferences vary, but no player will approve of a mixed bag of clubs built up from odd clubs with different types of shaft. Shafts from a single set should give uniform swing and elasticity, simplifying the switch from club to club during a game. It is less important to make sure both woods and irons come from the same manufacturer. If a club is still being manufactured, a set can be built up club by club, but buying a secondhand set complete may mean buying more clubs than you need. Opinions vary on the ideal combination of clubs, but no-one would suggest a beginner needs a complete set. A common selection would comprise numbers 3, 5, 7 and 9 irons, woods numbers 2 and 4, and the all-important putter to finish off the game.

When the putter has sunk the last ball on the 18th, and you turn towards the club house, look out for the market in secondhand golf balls operated less by the club professionals than by the small boys who haunt the courses gathering up "lost" balls and selling them back to the players near the club house. If the club professional chases the lads away, balls should soon turn up in local junk shops.

GUINEA PIGS *see* Pets

GUITARS *see* Musical instruments

GUNS

Laws govern secondhand gun sales, restricting who can sell guns, which guns they can sell, and who can buy them. It is illegal to sell firearms and shotguns as part of a business without first being registered with the police as a firearms dealer. This restriction applies not only to specialist gun dealers—even the local junk shop would need to be registered. The law does not apply to private sales.

Under the Firearms Act of 1968 no-one under 17 years old can buy a gun, even a low-power air weapon for which no licence is needed. The system of gun licences is explained in a free leaflet produced by the Home Office and available from police stations, called *Firearms: what you need to know about the law*. The essential point is to learn the law before you try to buy a gun, as you will probably have to obtain a certificate from the local police before you can walk out of the gun shop without risking three years in prison. The police can supply two types of certificate: a firearms certificate and the more usual shotgun certificate. Firearm certificates are never given without good reason, although membership of a gun club is normally considered reason enough. Gun club membership also satisfies security requirements, as the gun could be kept safely locked up at the club. A club's notice board and grapevine can be useful sources of secondhand guns, and buyers can also benefit from other members' advice on selection.

The police are entitled to refuse certificates if the murderous gleam in the applicant's red eyes makes them fear for the public's safety. A criminal record or a past full of fights and intemperance rule you out. Although requirements for shotgun certificates are less stringent, criminals remain ineligible.

The gun dealer has to make sure that the guns he sells are "in proof" and therefore safe. The proof system was introduced in the nineteenth century to protect the public from the dangerous products of unscrupulous or incompetent gunmakers. A new gun must be checked before sale and marked on the barrel. It is illegal to possess a gun which is out of proof, and there is a £1,000 fine for selling one. Nevertheless far too many secondhand guns change hands out of proof and continue to be used in a dangerous condition. The buyer cannot really be sure of the condition of a gun which has not been recently reproofed, unless he insists on a check by one of the two places where proofing is carried out. These are the Proof House, 48 Commercial Road, London E1 and the Birmingham Gun Barrel Proof House, Banbury Street, Birmingham 5. After purchase you can send the gun direct to a proof house or ask a reputable gunsmith to check it. After looking for obvious signs of damage, the gunsmith will usually send it to the proof house on your behalf. A visual examination, even firing, cannot reveal all problems. Obvious and serious rust or damage to the barrel will almost certainly put a gun out of proof, but pitting of the metal inside the barrel is difficult to spot.

It is prudent to ask the seller to fire the first shot with a secondhand firearm during the sales demonstration. If you are an inexperienced or poor shot, take a hot marksman with you to test the gun's accuracy. If a shotgun will not fire straight, the barrel is probably bent, and a repair will be an expensive job for a skilled gunsmith.

A warping wooden stock can force the barrel out of alignment. Restocking is possible but very expensive.

The barrel end of a shotgun can be rechoked: fitting a choke is expensive, but partial or complete choke removal is quite common. The life of old or damaged guns can sometimes be prolonged without the expense of a new barrel by "resleeving", fitting new tubes to the old breech. This process affects the gun's balance.

Guns periodically need reblacking or blueing, fairly simple processes to replace the protective coat on a barrel, preventing rust and neutralising the barrel colour. This stops light reflecting off the metal to warn prospective victims that they are about to be killed.

Antique guns are exempt from the legal requirement of a licence, but problems have been caused by the failure of the Firearms Act 1968 to define precisely what an antique weapon is. In practice, the police normally expect you to have a firearms certificate for any gun which can be loaded with a self-contained metallic cartridge.

Besides the specialist gun dealers, the specialist magazines are often useful sources of used guns. The monthlies *Airgun World, Sporting Gun* and *Guns Review* have classified sections advertising private gun sales.

H

HAIR DRIERS

A hair drier either works or it doesn't, and broken hair driers are not worth buying. Almost any repair on top of the secondhand purchase price could easily make it cheaper to buy a brand-new appliance. Besides, many driers are literally impossible to repair and will be irrevocably broken if any repairs are attempted. For example, the drier may, in common with many other small electrical appliances, be enclosed in a moulded case which prevents access to the working—or

199

broken—parts. In a sense, this kind of inbuilt obsolescence can be viewed as an effective safety device.

Cracks in the case can be repaired by epoxy resin or plastic adhesive, but such repairs are seldom pretty.

Overheating caused by a blocked air inlet or nozzle can lead to a complete and irreparable melt-down of the plastic, particularly if the fan stops turning. There should be a safety thermostat to prevent overheating. This can be tested by covering the air inlet grille with your hand: the motor or heating element should cut out within seconds. If the drier begins to feel hot or smell odd, switch off fast and start looking for another.

A hair drier is quite a complex appliance, and not a very robust one. It is a sort of combined toaster and fan. As in a toaster, the heat is provided by one or two elements, while an electric motor drives the fan which pushes the air towards your hair. The drier's efficiency can be tested by trying it out at three settings—cold, warm and hot. A hand held over the outlet should feel a noticeable change of temperature, but the temperature should not fluctuate within the single setting. If it won't heat up, an element is probably broken. If it is very noisy, the fan is no doubt damaged, and this will cause extra wear on bearings. Ideally the drier will be tested on wet hair, so examination may be best kept until a rainy day.

If the drier has a plastic flexible hose, look for holes and tears in it; they can be repaired with adhesive tape or vinyl adhesive. The flex on old driers is often in bad condition. Besides being frayed by rubbing, it may have worked loose from the terminals. The standard test is to turn the drier on near a switched-on radio and to waggle the flex, listening for crackling on the radio to betray a poor connection. Before using the drier, dust it inside and oil its bearings.

HAMSTERS *see* Pets

HANDBAGS

Bags must open and bags must close—buyers should test both functions on secondhand handbags. Zips and locks should work, handles should not be about to fall off or snap, nor should any hinges. All these faults can be repaired, but damage to leather, whether in the form of scuffed and dented corners or overall cracking due to age, may put the bag beyond repair. Dry and perished crocodile can't be rejuvenated any more than the skin of old humans can be made childlike by beauticians, so don't buy cracked croc. A lot of crocodile is phony: look for the irregular rough-edged scales of the real thing. It may be worth while having a new lining, handle or catch fitted to a fine but faded bag, but finding a person prepared to repair a beaded bag could be difficult. Self-help is possible, but very time-consuming if a lot of beads are missing and unsatisfactory if the originals can't be matched. The Warehouse in Neal Street, London WC2 has a remarkable range of modern glass beads, including silvered ones and tiny ones in many colours and degrees of opacity.

Diy repairs can often save a good bag cheaply if perfect elegance is not essential. Strips of leather stained to match or contrast and held on by neoprene cement or hammer-on rivets will cope with the common causes of handle failure.

Some patching and re-stitching can usually be done cheaply by cobblers unless the work is very delicate. Certain traditional cobblers will also stock Neat's Foot Oil, which will keep leather supple and moist, though it will often darken the colour. Tough leather should come clean with saddle soap, but delicate leather such as kid can be very hard to clean. Buyers can be badly caught out by grubby secondhand pigskin, which many experts say cannot be cleaned at all, looking greasy whatever treatment is tried.

HAND DRILLS *see* Tools

HANG GLIDERS

To harness yourself to a secondhand hang glider and jump off the nearest cliff seems like an act of extreme faith and folly. Recognising the very real dangers of used hang gliders, the safety-conscious British Hang Gliding Association (BHGA) print a public warning over the "Small ads" section in their official magazine *Wings!*.

"For your own safety," it runs, "if you are purchasing a secondhand glider, check that it is a registered BHGA model, see it test flown, test fly it." The order of these two procedures is important. If the seller won't trust himself in it, the purchase should go no further. The BHGA advise a thorough inspection for damage and wear to critical parts and recommend seeking advice from the Club Safety Officer if you have any doubts. Check whether a suitable and sound bag is included in the price. Helmets and other more specialised equipment such as altimeters and airspeed indicators may also be on offer.

Wings! has placed restrictions on advertisements for gliders which haven't gone through the British Airworthiness scheme: Advertisements are placed by BHGA members, whose gliders will in the past have been tested and approved, so the magazine is a relatively safe source of secondhand gliders. Companies dealing in secondhand hang gliders can also be traced through the magazine.

Before buying any glider, a pilot should learn the right way to handle them in a recognised school, and then join the BHGA.

HATS

When old felt hats become too old hat, and their owners discard them in the jumble pile, they are often retired to coastal resorts, to gain a fresh lease of life in the seaside air. The original shape is pressed out of those elegant 1930s felt creations, and they emerge from the treatment room as cowboy hats bearing a "Kiss Me Quick" label, ready to be sold to a day tripper stumbling along the prom looking for a mate. Charities such as the PDSA derive part of their income from turning baskets full of musty felt rejects into seaside souvenirs.

HEADPHONES *see* Audio equipment

HEDGE TRIMMERS

Hedge trimmers are similar to other popular power tools. The most likely source of trouble will be worn brushes. Replacements should be readily available from manufacturers' service agents. If the cutting blades have caught on a stem too thick to cut, the armature may have suffered damage. Signs of wear may show in the blade-driving block: if the slot is worn, replace it. A well-oiled blade is a good sign, as oil lowers friction and therefore wear on the motor. Cables should be checked carefully, as they can easily be slashed during use.

HOLIDAYS

Holiday cancellations are depressingly common, but cut-price secondhand buys are a rare and potentially dodgy consequence. Holidays cancelled due to illness, accident or simple fear of flying are just put back on the market at full price. The only advantage such a system offers the public is the possibility of a late booking on an otherwise fully-booked tour.

Some major tour operators will reduce fares in an effort to offload unsold seats at the last minute, but they frown deeply on any transfer of a holiday between friends which bypasses the tour operator. A "name-change" system operates occasionally, but brings no financial benefit to either buyer, as the hapless cancellor has to pay the appropriate cancellation fee and the new traveller pays full price. Private deals between friends usually break the terms of the contract the original booker entered into by signing the booking form. Somewhere in small letters the transfer is usually banned. The agent is entitled to his pound of sunless flesh from the disappointed holidaymaker and a new contract with the new buyer.

It is unwise to risk unapproved air travelling on another person's ticket unless the two names match very closely, as both ticket and passport may have to be presented and compared at the check-in desk.

Recently the best source of secondhand holidays has been the so-called "bucket shop". These advertise extensively in *Time Out* magazine and the Sunday newspapers. They are the "late booking" specialists who deal in unsold seats on major charter flights and national airlines. Their prices often represent enormous savings on any other booking method.

Rather than reduce prices directly to the public and risk the wrath of early bookers, certain tour operators will fill empty seats and beds via the anonymity of the bucket shop. Holidays and flights bought here will be no different from those sold in the glossy brochures. A complete package holiday, with hotel and meals included may be on offer or it may be possible to buy the return flight alone.

Certain bucket shops were once major outlets for unloading stolen tickets, but now the tickets are more likely to come from the airlines' agents, who often make use of them. Despite intergovernmental price-fixing agreements, the airlines themselves are rumoured to use the bucket shops. The system's legality has not been attacked in the courts since 1971. Most bucket shops are perfectly respectable and reliable organisations. The minuscule minority of sharks have their every bite at a stranded traveller magnified by hostile publicity from the travel establishment.

The longer a particular company has been in existence the more reassured the first-time secondhand buyer may feel. A few pounds deposit is often needed as proof of good faith, but it is a universally valid precaution to hold back your money until the ticket itself is produced on the desk in front of you, with flight number and airline marked. Paying in advance is inviting the bucket shop dealer to take a very long holiday at your expense.

HOMING PIGEONS

Newcomers to the world of pigeon racing may be legitimately suspicious about the idea of secondhand homing pigeons. This may, after all, be the hundredth time an unscrupulous dealer has sold the same highly-trained bird, which just keeps on returning home after every sale. Old pigeons can be persuaded to adopt a new home, but the process can be too difficult and time-consuming.

The market in secondhand birds is a lively one, and pigeons quite often move three or four times in their seven-year lifespan. With each change of ownership the bird must be reringed—at minimal cost—by the Royal Pigeon Racing Association. All sales must pass through them. The vendor fills in a transfer form which is then kept in the Association's office until signed by the purchaser. The Association can be contacted at The Readings, near Cheltenham, Gloucestershire (tel: Churchdown 713529).

All this effort is generally worthwhile only at the top end of the pigeon market, where birds are bought for breeding, and prices may top £1,000. Unless you are determined to take up the challenge of changing a pigeon's ways, it is far simpler, and probably cheaper, to buy a young bird.

HOSES *see* Garden tools

HOUSES

Britain's estate agents can expect to sell 750,000 secondhand houses every year. Many of these houses are disaster zones, with repair bills pouring in faster than rain through the holes in the roof. Only three in every ten buyers are prudent enough to take a surveyor's advice before signing the contract. The majority feel they can't afford a surveyor when every pound is needed for the deposit. The worst way to economise is to employ one of the many unqualified surveyors lurking in the 'phone book. The costs of a proper professional survey can be cut by using the building society's

surveyor. The societies are now more willing to reveal their surveyor's name.

It is important to discuss and agree on both the price and scope of a survey at a preliminary meeting with the surveyor. Checks on the electrical, plumbing and underground drainage systems are by no means automatic and could cost extra, even in a so-called "full structural survey".

There's a limit to how far a reputable surveyor can rip a house apart to look for hidden faults, especially if the house is still occupied. Only the demolition man does a thorough structural survey, but even the amateur can spot bad signs by taking a couple of hours to look logically over the building.

The diy survey should take place in daylight. The only tools needed are a tape measure, a penknife, a torch, and binoculars to examine the chimney stacks and roof, which is where the survey begins.

Roof Use binoculars if access is impractical or alarming. Some roofs can be checked from inside the loft space, where the risk of rotten timber should make surveyors tread carefully. The torch will normally be needed. Look for missing or slipped slates, and slates held at the bottom by lead or copper clips: these are signs of tired nails breaking up and making an expensive new roof necessary. Cracked and crumbling slates can be replaced. A sagging roof apex is a bad fault. Insecure ridge tiles and cracked flaunching could let in damp. Bubbling surfaces on flat roofs soon crack and should be replaced before damp damages the ceiling below.

Chimneys Leaning chimney stacks need rebuilding. The pointing must be sound, as stacks are very exposed to wind and rain. Rain often penetrates the junction of stack and roof, leading to stains by the chimney breast indoors. If fireplaces have been blocked up, the chimney pots should be covered and the chimney breast ventilated by an air brick.

Gutters and rainwater pipes Leaking gutters are best seen in wet weather, but may be betrayed by saturated or mossy patches on the wall below. Dirty marks around the joints of modern plastic gutters usually mean leaks. The guttering should be held by brackets at least every three feet. If the wooden fascia behind the gutter is rotten, trouble will follow. Cast-iron gutters rust and fail in time. Check cast-iron pipes closely for corrosion, especially at the back where painting is often neglected. Prod suspicious patches with a penknife.

Outside walls Cavity walls, with a two-inch gap between the two layers of brick/blockwork, have replaced the less desirable nine-inch-thick solid walls found in most pre-war houses. Measure the wall thickness at a window opening (allowing for the thickness of plaster inside) to determine which type of wall it is. Walls must be upright and free of cracks—vertical cracks are especially worrying indications of settlement. If the pointing or bricks are crumbling away, repair will be a long diy job or an expensive professional one. Bulging rendering has detached itself from the wall and will trap water.

Damp-proof course A good damp-proof course (dpc) is vital. It stops rising damp, which often shows first as stains above the skirting boards indoors. The dpc is a course of engineering bricks, felt or slate running between two brick courses some six inches above ground level. A slate dpc can crack and become ineffective if the house settles. If the dpc is bridged by soil or rubbish piled against the wall or by a new path or patio, it can be ineffective. A recent dpc may still be under guarantee.

Internal walls The state of the decorations is unimportant, as pre-sale redecoration is usually designed to hide faults, and is rarely to the buyer's taste anyway. Old decorations allow damp patches and cracks to show. If you suspect that important structural walls have been removed in the interest of open-plan design, take professional advice. Examine skirting boards carefully for the horizontal crazing which means dry rot has taken a grip. A combination of poor ventilation and damp causes dry rot. Expect the characteristic musty smell where air

bricks have been blocked off, in still cellars and damp cupboards. It is worth asking a timber preservation company to inspect the property (the survey is free) and estimate for eradicating dry rot, wet rot and woodworm.

Windows Windows rot, warp and stick. Open them all to test the action. Rattling, rotten windows let in cold, noise and damp. Poorly-painted frames rot. A prod with a penknife should reveal wet rot. The wall above windows needs strong and stable support. Double glazing is a debateable investment, but it is good news if someone else has paid for it. Bay windows are often built on bad foundations and start leaning away from the house.

Doors Check that all doors fit neatly in their frames. Warped doors are almost impossible to repair. A twisted door frame could be the sign of settlement.

Floors It is often impractical to lift carpets and floorboards, but a timber preservation company should check the floor out. Joists can rot away where they sit in a damp outside wall and may be seriously weakened by worm. Bouncy floors are possibly unstable, but squeaks can normally be cured by a few nails.

Staircase Creaking stairs are more of an irritation than a danger, but really rickety and uneven stairs with trembling handrails and a marked slope away from the wall should be professionally examined.

Plumbing An amateur will find the water system hard to examine in detail. Look for lead pipes which betray an ancient system, and check old cisterns for corrosion. Try all taps and listen for hammering and other sound effects. Cracks in underground drainage systems can cause unpleasant problems in old houses. A plumber will carry out a special drainage test.

Electrical system Pre-war wiring is dangerous and should be replaced. Signs of obsolete systems are a spaghetti of cables around a wooden fuse box, round-pin sockets and rubber-sheathed cable. The system can be checked by a NICEIC-registered electrician.

Lighting Gloomy stairways are dangerous. In other rooms bad lighting is just inconvenient.

Insulation Since insulation saves money, and it must be fitted if you apply for an improvement grant, it is better that someone else should have paid for it already.

Heating system Fuel costs vary from year to year, so fuel flexibility is a virtue. If the fireplaces or chimney breasts have been removed, this flexibility is reduced.

Garden Outside the house, check over the condition of outbuildings, paths and fences.

Legal arguments about cutprice conveyancing seem set to continue. Nobody disputes a person's right to carry out conveyancing on his or her own behalf, though some solicitors are outrageously snooty about public intelligence. You can assess your own chances of carrying the conveyancing through by reading one of the guides to the subject, such as

Michael Joseph's *The Conveyancing Fraud* or the Consumers' Association's *The Legal Side of Buying a House*. A good, brief, cheap guide to *Buying a House or Flat* is published by the Bedford Square Press, 26 Bedford Square, London WC1.

The major rule of house buying is never to agree to buy, especially in writing, until all the contractual and financial details are complete. Protect yourself by adding "subject to survey and contract" to all mentions of the purchase.

HOUSEBOATS

A floating home offers no escape from housing problems. You can't own the water, so there's usually a landlord to be dealt with. Rates have to be paid at commercial rather than the lower residential rate. Life on the water just adds super-damp foundations to the worries of the landlocked householder. In many ways life is less secure afloat. Houseboat dwellers have no security of tenure stretching beyond a maximum three-year licence. In practice most people renew their licence monthly or annually. Mooring fees add a further ever-rising expense. They can—and do—rocket horribly, and those who can no longer pay must go. Prices rise with inflation and proximity to London. Residential boats on the Thames seem to have more trouble than those moored on canals, where the landlords are the British Waterways Board (BWB). The BWB publish an annual list of charges which will be sent to any enquirers by the Craft Licensing Supervisor, BWB, Willow Grange, Church Road, Watford WD1 3QA. The list contains details of Houseboat Certificate fees and mooring fees.

The occupants of boats have no rights to the land the boat is moored to beyond the basic right of access to the boat. Sympathetic landlords allow tenants to use the bank as their garden. Services at the mooring vary from site to site. Tap water is nearly always available, as are toilet facilities, but electricity and access to a telephone are less common.

A new narrow boat can cost as much as any other type of house, but empty hulls may sell for £3,000–£7,000. The self-help urge is strong among the houseboat people, who happily take over such shells and convert them into something grand.

Idle boats can quietly moulder away unnoticed, so a survey is essential before buying any secondhand boat. The survey should be carried out by a surveyor familiar with the very particular problems of residential boats rather than by a general marine surveyor. The boat need not be dragged onto dry land for the survey—modern electronic equipment has made even underwater surveying of steel boats possible. In general, steel or glass fibre hulls will need less maintenance than the timber used on most older boats. Major structural defects below the waterline can be very expensive to put right, but visible problems are usually within the scope of the competent handyman.

The state of a secondhand boat is less important than the continuity of its mooring. The boat itself can always be swapped for another, but without an established residential mooring, you are sunk. Moorings are scarce and expensive. The new marina developments tend to resist long-term residential moorings.

A Certificate of Mooring will confirm the legitimacy of the mooring but is not in itself enough to reassure the wary. It is important to have a statement in writing from the letting authority confirming that the Certificate will be transferred to you and giving the precise contractual terms of the continued mooring.

The market in secondhand houseboats has never been lively, with the curiously high level of demand often leading to sales before boats are publicly advertised.

Good sources of information are therefore vital to the houseboat hunter, and there is none better than the purpose-designed Residential Boat Owners' Association, who float % Eridanus, Benbow Way Mooring, Uxbridge, Middlesex. The Association's newsletter lists boats for sale, and they also maintain a list of prospective buyers. Their extensive knowledge is willingly shared with members, who may for example need a recommendation for a surveyor prepared to travel anywhere in the country, or the name of finance companies known to be sympathetic to the needs of secondhand houseboat buyers. Building societies refuse mortgages other than the 5–7 year marine mortgages financing boats registered with Lloyd's.

A large selection of secondhand canal boats of all types, from the luxury of full central heating down to ex-army wooden pontoons with conversion plans, is on offer in the classified ads of the monthly *Waterways World*.

The "for sale" columns also include moorings and equipment; readers will normally find the names of several specialist surveyors plying for hire.

IRONS

Electric irons last a long time, but once they break, they are not worth buying. The cost of repair will almost certainly be uneconomically high.

A common cause of failure is a frayed flex, suffering after being dragged over the rough edges of an ironing board for years. Simple flexes can be replaced at home, but the method of connection is not always obvious. It is crucial to get the proper heat-resistant replacement. In modern irons the element is embedded in the sole plate. This is rarely worth replacing when it breaks, as a typical new plate costs half the price of the whole iron. Sometimes the job is not only too expensive, it is also impossible.

The only other significant part of an electric iron is the thermostat. Once this has broken, leaving the iron stuck on very hot or very cool, only an expert can bring the appliance back to useful life. The iron will have to be recalibrated and this costs a lot. On some irons, a neon light will indicate whether the thermostat is doing its job, but on others the thermostat must be tested at several settings next to a radio: there should be an audible click on the radio as the thermostat switches. The controls should not get too hot to handle even at the highest settings.

The iron's handle could be cracked, broken or uncomfortable, and the sole plate could be clogged up with filth. Aluminium sole plates are lighter than chromium-plated ones and also more likely to be scratched. Brown stains on the sole plate can usually be removed by a rub with very fine steel wool dipped in methylated spirits. Blue stains are a more serious problem, as they are a sign of overheating. If the iron has a thermostat, the blue sole may mean it is about to collapse, but if there is no thermostat, the iron could have been quite seriously damaged and is really not worth gambling on.

A steam iron may be furred up inside, especially if it has been used with undistilled water in a hard water area, which is extremely likely. Shake the iron and listen for the sound of maraccas to indicate mineral scale sloshing around inside and reducing the iron's efficiency. Irons can be cleaned out with a spe-cial chemical such as Sunbeam, to dissolve scale.

Performance may be improved by unscrewing and removing the centre of the sole plate, brushing out scale and replacing the metal mesh de-furring filter—it's a two minute job. A badly scaled iron is unlikely to come completely clean, and there's no guarantee that it will work any better after a descaling. A steam iron can be tested by leaving it full of water for a few minutes to check for leaks and then switching on to check that the steam emerges from the right place—and only the right place.

Before buying a very old iron, check that the manufacturer is still in existence. Long-discontinued lines are hard to find parts for.

IRONING BOARDS

Even in a permissive age, the love of ironing is widely considered a perversion. To enjoy standing with iron in hand by a worn and unstable ironing board, which wobbles around at the ideal height to produce backache, is positively masochistic. Whether buying new or secondhand, it is essential to buy an ironing board offering a comfortable working height, and this height varies from person to person. Ergonomists claim the ideal is to have your elbow on a level with the top of the iron handle. A board with adjustable height is handy for sharing the work around. Every position should be tried, as some may not hold the board steady enough.

Stability is a problem with old boards, as fixing screws can work loose. As long as they haven't fallen out, tightening up is easy. If they are missing, standard screws should fit.

The condition of the cover is significant, and not only as an indication of the past use the board has had. Dirty covers don't take kindly to washing, and finding a replacement of the right size for a worn cover may prove surprisingly hard. Flashy but usually ill-fitting covers cost only £1 from street markets and are the seller's perfect weapon in the struggle to sell a damaged board. Covers must be removed from any board to examine the base beneath. It may be warped with damp if it is made from plywood or chipboard, and plywood is also prone to woodworm. Both types of wood can be charred by hot irons or broken during karate practice.

The condition of the iron-rest should be plain to see. Asbestos remains the most popular material for iron-rests. For health reasons it is vital to reject any rest which has begun to crumble.

Maltreated steel bases may be going rusty, and this can permanently stain clothes during ironing. Rusty metal can of course be treated with a rust remover.

A sleeve board is a useful additional feature with a secondhand ironing board.

J

JEWELLERY

Only the most ignorant of secondhand dealers is unaware of the hallmarking system, so gold and silver are unlikely to go unnoticed in their stock. Unwary buyers may be fooled by the practices of cunning jewellers, who for centuries have been disguising baser metals as something grand by using hallmark-like marks. Arm yourself with an excellent free booklet published by the Assay Office of Great Britain. This explains the system and illustrates hallmarks through the ages, year by year and town by town. Send a 4″ × 9″ sae to the Publications Department at one of the four Assay Offices — Goldsmith's Hall, Gutter Lane, London EC2V 8AQ; Newhall Street, Birmingham B3 1SB; 137 Portobello Road, Sheffield S1 4DR and 15 Queen Street, Edinburgh EH2 1JE.

Objects manufactured before 1900 need no hallmark. Certain other objects made before 1975 — when platinum hallmarking was introduced — are also exempt; these include gold rings (except wedding rings), gold and silver watch chains and gold pencil cases. Foreign pieces are not necessarily marked.

Damaged jewellery should be cheap, and for good reason: highly skilled jewellers can still be found with the time and the tiny tools to repair practically any piece well, but costs can be very high. Professional repairs are only worth considering on pieces of high value. A professional repair such as resetting or remounting can sometimes be financed by omitting some of the original's metal or stones and selling them separately. Diy repairs can ruin good pieces but are often satisfactory on cheap jewellery.

214

Beads, for example, are easy to restring using nylon thread, although tensioning knotted strings correctly can be tricky. It is usually wise to assume a secondhand necklace has a weak string. Stones can be cleaned at home by a simple wash and brush up in a plastic bowl of warm water and washing-up liquid using a soft toothbrush. Rinsing small pieces under the tap without the plug in is inviting disaster. Don't wash porous stones such as turquoise or opal.

Breakages need not deter you from buying. Epoxy resin adhesive (usually known as Araldite) will stick parts together and can grip a stone which has come loose in its setting or hold a new link on an old cuff link. Missing pieces can sometimes be built up using Araldite, colour match being achieved by adding powder pigments sold by art shops.

Most fashion jewellery is made of a soft white metal which is easily bent out of shape but almost as easily hammered flat. Hammer on the back if possible.

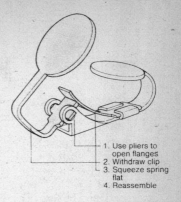

1. Use pliers to open flanges
2. Withdraw clip
3. Squeeze spring flat
4. Reassemble

Broken bracelet clasps are rarer than ones worn loose through use. The clasp arm is normally easy to bend back to shape with small pliers and care; replacements can be bought.

The springs of loose-fitting earrings are generally just as simple to bend into tension with pliers (see diagram above); the earring will probably have to be dismantled for repair. Pliers will also straighten pins on brooches and squeeze chain links closed.

(*See also* Silver.)

JIGSAWS *see* Power tools

K

KETTLES

The homely old copper kettle has become a desirable antique object, fought over by second-home owners rather than secondhand buyers. The cheap, whistling, aluminium kettle is a more frequent item in the junk shop. The aluminium kettle is soft, prone to deep dents and scratches and barely worth buying secondhand for more than a few pence. However, it can provide long and loyal service on the hob if it is not too distorted to stand flat, and there are no holes. Aluminium is horribly hard to solder, making repairs too tricky to contemplate if, for example, holes have burned through the bottom when the kettle has boiled dry. Fill it with water to check for leaks.

Stainless steel is a more resilient material than aluminium, although enamel could easily be chipped from an enamelled steel kettle. No electric kettle, even a steel one, is meant to stand on a hotplate: heat harms their feet and makes them totter.

Replacement feet are usually easy to find and fit as long as the fixing studs have not been knocked off.

Electric kettles have been heating British water for many years, and there is a good chance of finding a kettle with an immersed element dating from the 1920s. However, antique kettles are not worth buying secondhand except as art objects, as they were built without the useful switch which turns the kettle off once the water boils, saving the kettle from boiling dry and the element from burning out. Replacement elements can be impossible to find for ancient kettles. The design of many old kettles is wonderfully striking, yet they are frequently melted down for scrap. They are certainly worth rescuing from the scrap heap, if only to serve an active retirement as flower vases.

Modern electric kettles incorporate a safety cut-out to prevent a domestic replay of the China Syndrome. You can check that this feature is operational on secondhand kettles. The test involves switching on an empty kettle and seeing if the element burns out. Some sellers are reluctant to permit such a dramatic acid-test: an untested kettle is an unwise buy.

Replacing a burnt-out element is a simple job on most modern non-automatic kettles, and is theoretically simple on all. Professional repair men can mend a kettle in their tea break, but replacing an element can take an ill-equipped amateur all day and more. While replacement switches and elements are easy to buy for the popular Russell Hobbs kettle, a special pronged tool is almost indispensable to remove the old element. Long-nosed pliers sometimes suffice. Anyone attempting repairs on this type of kettle should dismantle the appliance with care, as a captive nut can easily drop out and disappear for ever when the switch cover is removed. A dab of glue will hold it in position during reassembly.

Professional repairs are not expensive—an element can be replaced for under half the price of a new kettle; switches and thermostats may be even cheaper. If possible, a secondhand kettle should be boiled up before buying to check that the thermostat cuts out when the water boils, and not before. Sluggish old thermostats often turn the kettle off too early. During this test the boiling speed of the kettle can be timed against typical figures for a new kettle; a new 3kw kettle will boil three pints of water in under four minutes.

Even if no plug is available, and the kettle can't be seen working, there will normally be a handy water supply, and filling the kettle provides the best way to check for leaks. Ideally, washing-up liquid should be sneaked into the water, as this helps seek out leaks by breaking down surface tension. Leaks can be expected to ooze water around points where feet fixings, spout and element penetrate the metal body. The remedy may just be a new washer, but leaky spouts are too hard to repair. If the water hasn't leaked all over the floor in a minute or two, pour it away through the spout: the spout may be damaged in such a way that it dribbles boiling water over your clothes.

Check the flex. It should be both long enough to reach your socket outlet and in perfect condition. Any signs of fraying make a new flex absolutely necessary, and this can be a pricey, even impossible, matter if the flex connector is moulded on at the kettle end. With most kettles the connector is easily opened by removing a screw.

If the kettle can't be tried out, it is not worth paying more for it than you can afford to throw away. Furring is almost invariably present in old kettles in hard water areas. Chalk deposits build up on the sides and bottom and cover the element. This scaling can be pretty, but it slows down the kettle. Scale should not be hacked off with a knife, but burned off by one of the proprietary descaling products available from hardware stores. The descaler is normally added to warm water in the kettle and allowed to fizz away. The fumes should not be inhaled as they contain formic acid and are the equivalent of a face full of stinging nettles.

KITCHEN EQUIPMENT

Old smoothing irons, coffee grinders and jelly moulds have joined copper pans in the antique category, and prices have therefore risen. However, the humble traditional mincer remains both cheap and useful secondhand. Replacement plates are available for Spong mincers at about £1 each.

Tins, moulds, spatulas and whisks are among the best buys at the average jumble sale. If you like them, buy them, as the cost is normally just a few pence. Rust and holes are the only common enemies to look out for, although the entire idea of cooking the family cakes in a junk tin appals the fastidious. Others find comfort in the savings and still enjoy the cakes.

KITCHEN SCALES

Modern scales can measure the weight of a word on a

piece of paper, whereas some secondhand ones couldn't be trusted to register the presence of the *Encyclopedia Britannica*. Secondhand scales turn up regularly in auctions, junk shops and closing-down sales, as the country's small corner shopkeepers close down or turn to the unerring green digits of computerised weighing machines, and the nation's cooks go progressively metric.

It is most unwise to expect old commercial scales to be accurate. A tendency to exaggerate weight rather than underestimate it is predictable. However, even when a decline in accuracy finishes the shop-counter life of old scales, they can still command a high price among collectors of machines or kitchen gadgets and designers of country-style kitchens.

The accuracy of commercially-used weights will in the past have been the responsibility of the weights and measure inspectors. They traditionally made an annual descent on a village to verify every merchant's scales, adding lumps of lead to a weight when over-enthusiastic polishing had caused a decline in weight. The inspector's code number can be seen punched into the weight. This number is officially obliterated by a star-shaped mark when the weight falls horribly below expectations. On the weight's base will appear the final two digits of the year in which it was last approved; for example a circled number 26 stands for 1926. The relevant monarch's cypher—for instance VR or EIIR—may also appear, topped by a crown.

The commonest type of weight is the nest of metal cylinders fitting together to make a cone. The more attractive—and more expensive—style is the set of bell-shaped weights with handles. A normal set of commercial weights will contain ¼oz, ½oz, 1oz, 2oz, 4oz, 8oz, 1lb. Higher weights are uncommon if the scales were designed for a sweet shop or tobacconist.

Imperial weights are becoming less desirable as weight-watching in Britain goes metric. Baby-weighing machines marked in the imperial scale have become a dead weight on the secondhand market, and lovers of the imperial system may find bargains. Domestic kitchen scales are unlikely to bear any inspection stamp to indicate that they were ever accurate, but accuracy is not necessarily crucial at home, unless you want to double check the 3 lb of carrots bought from an untrustworthy trader.

The balance type of scales can be checked for accuracy by putting objects of known equal weight on each side of the balance. The weights used with such scales can also be checked against a counterbalance of known weight. A new set of weights can be bought for approximately £7 if the original weights are missing or unacceptably wrong. New sets can be bought in imperial or metric sizes (the ranges are 5g–1kg and ¼oz–2lb) from specialist shops such as Bush and Hall, 40 Theobald's Road, London WC1. Other parts for old balance scales are almost impossible to find.

Scales with a dial are a less reliable secondhand buy, being distinctly less robust than balance scales. As long as the pointer is not missing or twisted, they can be tested for accuracy by weighing something of known weight. The test can be repeated several times to make sure that the dial is consistent and the pointer can move freely.

L

LADDERS

Once a week, on average, someone falls to their death off a ladder in Britain. Most falls happen when the ladder topples over, often because it was wrongly put up. Enough accidents can be blamed on faulty ladders to make testing a secondhand ladder a hazardous enterprise. Nevertheless it is necessary to test the level of comfort and the extent of swaying before you buy, and the only way is to climb the rungs. Fortunately, dangerous ladders can usually be spotted before the climb begins.

Timber is traditionally the most popular material for ladder construction, but the much lighter, cheaper and warp-free aluminium alloy is replacing it rapidly for both stepladders and extension ladders, indoors and out. Wooden ladders are therefore more likely to turn up secondhand, displaced in their owner's affections and toolshed by aluminium.

Never buy a painted wooden ladder for anything but a climbing frame for plants. Dangerous faults can develop unseen under paint, and paint may even be used by the unscrupulous or the ostrich to hide flaws. A more obvious sign of hidden damage is string wound around the ladder's stiles: it is safe to assume that such whipping covers split wood.

Bad hanging can bend ladders: look along the ladder for signs of warping. The wood used for ladder stiles should be straight-grained and knot-free. All splits make purchase unwise. Both stiles and rungs should be cut along the grain, not across it. A hammer is a useful aid to rung examination—tap each rung with the hammer, look-ing for splits to open and listening for the dead sound of damaged wood. Don't buy a ladder with faulty rungs, as these must be replaced only by an expert, and experts are expensive. If you suspect that amateur repairs have been carried out, reject the ladder.

Well-made traditional timber ladders have hardwood rungs that do not go right through the stiles. If the rungs can be seen from the sides, the ladder may become unstable after a tough life outdoors.

Steel tie rods are fixed under wooden rungs to give strength. These can rust away and the screws or rivets holding them in position can work loose or drop out. Screws may prove hard to tighten. Tie rods are not needed on aluminium ladders.

Aluminium rungs come in several shapes and are widely considered safer and less harsh on the feet than round wooden rungs. Aluminium rungs may be set in wooden stiles—if so, check for signs of splitting caused by swelling of the wood where rung meets stile.

The joint of stile and rung is often fixed with rivets on an aluminium ladder, but flanged joints are preferable. The entire section of an aluminium rung should be supported at the joint. The heads and feet of aluminium extension ladders need non-slip shoes covering the ends if these are not reinforced. Shoes can be bought separately and cheaply.

Extension ladders should be assembled to check the condition of the pulley mechanism and the ease of movement.

The sliders and hooks are held by rivets or bolts which should go right through the entire stile. They may have worked loose and present real danger, especially if tightening proves impossible. It is senseless to buy without tightening them up. If the sections of an extension lad-

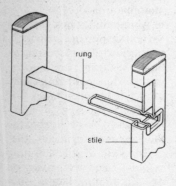

a secure flanged rung-joint

der are designed to be used separately, take the ladder apart and put it back together again.

The correct working position for platform stepladders is fixed by a stop on the platform. Other stepladders are held at the right angle by ropes, chains or struts. These are easily replaced and essential. It is just as important and—as long as the wood is not rotten—just as simple, to fix new cross supports between the uprights of the stepladder where old ones have snapped. Without a full quota of braces, the ladder may fall down and will certainly prove rickety and unstable.

LAWNMOWERS

The price of secondhand garden machinery follows the rhythm of the seasons—it rises with the sap in spring and reaches a low point in midwinter. But winter is not always the best season to choose a used lawnmower, because there's no grass to try out its cutting efficiency and ease of handling. By the time the grass needs cutting, any guarantees are long lapsed.

The risk of problems with

untested equipment can be offset by buying a machine from a specialist dealer in garden equipment. The price here will on average be higher than in a private sale or an auction, but the specialist normally overhauls the mowers before selling them. Dealers may also be able to supply an owner's handbook for the mower, generally a handy little document explaining routine lubrication procedures, whether to use oil or grease, etc. As always, it is sensible to check out future spares availability with the manufacturer before buying.

No mechanical wizardry is needed to spot some of the most serious problems a secondhand lawnmower may hide. With most kinds of appliance general outside appearance is an unreliable guide to the condition of the innards, but in this case it counts for something. Poor maintenance leaves the blades and deflector plates clogged with grass, adjustment nuts seized up with rust, and the blades damaged.

The front roller must be easy to spin and fully adjustable, to cope with varying conditions on the lawn. An adjustable spanner is a handy tool to test the adjusting nuts for seizure. A straight edge such as a metal ruler held against each blade will show up any distortion, which may be a sign of ill treatment or poor metal. Minor burrs can be ground out of a blade, but if the blades on the rotating cylinder are warped or badly chipped they will need replacing. Similarly, if the fixed blade at the bottom of the machine has become rounded it too is useless.

Cutting efficiency can be checked by loosening the lock nuts holding the blades and adjusting them until the blade just touches the static bottom blade along its whole length. As the cylinder is slowly turned, it should maintain a constant distance from the bottom blade. Otherwise expensive regrinding or replacement may be needed. A sharp and well positioned blade will slice cleanly through a sheet of paper. Try this test on your list of spares suppliers: if the list remains intact, you'll need it, though spares may no longer be available for many models. Blades can easily be reshaped to some extent by smearing coarse grinding paste on both cylinder and static blades and rotating the cylinder *back-wards*.

If the blades won't turn at all, there's probably a fault in the freewheel. This takes time to repair but is not a very demanding or expensive diy job if spares are available.

Worn cylinder shaft bearings are a common cause of poor cutting. They can be checked out by trying to move the cylinder up and down—if there is any play, a tedious and lengthy repair job is indicated.

Tell-tale signs of wear on chain-driven mowers should be revealed on the sprockets. If the teeth have become hook-shaped or rounded, this is a sign of heavy use. Belts, which often give a similar clue to past use, are very simple to replace, as long as an exact replacement can be bought. Chains are tougher than belts but they stretch with age and hang loose on the sprockets. Links can be removed to shorten the chain.

Rotary mowers have blades

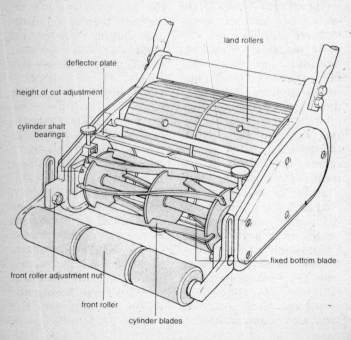

land rollers

deflector plate

height of cut adjustment

cylinder shaft bearings

fixed bottom blade

front roller adjustment nut

front roller

cylinder blades

rotating in a horizontal plane underneath the machine. A single blade must be perfectly balanced to prevent bad vibrations damaging the engine. If the machine shakes in use, even when the blade is removed, the engine may already be ruined. The heavier end of a blade can be filed down to restore the balance after sharpening. Sharpening is not practicable on blades with detachable cutting edges bolted on, but these are easy to change. Other models have short blades bolted onto a rotating disc; these may need replacing.

The air filter may need cleaning out, and the throttle cable and wheel bearings may need a little oil, but rotary mowers are relatively simple machines. As long as the lever or screw for adjusting height of cut is still operable, and the engine starts up and drives the blades, the mower should be a reasonably safe buy.

This is a sound principle for all power mowers. Test the engine by starting it several times and running it at both low and high speeds. Bad noises in the engine should put anyone off, and blue smoke pouring from a four-stroke engine probably means it is worn. Once the engine is warm, compression can be checked by operating the starter very slowly, feeling for increased resistance as the piston is forced over the top of the stroke. If you can't feel the force, the engine is worn.

It is certainly unwise to buy any mower whose engine won't start. The problem may just be maladjustment or a broken starter handle, but without technical skill proper judgement is difficult. A petrol-driven motor is just as unfathomable a machine as a motor car, with clutch, carburettor, points, plugs and all the other mysteries. To buy a car that won't start is not wise unless you have the knowledge. A mower is no different, but cheaper.

The growing popularity of reliable lightweight electric mowers is quite understandable. They are both cleaner and simpler to operate. The likeliest cause of motor failure is worn carbon brushes, which are easy to renew. The handlebar switch may be broken, but this too is easily replaced. Unbalanced blades can lead to engine wear. The commonest problem is a slashed cable; as these tend to be very long, replacement can add considerably to cost. Cable length can be increased only by using a specially-designed waterproof connector for outside use, not an ordinary household job which could provoke a short circuit on damp lawns.

Battery powered mowers are relatively rare. They are similar in principle to all other mowers, but may involve unwary buyers in extra expense if a completely flat battery needs replacement. A separate charger may be needed, although some have one built in. Acid spills can damage the mower.

On any mower, remember to ask about the grass box.

LIGHT FITTINGS

In 1878 Paris By Night was flooded in electric light for the first time. Following the French lead, English country houses and public buildings such as the Post Office's Glasgow sorting office switched on to electricity during the 1880s. Despite the high cost of light bulbs at the time—the early incandescent lamp cost 5/-(25 pence) each—electric lighting grew in popularity, although it was only in the second quarter of the twentieth century that the electric light established its supremacy over gas lighting in the nation's homes.

Light fittings from the inter-war period are now commonplace in secondhand shops. They are often extremely stylish and extremely dangerous, as the Art Deco age was unconcerned with such safety precautions as an earthing terminal, even if the metal parts were prominently exposed. Only in 1975 and 1976 were safety regulations introduced requiring equipment to be either earthed or double insulated.

It is not easy to establish whether an appliance is well earthed or not, as the terminal could be inaccessible, on the base or the lampholder itself.

Besides a lack of earthing, old light fittings could have equally old wiring, with brittle insulation. It is sensible to have all secondhand fittings checked out, and perhaps rewired and earthed, by an electrical contractor before they are linked up to live cables.

Although a potentially dangerous old lamp should

be made electrically inoperable before being sold, this precaution is almost unknown to secondhand dealers. Reputable lighting dealers are worth seeking out, though the chances of a bargain from a specialist are slim. The most famous dealer of all is Christopher Wray at 600 Kings Road, London SW6. All Wray's lamps pass through the renovation department before being offered to the public, and every electric light fitting is safely earthed. Wray's also carry an impressive array of spare parts for old lamps with smashed shades, globes and funnels.

LIQUIDISERS

Liquidisers are sometimes known as blenders, and this confusion of names helps explain why they are so often given as duplicated and unwanted presents which are quietly sold off secondhand by ungrateful recipients. Good quality blenders are often found on the secondhand stalls.

A blender/liquidiser consists of a container mounted on an electric motor. The motor turns the cutting blades which liquefy and mix food.

They are particularly good at producing purées and soups. Coffee mill attachments are sold for some models, and should make a difference to the value of a secondhand appliance.

The price of new blenders varies vastly, but few secondhand machines are worth the expense of a repair. Cutter blades may be an exception, as they are often simple to replace, but others are held by an inaccessible rivet and are all but impossible to adjust or replace. It is usually a job for the professional, and a new machine may be cheaper in the long run, especially if time is included in the calculation.

Because repair is rarely worthwhile, it is vital to try the appliance out before buying. Testing is simple. After examining the flex for wear, try the switch in all its positions. If a switch position doesn't work, the problem is likely to be a dud resistor, but only an electrician can confirm this. If the appliance works at all, its most noticeable feature is usually noise, which may prove so unbearable that you call the purchase off.

The motor is the main

cause of problems with old blenders, especially as many models are not meant to be run for more than a few seconds at a time, to prevent overheating, and many hard-pressed cooks ignore this instruction. Food can complicate motors by penetrating the housing through a poor seal, giving the motor severe electrical indigestion. Dirty appliances are probably problematic. On much-used blenders the motor bearings or carbon brushes may be worn. The motor windings may be burnt out, in which case the appliance just won't work, though it will probably smell very hot.

Some containers are made of easily-broken glass. These are in a very vulnerable position perched on top of the motor, and it is important that spares should be avilable. Buy one for discontinued models while you can. The alternative to glass is plastic, which is more durable but which gathers unattractive stains and scratches in time.

LOCKS

Locks have a long history going back to law and order in ancient Egypt. The main types of lock keeping today's undesirables out are 19th-century inventions, typified by the Chubb and the Yale. Old locks are sold occasionally at auction but are more frequently discarded.

A used lock has usually lost its key; whether the lock is sold separately or fixed to the furniture it's meant to guard. A keyless lock is a doubtful asset, as there can be no certainty that the lock will ever work again. All repairs are possible, but a locksmith's time is too expensive to make any repair to an inexpensive modern lock worthwhile.

The main problem is likely to be finding a key to fit. Locksmiths can make new keys for old locks without working from an original key, but they may have to take the lock's innards out and either replace them or adjust the levers and then make a key to match. This might be more expensive at the end of the day than buying a new lock, and is normally more trouble.

However, the rejigging of the levers will at least reassure the security-conscious by rendering useless any duplicate keys held back by an old owner with a penchant for burglary.

The more old-fashioned type of locksmith may be willing to cut a key to match the existing lock's pattern, and this will not necessarily cost more than twice the price of a normal duplicate key. Keys for rare and tricky locks could be much more costly.

Locksmiths can be located through the "Locksmith" section of the *Yellow Pages*; most will be discouraging, but perseverance usually brings success in the end.

If you buy a door with a lock already fitted in it, but no key, it is probably worth paying for a new key to be made rather than risk an expensive and difficult refitting with a new lock of different dimensions. If the old lock won't come out of the door, a house visit from the locksmith will add to the cost of the key.

Oily locks are not to be trusted. Oil will ease the working parts of stiff locks for long enough to sell them, but after a while the oil attracts dust and the lock can be ruined.

Instead of a secondhand lock to replace an insecure original, it may be more cost-effective in terms of burglar-deterrence to buy a new escutcheon to display on the front door. For a few pence your keyhole can be covered by a name to deter all but the most determined criminals.

LOUDSPEAKERS *see* Audio equipment

LUGGAGE

A broken zip is the likeliest fault in secondhand luggage, followed by damaged locks, snapped handles and frayed stitching. All these problems can be put right, often quite simply, but their impact on the price makes considerable bargains commonplace. Simple repair jobs come within the scope of the neighbourhood shoe repairer or even the enterprising do-it-yourselfer, who should find few problems in fixing a handle or riveting reinforcement pieces on damaged corners.

Most shops selling cases quite understandably refuse to mend goods they didn't supply. The seller may know where the case came from, indeed the truly efficient will even have a receipt to prove it.

Traditional craftsman cobblers have the necessary skills to mend leather luggage and may be willing to try. Finding one of the increasingly rare repairers may be easier outside major cities, as country town saddlers will often use their hand-stitching skill to mend leather suitcases. The yearbook of the Society of Master Saddlers has a county-by-county list of all its members. The yearbook is obtainable from the Secretary at 9 St Thomas Street, London SE1.

Locks are little use without keys, and few cases come with keys attached, even fewer with the right one. The manufacturer should have replacements, but even if the manufacturer's name is still legible inside the case, it is unwise to assume they did not go bankrupt years ago. The luggage department of certain major stores may hold the key for their own merchandise. Shrewd secondhand buyers ignorant of a case's origin can approach the department store with a story about the case being a present believed to come from them and now found to be keyless—this saves embarrassment if it transpires that they never stocked such things, and it may locate a key. Harrods estimate that they can normally supply keys up to five years after the last date of manufacture. It may of course be simpler to fit a new lock, particularly if the case will open to give access to the tongues holding the lock in place.

Soaked and rippled cardboard cases are too weak to be of use. Once their decorative top surface begins to wear away, their days are numbered. Plastic is waterproof but torn plastic is not worth bothering with, as few repairers will touch it. New glues such as Vinylweld make diy plastic repair possible.

Dry old leather is weak and brittle, a bad secondhand buy, particularly if the case is intended for the rough treatment handed out by airport baggage handlers. Well-cared-for leather is supple and lustrous. Dirt can be cleaned off by a wipe with a damp cloth and pure soap flakes; let the case dry out naturally, as heat can crack leather. Complete the clean-up with a little hide food. Travel-weary leather suit cases like hide food, a creamy emulsion with fat liquors to nourish and preserve.

Ceebee Food or Leafood by Bridge of Weir are two brands available in major department stores. Let the hide food dry after application and then polish it off. Alternatively try transparent shoe polish or Neat's Foot, a pure oil from the heel of a cow, sold by the increasingly rare traditional cobblers and saddlers.

Cases left in damp attics can get mildewed. Rather than washing mildew off, which might leave stains on the leather, wipe it off with a dry cloth. White of egg sometimes shifts mildew stains.

Auctions can be a source of almost-free secondhand luggage, as lots of clothes, books, pans or oddments often come packed up in good yet unnoticed cases. However, the most reliably excellent sources of secondhand luggage remain the Lost Property operations of the various transport authorities, as cases rank with raincoats and brollies as prime candidates for an extra ride.

M

MICE *see* Pets

MICROSCOPES

Sherlock Holmes' famous magnifying glass was an elementary microscope, being an optical device for examining small objects, albeit clues of mammoth significance. Today's scientifically-minded super-sleuth would be more likely to fight crime with a sophisticated £40,000 electron microscope. The scope of the average buyer of secondhand equipment lies between these two extremes.

The popular general-purpose light microscope has its eyepiece and objective mounted in a tube. The classic monocular microscope, over which generations of students have squinted, has been superseded by a binocular type which doesn't tire the staring eye so fast. A third type——the dissecting microscope——consists of two separate microscopes mounted side by side: their magnification power tends to be low.

Magnification power varies with purpose, and the best test of a secondhand microscope is to try it out on the kind of object it will be asked to magnify in future. At this stage it may become apparent that the microscope's all-important mirror is broken or missing. These are not made to a standard size but can be replaced at reasonable cost by specialist suppliers: the absence of a mirror need not deter the buyer. If a lens is broken, on the other hand, the microscope is not normally worth buying at any price, as repair costs have been magnified enormously in recent years. As long as the lens is not cracked or chipped, it should be acceptable. The test should reveal whether the focusing system is operational and this involves verifying that the rack and pinion for both coarse and fine adjustment are secure and don't slip.

Standards in the world of microscopes have been set and maintained augustly for over 100 years by the Royal Microscopical Society. As early as 1859 Richard Beck was writing in the *Transactions of the Microscopical Society of London* his "Remarks on the 'Universal Screw'". At that time the thread on objective lenses was standardised throughout the world, and by the turn of the century the diameter of the eyepiece was also fixed. Mirrors and focusing mechanisms have never been standardised and are virtually never interchangeable. This is particularly true of the more expensive makes—which tend to use their own system—and old microscopes from the days when each firm had its individual taps and dies to hand-chase its own screw threads.

Early microscopes are solid brass, and brass is worth having. Brass stands will probably have been deliberately blackened during manufacture, but the underside of the base is rarely treated and can usually be examined to identify the metal used. Modern microscopes are less likely to be all-brass, but brass moving parts remain a sign of a well-made instrument. Brass parts may be hidden until the sliding parts are separated to reveal the inside surfaces. Cast aluminium alloy is the perfectly acceptable modern alternative to brass in the body of the microscope.

Connoisseurs scorn instruments made of mazac, an unsavoury metal prone to crumbling away. Italian microscopes frequently employ mazac.

The great Japanese and German names in camera manufacture tend to dominate the microscope market, with many of today's cheaper instruments being imported from Russia. Russian spare parts are universally acceptable, and are commonly used during repairs. Russian and rival Chinese models are reliable, although a recent Chinese experiment with plastic handles outraged traditionalists in Britain: the practice ceased.

Thoroughly reliable suppliers of secondhand microscopes can be found. One such is Brunnings (Holborn) Ltd of 133 High Holborn, London WC1V 6PX, who sell, repair and love secondhand instruments. They offer a year's guarantee with their

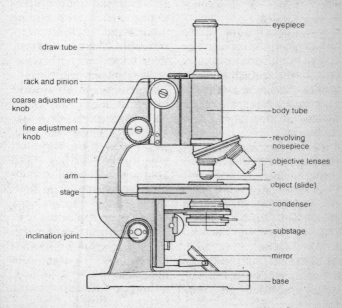

draw tube — eyepiece

rack and pinion

coarse adjustment knob — body tube

fine adjustment knob — revolving nosepiece

— objective lenses

arm — object (slide)

stage — condenser

inclination joint — substage

— mirror

— base

microscopes and will also supply replacement parts to repair old and neglected ones. They never turn away a microscope without at least pointing the owner in the right direction.

Sarose Scientific Instruments Suppliers, 2 Manor Road, London W13 sell renovated secondhand microscopes together with other secondhand laboratory equipment. They offer a reassuring two-month warranty. Other companies listed in the *Yellow Pages* as "Laboratory Equipment Suppliers" may also sell secondhand microscopes.

Several magazines carry occasional advertisements for secondhand microscopes. Among the specialists, *Laboratory Equipment Digest* and *Laboratory News* are worth looking at; *Nature* may also be fruitful.

People looking for or enthusing over microscopes could contact the admirable Quekett Microscopical Club (founded 1865), which can be found % the British Museum (Natural History), Cromwell Road, London SW7 5BD. This unique club welcomes amateur enthusiasts as much as experts. Members circulate each other with requests for microscopes, lenses, books etc., and the club publishes both an internationally respected journal—*Microscopy*—and a very informative *Newsletter*.

MICROWAVE OVENS

The long-term effects of microwaves are unknown; optimists argue that the lack of exposed hot surfaces on microwave cookers makes them safer than conventional cookers, which annually burn cooks in their thousands. However, the thought of untamed microwaves zipping around the kitchen understandably scares a lot of cautious cooks away from secondhand microwave cookers. The danger of microwave leakage is undoubtedly higher on old appliances, which may have been mistreated, and this makes them very bad buys for the nervous. Even bold and undemanding buyers may have problems finding a suitable secondhand cooker. The appliances have not been around long enough to have reached the secondhand market in significant numbers. If one is located, a simple examination can cut the risk of waves leaking over the kitchen floor. The local council's environmental health department may be prepared to give a cooker a free safety inspection once it is installed in your home, but it is doubtful if any will advise on whether or not to buy a particular used one. Hiring an engineer to check it for you is too expensive to contemplate. Diy examination should concentrate on loose doors, rusty door hinges and broken see-through door panels, all bad signs.

Steer clear of dirty cookers. Food accumulating around the door seals could lead to leaks, and signs of charred food glued to the cooker's insides should be as offputting as they sound, for they can be very hard to remove and could impair the cooker's efficiency. A clean cooker also has its possible risks; if it has been scoured with abrasive cleaner, the surface could be damaged, so ask the seller tactfully which cleaner has been used. The instruction book will explain how to clean the cooker and how to make it work. It is a document worth having.

Microwave cookers need no special wiring and can be plugged straight into a normal socket outlet using a 13 amp plug, so a demonstration should usually be perfectly possible and is worth demanding. An interior light indicates that the waves are being generated. The cooker should not be tested by switching it on empty, as this can damage the all-important magnetron which generates the waves. Serious damage can be caused by any metal objects in the cooker. The ideal test of a cooker is to give it something to cook. An oven-ready frozen meal is perfect, for it takes only a couple of minutes if the cooker is working properly, and you can then share a celebration snack with the seller if all goes well. Bread or water are a more frugal substitute. Try out all the switches and check that the turntable is working if it should have one.

If you buy now and regret later, you can take out an insurance policy for the cooker with the manufacturer. Arranging an insurance policy for yourself may be more difficult.

MIRRORS

With a secondhand mirror, it's not what you see, it's the

way that you see it. Even the professional mirror man judges quality mainly by looking into the glass. The most noticeable form of decay in an old mirror, short of a large crack, is peeling of the silver backing. This leaves unappealing dark patches on the surface and causes a progressive loss in reflecting power. Mirrors which have hung for years in damp bathrooms, restaurants, hairdressing salons, ships and seaside amusement arcades will have had a particularly punishing life.

Resilvering can be carried out by specialists, but the number of local glaziers willing to take on this work is dwindling fast. Resilvering costs have become so high that the only mirrors worth buying in poor condition at any price are those with unusual or beautiful glass, etched and patterned surfaces or perhaps simple bevelled edges. A dim reflecting surface is of course a less serious problem if the chosen mirror is not meant to be looked into.

Before a mirror is resilvered, the old flaking surface has to be stripped away in a hydrochloric acid bath. The naked glass is then cleaned with ammonia. Scrupulous cleanliness is crucial, as any specks of dirt left on the surface will lift the new silver off.

Some old mirrors are beyond repair, as a chemical reaction has stained the glass itself. A reputable shop should spot this problem and point out the danger of wasting your money before they agree to attempt resilvering.

A cracked or gloomy mirror—like a torn or shoddy painting—may be worth buying just to throw it away and keep the frame, as long as the price is low enough. A cheap glass-cutting tool also makes it possible to cut a large cracked mirror down to fit a smaller frame.

Metal mountings should be examined for corrosion, and wooden frames should be checked for signs of woodworm. Woodworm love the plywood backing of a typical mirror. A new piece of mirror glass can be cut to any shape and fitted by a reasonably competent glazier, usually for considerably less than half the price of resilvering the original.

MOBILE HOMES

New or secondhand, buying

a house is supposedly the biggest and the best investment most people can make, as house prices just keep moving up. However, a financially sluggish exception to this rule is the mobile home, where prices tend to drop as the home grows older. The problem lies in the soil: the buyer of a mobile home doesn't own the land on which his home is temporarily propped, just the right to be resident there for a certain time.

Before 1975 the mobile home owner had a miserable existence, at the mercy of the site owners. Site owners were also retailers of mobile homes, and they could refuse, quite legally, to allow residents to sell their homes secondhand to the highest bidder when they wanted to move on. The departing owner had to sell the home back to the site owner for a joke sum. The home was then transported off site and sold at a profit by the site owner, probably to a holiday site operator or a construction firm wanting temporary accommodation for its labourers. The incoming resident would then buy a new home and the site owner would pocket a second profit.

Obviously the higher the turnover of tenants the greater this profit, which led the housing organisation Shelter to speculate in 1975 that this might explain the site owners' preference for aged tenants.

Since the 1975 Mobile Homes Act the occupier can sell the home on site to the highest bidder, and this has created the market in second-hand mobile homes. Site owners must now offer owners who rent pitches a five year agreement in writing, renewable for three years and including the right to sell to a third party after offering the home at a fair market price to the site owner. The site owner has the right to veto any particular individual, but permission to sell cannot be unreasonably withheld. Under the 1976 Mobile Homes Discounts and Commissions Order site owners are compensated for their deep loss by a 15 per cent commission on the sale or, alternatively, a 15 per cent discount if they buy the home themselves.

Homes and sites are sold independently, and finding a suitable site is often the greater problem. Planning permission for mobile home sites is not readily granted by local authorities, who are often snooty about the desirability of sites. Pressure on available sites is therefore high, and the price of a pitch can run into thousands of pounds. Rent will also have to be paid. Secondhand homes are understandably very much cheaper if no pitch is included, but no home is worth buying without a pre-arranged pitch. Moreover, transport costs can be very high to move a home around the country to a new site, and some old homes may not stand the strain. Local authorities may make stipulations about the type of homes allowed on a site. This is worth checking out before buying a possibly useless home. The commonest demand is conformity with British Standard 3632. Site rules may insist on replacement of old homes every seven years or so. Some sites are, in any case, revolting.

Examining a mobile home is similar to checking out a secondhand caravan. The overall structural soundness and standard of design are more important than the condition of fittings which can be easily replaced. Many manufacturers have gone bust over the past decade, so explanations of problematic points may be hard to come by. Owners' manuals are extremely rare even for new mobile homes: they must be collectors' items for old ones.

Financing the purchase can be tricky. Mobile homes are traditionally bought for cash, often by retired people who have just realised their life's savings. Indeed, many sites still stipulate that pitches are for "middle-aged and retired people only, no children or dogs". Building societies are reluctant to lend on mobile homes, particularly when funds are low. Short-term borrowing at high rates of interest is therefore the regrettable norm. Several well-known finance houses offer schemes.

For many people the search for a mobile home begins with a summer caravanning holiday. Home-based hunters can scour the classified advertisement section in the monthly magazine *Mobile Home and Holiday Caravan*. Several specialist agents advertise in the magazine.

MOTOR CYCLES

Motor cyclists are notoriously

accident-prone, and any used bike could be on sale because a broken rider has reverted to public transport. Buyers should be especially wary of bikes which the newly-motorised sixteen-year-old would ride, as they are the great abusers and crashers of motor cycles. Approach any sporty 50cc "special" with care.

Other little bikes can be an excellent secondhand buy. The machines which no self-conscious sixteen-year-old would be seen dead under are very simple, and as long as they are repeatedly fed with oil, they should have a long and frugal life. The traditional "clean" alternative to a motor bike—the scooter—is too often structurally damaged to be a reasonable secondhand buy.

It is wise to assume that any bike has been smartened up for sale, with oil leaks wiped off the engine, a worn seat recovered and perhaps a rusty tank resprayed. Bikes damaged in accidents may bear visible scars which a preliminary off-the-road test can reveal. Paint or metal may be scuffed on foot rests, pedals or handlebar ends, the petrol tank may be dented, and the frame may even be twisted.

Push down hard on the bike and let it bounce back up—the shock absorbers should damp out the bounce immediately. With the bike on its stand, spin the wheels to see if they revolve smoothly, and check tyres for even wear and good tread. The front forks should be rigid and secure. It should not be possible to wobble the wheels from side to side or up and down.

Check the chain and the rear sprockets. Poor maintenance and hard riding wear down the sprocket teeth or make them hook-shaped, particularly on big bikes. Replacement is neither very expensive nor difficult, but small repair bills soon mount up to major expense.

With the bike motionless, apply the front brake and try to rock the handlebars to test the head bearings—there should be no movement. The brakes cannot be properly tried out without a test run, although most big modern bikes have disc brakes, which are easy to check over for score marks in the metal. Drum brakes are harder to inspect and can really be tested only in action.

The last test before taking the bike on the road is to start it up. A good bike starts fast. Dealers will not normally allow inexperienced riders to take a bike on a test run, and many operate a complete ban on bikes leaving the premises before they are sold. This is in response to the widespread practice of taking a bike for a test and never coming back. Although the bike can be traced through the frame number, thieves make their profit from selling the expensive accessories and ditching the frame.

If a test run is allowed, use all the gears and check for the clutch slipping. If possible, abuse the bike a little to test its resilience, always remembering that you may be about to buy it. Experience is needed to interpret odd noises from the engine.

After the ride, look the engine over carefully for oil leaks, especially oil weeping from the cylinder head jacket. If you can locate the place where the bike has regularly been stored, examine the ground for ominous black oil smears. If a test run is refused, let the bike idle for as long as possible to warm the oil and give leaks a chance to show. When the engine is warm, there should be no smoke from the exhaust when you rev up.

Bikes sold privately are normally cheaper than the dealer's, and private sellers usually expect a certain amount of haggling over price. Dealers are usually very reluctant to lower their prices. However, the law makes it illegal for them to try and push the price up by little extras such as number-plates. A secondhand crash helmet may be offered with the bike. Old ones may be very dangerous, as the British Standard specification was upgraded in 1980 when the strength requirement for chin straps was doubled. All crash helmets must have a BS Kitemark.

Shops selling both new and used machines often offer worthwhile warranties on secondhand bikes. Guarantees should cover both parts and labour and carry no mileage restrictions. A dealer should also be willing to put right any faults you spot before the sale. Tell the dealer what you want to use the bike for and ask him if the bike you have your eye on would be suitable. Take a friend with you as a witness to what the dealer says. Dealers cannot get out of their obligations under the Sale of Goods Act and the Trade Descriptions Act.

Typical prices can be checked out by consulting the monthly magazine *Which Bike?*, which carries an informative guide to secondhand bikes as well as a price guide to new machines. *Motorcycle News* (weekly) has a good classified section of bikes for sale.

MOUNTAINEERING EQUIPMENT

The wrong time to realise you have bought a bad length of rope is when you are dangling from three fraying strands with an Alpine precipice snapping at your heels. Wise heads in hard hats all advise against paying for any old rope. Rope of all kinds can be damaged in ways impossible for even the experienced climber to spot.

Other pieces of mountaineering equipment change hands successfully, but in very small numbers. News of equipment for sale rarely filters out of the climbing clubs and climbers' cafes of Britain. Few items are ever advertised in the back pages of climbing magazines. Joining a club is the best way to find used equipment, but even here both wariness and expertise are needed to sort out the safe from the sorry. Although climbing equipment is designed with safety very much in mind—British Standards cover helmets, rope, karabiners and ice axes—items do get damaged. Even the sturdy karabiner will wear out in time.

MUSIC CENTRES *see* Audio equipment

MUSICAL INSTRUMENTS

To buy any musical instrument without playing it is like buying a secondhand car without a test drive. If you can't play the instrument yourself, you need the help of someone who can, as secondhand instruments can cost as much as used cars. Even an unexceptional secondhand flute could cost a good week's wages and few people can afford to throw that much away on a bad instrument. Repair to damaged instruments are often impossible or impossibly expensive. They can easily double the purchase cost.

An apparently squashed or even cracked instrument sold cheap could prove to be a bargain, as obvious damage need not impair sound. Playing the instrument is an obvious acid test, but no guarantee of satisfaction, as damage could be hidden. For example, sticking valves on a brass instrument may only need oiling, but they could mean expensive repairs are needed. Conversely, a clarinet may not play at all simply because the reed is too hard; it could be a good buy, as reeds are cheap.

Musical instruments form a rare group of products not yet hit by inbuilt obsolescence. Woodwind instruments deteriorate with age, and recorders in particular are not built to last, but most manufacturers still strive for durability. Bad handling is a more likely cause of problems in a secondhand instrument than poor manufacture. Violins and guitars are no-

tably bad exceptions, with their faults often hidden beneath a high varnish.

Experience teaches the musician the sound of problems, and this experience can prevent expensive mistakes. Music teachers will usually carry out a "survey" on an instrument on a student's behalf. Teachers also act as unpaid middlemen, finding secondhand instruments for their students and passing the word around college on behalf of musicians with instruments to sell. Teachers are both the largest and the most reliable source of instruments. Their suppliers are usually pupils selling an old instrument to buy a better one or professional musicians whose livelihood depends on looking after their instruments. They will normally point out faults that need attention and will not hide botched or esoteric alterations to the instrument which you may not like.

Your own teacher's advice usually comes free, but teachers and musicians will usually turn their skill to part-time surveying on anyone's behalf, for a fee. A local library can often supply the address of a teacher specialising in a particular instrument, but the obvious source of teachers is a school: music colleges, evening institutes and local schools will all have music departments. Teachers often advertise in local papers and music magazines, or put a card in the newsagent's window offering their services. Music centres such as the Early Music Society, or the Jazz Centre Society can offer specialist help, as can cultural organisations such as the African Centre.

The resourceful pupil can advertise his or her needs on the noticeboard of a music college, or just ask around. In the jazz, rock and folk music fields, it is reasonable to approach a performer you admire after a performance in a pub or club and ask for help. Formal adult education classes have the advantage of low cost and provide an easy way to find whether you are really interested enough to want your own instrument.

Few shops sell only secondhand instruments, but most shops selling new instruments also have secondhand ones passing through as people reward their improved technique with a new instrument. A reputable dealer is worth seeking out. For example, the very reputable Bill Lewington's woodwind shop in London's Shaftesbury Avenue, which is infested with musicians, will offer a two-year warranty guaranteeing that the instrument will remain playable. All instruments are thoroughly checked over in their workshops before sale.

Lower prices rule at auction. The major auctioneers, such as Sotheby's and Phillips, hold periodic sales of musical instruments, but these are largely antiques and are not necessarily playable. Technical developments alter the shape of musical instruments over the centuries, and professional musicians turn to the new improved models. Fashion too can have its influence. For example, single French horns are cheap because professionals prefer the double horn. Old woodwind instruments may be pitched above the international standard and are not worth buying.

Bargain buys are sometimes found in the trusty *Exchange and Mart* and in local newspapers. A better class of instrument is often sold through the more august classified section of *The Times* or the *Sunday Times,* where for example the high price of a quality piano justifies the high advertising cost. Music magazines are worth scouring, while a specialist magazine such as *Early Music* can often satisfy odd needs.

Pianos now pass through junk shops in large numbers as the modern public will pay large sums for instruments which twenty years ago would have been cast jangling onto the scrap heap. Avoid junk shops unless you are confident in your judgement or your judge. Pianos don't improve with age, use or neglect, and many junk pianos will never play properly again after years in damp rooms or the dry heat of central heating. Nevertheless, these instruments are often bought by the uninformed and unwary

upright piano with front and panel down, hammers rising

without any trial, when simple precautions will weed out the worst.

Buy a "C" tuning fork and check the pitch of the C on the piano. If it is flat, this could be the result of loose tuning pins or a lazy tuner. Even such a routine maintenance job as piano tuning can be very hard to arrange, as the number of piano tuners in Britain has dwindled so far that entire towns are now left to their own discordant devices. Inexpert rogues have taken up the tuning fork to profit from the shortage, damaging pianos as they go. Reputable tuners have the letters PTA (Piano Tuners' Association) after their name. Tuning should be done several times a year, and many secondhand pianos have been untuned for years. They may have decayed beyond redemption. Avoid very low-pitched upright pianos, as their ageing structure will not stand the strain of an average 16 tons pull which properly tuned strings exert. Old strings may also snap with fatigue and neglect. Pull the front panel forward and look at the sounding board under the strings, made up of narrow pieces of wood glued to-

gether: long white lines mean a cracked board and loose tuning pins. Look hard for cracks around the pins, and avoid any instrument with a damaged soundboard. Cracks in an iron frame cannot be repaired.

Well-made pianos are "overstrung", with strings crossing diagonally. The hammers and dampers should all be there and be free of deep depressions where the strings have struck a thousand tunes. Badly-seated dampers cause buzzing notes, and bad wear means expensive repair.

Even the musically clueless can press a piano key, first hard, then soft, then repeatedly. If any key sticks or fails to sound, try another piano. Like any wooden instrument, a piano can suffer from woodworm attack. If you like the sound and the piano works, get a second opinion from an expert before buying it.

Guitars Very bad guitars are a popular buy in general secondhand shops. Apart from cracked wood, which really relegates the guitar to firewood status, the most likely damage is a warped neck. Look along the line of the neck for signs of distortion. Warped instruments are not worth owning. The strings place enormous strain on the neck, and many can't stand it. As a result the strings lift away from the fingerboard, making it hard to hit the high notes. Frets can be worn flat and turn the guitar into an unwanted buzz machine or Hawaiian guitar. This condition can be repaired but it adds to the price. Look out for grooved frets, a sign of a much-used instrument. Any guitar which gives good harmonics when the strings are touched lightly at the twelfth fret should be all right.

There is a rapid turnover of used and abused electric guitars, as bands form and fail constantly. The condition of the pick-up on a second-hand electric guitar is not the buyer's main concern. As with acoustics, neck damage is the major problem, especially with early Pete Townsend guitars. Most electrics will have been adapted electrically by a previous owner, and they can just as easily be adapted to a new owner's needs.

N

NAILPUNCHES *see* Tools

NARROW BOATS *see* House boats

O

OIL HEATERS

Secondhand oil heaters are a bad risk, with an unenviably high and lethal accident record. They tend to be used in small rooms by old people and large families on low incomes, who consistently burn their homes and lives to ashes by knocking dodgy fires over. The dangers have been reduced by the Oil Heaters (Safety) Regulations 1977, introduced after a Home Secretarial admission that there were three million incendiary bombs in British homes. The new regulations put the more dubious manufacturers out of business, but their lethal legacy could still be up for sale in a junk shop. Even though the regulations apply to secondhand sales, the non-specialist shop with just the odd old heater going through is unlikely to bother with them. The sanctions of the criminal law are no consolation if your house and family are carbonised.

Used oil heaters are an insane risk unless they come from a specialist dealer likely to know his legal obligations and to back up the knowledge with a pre-sale overhaul. All secondhand heaters should be rejected unless they are in strikingly good condition and accompanied by warning notices and instructions.

There is no way a consumer can be sure that a particular secondhand heater is no death threat, or even whether it was made before the regulations came in. If there's any doubt about a heater's safety, take it to a service agent appointed by the Paraffin Heating Advisory Council. The Royal Society for the Prevention of Accidents (ROSPA) insists that any secondhand heater, whether paraffin, gas or electricity, should be overhauled before it is used, and the cost of this overhaul could push the price up towards that of a new heater.

Added to the potential dangers is the positive irritation of the clouds of black smoke which so often make the secondhand oil heater look like a North Sea oil blow-out. Rooms frequently have to be redecorated.

Before using any old heater, check that there is no build up of dust in the burner which might restrict air flow. Safety can be improved by renewing the wick—ask your dealer if replacement wicks are available before you buy—screwing the heater to the floor, keeping it out of draughts and throwing it away if there are small children or mad pets around. A leaflet on safe usage should be available from Citizens' Advice Bureaux or local housing departments.

OPERA GLASSES *see* Binoculars

P

PANS

Only death or bad damage seem to separate people and their pans, unless a change from gas cooking to electricity means a different weight of pan is needed. Very old and battered pans are therefore the rule in the second-hand market. Mutilated pans are common items in the jumble sale, normally dented beyond any hope of their ever lying flat and balanced on the stove again.

Check any pan for a level base. Cooking in a warped frying pan is irritating, and can even cause accidents. Cheap pans are usually made of thin spun aluminium, which is for use on gas only, and they are very prone to buckles and bends. Thick bases are stronger. Dents *can* be hammered out but it is surprisingly hard to get it right. A ground or machine base is a good sign—ground bases have a roughish texture, and concentric circles give away a machine base.

Copper saucepans command high prices at auction and now feature in antique shops. Bargain copper-lined or copper-based saucepans are likely to need relining with tin or silver. Specialist kitchen shops can arrange this and prices are not horrific—about £5 for a 9in saucepan.

Imported enamel pans were the focus of a heavy-metal scare in the 1970s, when it was learned that some could release cadmium into food during cooking. Safety regulations ended the scare in 1976, but nervous owners of doubtful pans may have exchanged them for safer home-grown alternatives, so beware of reddish or orange enamel on the saucepan's inside—it is perfectly safe outside. All new enamel saucepans are safe. The classic white enamel ware with blue or black rims was always safe, but beware of chipped enamel pans as they can leave rust in your dinner. Food also sticks fast to the rough surfaces of chipped or crazed enamel pans, making them very tedious to clean. If the enamel is baked on aluminium rather than on the more usual cast iron or steel, look out for pitted metal where the enamel has chipped off, as this could be a health hazard.

In 1972 new regulations outlawed saucepans with a high lead content. The names of the guilty manufacturers were not released, and such pans are hard to spot. In the very unlikely event of one turning up, the seller can be prosecuted if he sold it in the course of business, but in a private sale the buyer has no recourse for brain damage or being turned into a toy soldier.

Old pans may have holes. Leaks are especially likely where the handle rivets pass through the pan. Loose rivets can be replaced by well-equipped diy experts, or glued together by almost anyone. Plastic handles may break or burn. Pan retailers often sell replacement handles. Otherwise, a handle can be built up using two-part epoxy resin, and the handle of one pan can be married to the body of another. Loose handles are little trouble on most modern pans bearing the British Standard kitemark, as their handles will normally be fixed to a metal bracket by a long screw which can simply be turned tight.

Lids are often missing, but as pans are made in standard sizes there is a good chance of finding a separate lid in a junk shop. A loose or vanished handle on the lid can be replaced with a cork held in place by a screw—plus washer if necessary—driven through the existing rivet hole.

Non-stick surfaces were introduced in the late 1950s. The earliest coatings didn't last long and are normally ruined long before they reach the secondhand shop. Even modern ones are a poor risk secondhand. Spray-on treatments will make a temporary improvement but seldom last. Stains on porcelain-lined pans can be attacked with boiling water containing a tablespoon of borax. The same brew shifts stains inside aluminium teapots. Thick grime may come off with caustic soda, steel wool pads or in extreme cases a sanding disc on the electric drill! Always clean a new old pan well remembering that before being kicked out they are often relegated to humble and dirty jobs in garden and tool shed.

PARACHUTES

Secondhand parachutes have a special place in the unofficial history of Britain; they became a symbol of the wartime resourcefulness of the nation's women. The dark days of World War 2 were brightened by silk knickers and dresses cut from the cloth of salvaged parachutes, which were a highly valued commodity at the time.

Such a magical transformation is no longer possible, for today's parachutes are regrettably synthetic, usually made of nylon. However, the secondhand decorative tradition lives on: when old parachutes are declared "out of life" and no longer capable of supporting a floating airman, they may be used to decorate mess halls and hangars at party time. Others become marquees, and some are donated to play groups to become anything at all. Some have their life usefully prolonged at gliding clubs by conversion into wing covers.

No legislation puts a time limit on a parachute's life, but responsible manufacturers refuse to inspect and repack equipment beyond a certain age, approximately twenty years. The "drop by" date should be stamped on a label on the bottom of one of the parachute's panels. The label could give the date of manufacture, the serial number and other details making it possible to identify any parachute.

The RAF is the major user of parachutes, but is no source of secondhand equipment. During the 20–30 year shelf life of an RAF parachute it is periodically inspected and repacked, but when its time is up, whether it has been used or not, it will be cut into pieces to prevent a foolhardy skydiver damaging himself.

Secondhand parachutes can be bought and are understandably much cheaper than new ones. Examining a parachute doesn't differ radically from inspecting a pair of old jeans: there should be no signs of fraying, the material should still be strong and the seams sound. However, you rarely put your life at risk by jumping into a pair of used jeans. A secondhand parachute is potentially a winding sheet, and expert advice is therefore crucial. This is usually found by joining a parachute club. Joining a club is in fact the only way to jump, as clubs can arrange both the training and the membership of the British Parachute Association without which jumping is barred.

PETS

Animal welfare societies provide a refuge for rejected pets of all kinds, from hamsters to horses. Suitable secondhand homes are sought for animals rescued from cruel or neglectful owners. Unfortunately, deprivation may have made them as deranged as human beings from a similar family background. To adopt a secondhand animal in such circumstances is to act with great charity and to ask for great trouble. The RSPCA has homes all over England and Wales. For the address of the nearest one, enquire at the London Information Office, 106 Jermyn Street, London W1 (tel: 01–930 5765). The very excellent PDSA publishes a highly informative series of free leaflets about animal care which any prospective animal owner could usefully consult. The eleven titles in this *Pet Care* series cover: Canaries; Dogs; Cats; Tortoises; Budgerigars; Rabbits and Cavies; Golden Hamsters and Mice; Aquaria; Horses and Ponies; Parrots; Gerbils. They are available from the Information Office at the PDSA, PDSA House, South Street, Dorking, Surrey, or from the treatment centres around the country. The PDSA relies on voluntary contributions.

Secondhand animals could harbour terrible diseases; indeed the sickness of parrots has become legendary. Animals can be very difficult to examine without the skills of a vet. For example, there is not much chance of putting a tortoise through its paces during the winter hibernation period, and it may have died inside its shell.

Certain basic health checks apply to most furry pets. Hamsters, white mice, guinea pigs, rabbits and the relatively germ-free gerbil have signs of illness in common. These include coughs and sneezes, runny noses, flaking skin, dull and running eyes, and diarrhoea.

Birds A cage bird's age is hard to gauge, however well the bird can talk. Signs of an old bird are an overgrown beak and hard scales on the legs. Young birds make better pupils for speech training, but a secondhand budgie may already know some very smutty phrases. Cage birds can have a tough time flying to Britain on an aeroplane. Ill health may show in bedraggled or missing feathers.

Cats The idea of a secondhand cat is inherently absurd, as no cat can ever be truly owned. However, cats occasionally deign to accept a new "owner", and some will just stroll in off the street and adopt a new address. Ordinary moggies are usually free of charge, with kittens available in great numbers in the early summer. At this time newsagents' windows are plastered with postcard pleas for "good homes for lovable kittens". Private homes are probably a healthier source of kittens than scruffy pet shops with a catty smell where disease could be rife. Cats' homes may have similar problems. Unhealthy kittens must be avoided, as huge vets' bills just add financial insult to the emotional injury of a sick cat. If the cat has not been vaccinated against feline infectious enteritis, the vaccination is worth paying for. Cat 'flu is less serious, and the vaccination more expensive.

The kittens in pet shops and market stalls are often unhealthy because of being torn from their mother before they were weaned. The probable result is expensive digestive trouble. Kittens unable to walk slowly and steadily over the floor are too young to be moved. A kitten should be kept with its mother until it has a full set of white teeth in each jaw.

Cats' characters vary widely. It should be clear if a grown cat has been made nervous or fierce by mishandling or too much playing with children. Kittens are harder to analyse.

Approach your chosen kitten slowly, by holding out a finger for it to sniff and stroking it before picking it up. If its tail goes bushy and it starts to hiss, look for another. Healthy cats and kittens have clear, bright eyes and clean ears that don't smell, pink gums and tidy coats.

Dogs The dog-dealing world is as murky as the motor trade, with evil dealers forging pedigree certificates like MOTS, and even giving dreary or stolen dogs a respray in a desirable colour before selling them in a street market. Remember that the dogs from the market will rarely be inoculated, and this necessary precaution will cost pounds.

Signs of ill health are coughs and sneezes, scurfy skin, ear scratching, and running eyes. Any one of these symptoms is enough to make a dog a reject.

Stray dogs are housed by welfare societies. Anyone can visit the dogs' home and check out the animals during the week they are kept before being released to new owners. If you choose a dog from the RSPCA, it may be neutered before it is allowed to leave the home. This is part of the society's effort to reduce the nation's population of unwanted dogs. Britain's most famous pound is the Battersea Dogs' Home. Some fifty dogs enter the Battersea gates every day. Most leave alive.

Queues form early in the morning when a pedigree dog is about to be released. All Battersea's dogs cost £7.50, a bargain for one of the top breeds. Large and small breeds tend to be expensive from a dealer, and they are often the unhealthy dogs too. Puppies are understandably popular, although no-one can know how large they will grow. Nor can the exact age be known. Eight weeks is the minimum acceptable age for weaning a puppy, and any dog over six months old needs a licence. It is all but impossible to spot a crazed dog from its behaviour in the bizarre environment of the Dogs' Home, so Battersea offers a "money-back" guarantee. Your £7.50 will be returned if you decide against the dog within a week. The Home cannot tell you whether the dog has been inoculated, so this should be done straight away. If you have an old lead and collar, take them along when you go to collect the dog.

Many of the dogs are in the pound for good reason. Surveys suggest that half the inmates have serious behavioural problems. As far as the buyer of a secondhand dog is concerned, arguments about whether the dog was born to be wild or was just driven mad by a bad home are irrelevant. The immediate problem could be a loony dog snarling around the house. The idea of giving a mal-treated dog a good home is appealing to animal lovers, but the effects of past mal-treatment are often hard to remedy. If the dog should prove awkward, it is all too easy to give it back to the pound and pass the problem on to the next well-inten-tioned person.

Such problems rarely arise with racing greyhounds, which are often left in the hands of the trainer. A grey-hound's past history is re-vealed in the form book, which is the major influence on price. Puppies straight from the breeder may cost as little as 100 guineas, but a Derby winner will be closer to £25,000.

Ponies Some animals can-not safely be bought second-hand without expert advice. Horses and ponies are often bought at auctions, where judgments must be made fast and buyers have little legal protection. Unscrupulous dealers regularly sell vicious and unsound nags to the in-nocent at very high prices. A knowledge of current market prices is of course necessary wherever you buy, but only a vet can really pronounce on the physical fitness of a pony. The vet must be paid to come out to the pony and put it-through a 1–1½hr vetting. This can cost a lot, but far less than the potential loss if you fail to notice at the time of the sale that the pony is broken-winded, blind and lame, with a weak heart and cracked hooves.

If a pony is being bought for a child, the acid test of suitability is to bring the two together and see how they get on. If the child cannot ride, it is a waste of money to buy a pony before sending the child to a riding school and giving the passion time to die.

A solid and mature Welsh or New Forest pony is a more suitable animal for the inex-perienced child than a lively young pony, however pretty. Any pony which gallops off when you approach it in the field is likely to be flighty. Forget any pony which kicks or bites as you catch it, halter it, lead it back to the stable and saddle it. The pony should be put through its different paces in all the circumstances it is likely to meet in future, from bridle paths and hills to open main roads.

Tortoises Most tortoises are imported, and most die during their first year in this country. Any which have survived their first British hibernation and come bright-eyed and clean-mouthed out of a crack-free shell in spring should be a good secondhand buy. However, there's no sure way of telling a tortoise's age.

PIANOS *see* Musical instruments

PICTURES

The nearest thing to an undiscovered Constable in 99.99 per cent of junk shops is a plain-clothes policeman looking for stolen goods. This is not because the nation's junk dealers have learned art history. Indeed, most tacitly admit their limitations as art critics by ignoring their pictures completely and putting a price on the frames instead, as these are simpler to evaluate.

Although considerably more refined, the scale of values in central London's art auctions is similarly grotesque. However, the viewing days at major art sales provide poor art lovers with an incomparable opportunity to admire wonderful pictures before they vanish into private vaults. The entertainment value of an art auction is very high, and the whim of the market increases the chance of finding a picture you like at a price you can afford. In a world where artistic standards and commercial investment are so intertwined, these must be the major criteria for judging whether a picture is worth buying. Without some knowledge of the art dealers' peculiar code, auction catalogues can be misleading. For example the phrase "bears date"—rather than "dated"—means that the date is very dodgy, while "bears signature" or "traces of signature", as opposed to just "signed", mean the artist's identity is in serious doubt. If the artist's surname is preceded in the catalogue only by initials rather than by the full Christian names, this shows the auctioneer is confident about the picture's date but less certain whether this artist really painted it. The artist's surname on its own merely means "in the style of" or "school of". "After" plus surname indicates a copy.

Besides being appealing and reasonably priced, the physical condition of the picture must be good enough for it to have a chance of survival on the wall. Broken glass is no problem, as lightweight picture glass is readily available from local glaziers, who can cut it to any size. The wooden backing board may present another equally minor problem, as this is a type of wood woodworm like.

Renovating pictures is an absorbing hobby, but the budding restorer's first attempts at saving the heritage are almost invariably disastrous. Valuable pictures should never be used for practice. A good book and a bad painting are the beginner's best companions. The latter are available in large numbers, and an example of the former is George Savage's *The Art and Antique Restorer's Handbook*. Damaged and worthless paintings are a bargain for a novice restorer, who can experiment freely and without anxiety on the works of long-gone Sunday painters, hacking them up to test the effects of various solvents.

Renovation is time-consuming and delicate work: only the very patient who enjoy working with their hands should attempt it. Repairing torn canvas and patching over holes is a skill few people master, but in time the competent can realistically expect to master the techniques of cleaning and revarnishing paintings when dirt and age have made the original varnish opaque.

Cracked varnish is not necessarily a sign of extreme age: it usually means an impatient painter has slapped on the varnish before the paint was dry, or it could be the mark left by a forger's needle scraping away for an "antique" effect. The clue to this common malpractice is often a pattern looking too regular to be natural crazing. Problems may arise as soon as the varnish is lifted, as the solvent may lift the pigment with the varnish. Experience suggests that greens and browns, for whatever reason, are more likely to lift than blue and white, so an oil-painted sky will present fewer renovation problems than a damaged landscape.

Finding a convincing colour match to repair damaged sections is notoriously hard, even for experts. Calling in the experts is not automatically a good move. The picture restorer typically charges hysterically high prices, and customers occasionally mutter about their tendency to paint in too much.

Very simple home restoring of prints and drawings is worth attempting (a rub with a little ball of moist bread, for example, may help lift grease and dirt), but any more radical treatment is liable to harm the picture. Mildew is troublesome once it has taken a grip, and even "foxing" stains can be tougher to remove than some manuals suggest. However, they are quite easy to live with. Water colours are best considered beyond restoration.

Before any picture can be restored it must be removed from the frame. At this point a buyer may decide the picture is best thrown away and the frame filled with something else. Professional restoration services can be used to mend and rejuvenate frames. The "Picture and Photograph Frame Makers" in the *Yellow Pages* may be able to help, but some jobs are very much within the reach of the amateur. Gold leaf is the traditional method of improving a frame, but is far too expensive for general use. It also needs a certain skill to be applied effectively. Old gilt frames can be touched up with Gold Treasure, a wax gilt which is rubbed on by cloth or fingers. Wooden frames can be gilded by painting on Liquidleaf Gold. Both products are available from craft shops and artists' materials shops, which are listed in the *Yellow Pages*. Chipped sections in gesso frames can be filled with Fine Surface Polyfilla before regilding.

A large and/or damaged frame can sometimes be cut down to make a perfect smaller one. When measuring up the frame for cutting to take a particular picture, measure on the *inside* edge of the frame, and take care to cut mitred corners at 45°. PVA adhesive will hold wooden sections together,

257

with the help of a clamp to hold the frame until the adhesive dries. Triangular metal sections fixed at the back will give corners extra strength.

PLANES *see* Tools

PILLOWS *see* Beds and bedding

PLIERS *see* Tools

PLUMB LINES *see* Tools

PONIES *see* Pets

POWER TOOLS

Electric drill Heavy-duty professional drills are used constantly and used hard; they are rarely sold secondhand until they are badly fatigued or stolen from the owner's toolkit on a building site. The average handyman's electric drill, on the other hand, sees only a few hours' active service every year and is often replaced by a more modern model while its condition is still good.

It can be difficult to repair a broken old drill, as spare parts may no longer be available. Cannibalizing another obsolete tool may be the only way of replacing a damaged part. Old drills will have heavy metal bodies, and this mass of exposed metal must have the protection of an earthing circuit. The only reliable test of the appliance's earthing efficiency is to slam a sudden and massive current through the earth circuit, a job which only a well-equipped electrician can undertake. Modern double-insulated drills do not rely on an earth wire to cut off the power when an electrical fault develops.

Even dust can be dangerous in drills. Uncleaned drills clog up with sawdust; if this dust is damp, it can wreck the insulation. Dirt inside the drill and blocked air vents in the casing can lead to overheating. Internal hot spots can also be caused by clumsy users who jam the motor. After lengthy misuse the motor on old drills could be burned out or on the verge of a burn-out. Modern motor windings are drip-impregnated during manufacture, a process which makes them less prone to overheating than older motors, which were dipped in resin and baked. Specialist companies will rewind old motors, but the cost is rarely justified.

Without plugging in a secondhand drill, it is possible

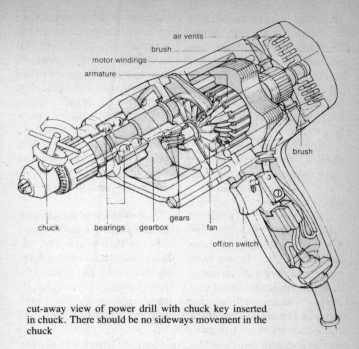

air vents

brush

motor windings

armature

brush

gears

chuck   bearings   gearbox   fan

off/on switch

cut-away view of power drill with chuck key inserted in chuck. There should be no sideways movement in the chuck

to check the casing for cracks and to examine the flex for signs of damage. Sander and saw attachments often carve through flex, and insulating tape on the flex probably hides nasty scars.

Using a sanding attachment usually means applying sideways pressure to the drill and this side thrust will strain the drill. If any movement can be felt when the chuck is waggled, the chuck bearing or armature spindle are probably due for replacement.

If the drill can be plugged in, try it out. The switch itself may be faulty, and although easy to replace, this fault makes purchase too risky. If the drill starts up, listen for a "metallic" noise from the innards. This usually indicates a lack of lubrication or a damaged bearing, but may equally be a sign of badly-worn gear wheels or motor. In theory all parts are replaceable—brushes, chuck, gearbox, switch and motor. Problems come with the cost of multiple repairs. For example, a burn-out could have led to ruined brushes, softening of the gearbox and cracks in the casing. Such a drill is best discarded.

Parts are on sale for diy repairs, but repair by the manufacturer brings the benefit of a guarantee. Certain Black and Decker service agents also sell guaranteed reconditioned tools, which have been put through high voltage and insulation tests which are beyond the amateur's capabilities. Black and Decker's repair policy came under heavy consumer attack in the late 1970s, when people were almost forced to buy new drills which they didn't want when the company refused to repair their old one. Customers with obsolete drills are now given the chance to buy a reconditioned tool of a later model for the notional cost of the repair which won't be done.

An electric drill is widely used as the basic unit to hang accessories on, and a secondhand drill could be a better investment if the manufacturer can supply it with a wide range of attachments, such as a sander, circular saw or jigsaw. It is not only the major manufacturers who are involved in drill attachments. There is, for example, the "Pulpmaster", which fits a standard drill: placed in a standard two-gallon bucket, it is used to pulp fruit; it will also break down newspapers and cardboard to make *papier mâché* and recycled paper.

The most basic attachment for any drill is a chuck key. It is easily mislaid and, although cheap, is worth having included in the price. The drill's side handle is also liable to get lost before a secondhand buyer is found.

Circular saw These are fearsome machines: they take the effort out of cutting wood and make diy amputation easy. The best thing to do with a secondhand circular saw is to have it serviced immediately. Unfortunately, an overhaul by the manufacturer can cost half the price of a new one, probably putting the overall secondhand price too high. Besides being potentially expensive, secondhand saws are potentially hazardous. Indeed, the first stage in testing a circular saw is to put on goggles to protect eyes from flying debris. Make sure no loose ties, jewels or hair are dangling from your person within reach of the whizzing blade. Any piece to be sawn must be clamped safely to a stable surface.

Rather than grabbing an old saw and trying it out yourself, it is more prudent to ask the seller to demonstrate it before you chance your arm, literally. A visit to a shop selling new appliances is a sensible prelude to secondhand buying, to familiarise yourself with the way the saw fits together and the all-important safety features without which the saw becomes lethal.

The first thing to check on a secondhand saw is the flex, which is probably slashed and dangerous. It is crucial to check that the guard is in position and operational, with the spring pushing the lower guard securely over the blade.

Blades are designed to cut a particular type of material, and only the right blade should be used. All old blades are likely to be blunt, and that makes cutting hard work, which in turn leads to jamming and possible danger.

Makers operate blade replacement services, giving a discount of some 50 per cent on new blades when an old one is traded in. This means that even old blades are worth having included in the price of the saw.

The bearings on a circular saw are put under huge strain when the saw binds in wood, which can easily happen when any twist is applied. A six inch blade effectively becomes a powerful six inch lever, and under such severe strain the saw motor can burn out. Modern integral tools are tougher, with larger bearings.

The soleplate can be adjusted to alter depth of cut. Fixing nuts fall off and may be missing from the soleplate. The nut holding the angle-of-cut adjustment may also have disappeared, and the entire rip guide is removable and therefore losable. Spare rip guides are sold for all saws.

Jigsaw When you are pondering the advisability of buying an integral jigsaw secondhand, the solution to your jigsaw puzzle may be a new jigsaw attachment for an electric drill. These are cheap, safe and will not have parts missing. Old saws can be dangerous and incomplete.

Jigsaws share many mechanical and electrical problems with other power tools, such as cut flexes, blocked air vents, worn brushes and broken switches. One serious problem peculiar to jigsaws is wear in the ram assembly and gear mechanism, caused by pushing the jigsaw too hard through thick wood, and itself causing the blade to wobble about quite considerably. This makes it almost impossible to cut a straight line. Repair is normally easily arranged, but can be costly.

New blades are very easy to find.

PRAMS

Many proud parents-to-be feel that the baby's pram should be as new and unique as the baby. Others worry how to choose a secondhand pram wisely. The best sign of security is the British Standard Kitemark, without which all secondhand prams are best consigned to oblivion. In 1978 safety standards were formalised by the Perambulators and Pushchairs (Safety) Regulations which say that a pram or pushchair must be stable and must have some form of brake and harness attachment points.

In the case of folding prams and pushchairs the regulations stipulate a locking device to stop them collapsing, backed up by an independently operated additional safety device. The regulations apply to any pram, even those made before 1978. This means, at least theoretically, that the only place there's a risk of buying a dangerous pram is in a private sale. Wherever you buy a pram, the regulations provide a good framework for checking it over.

Take the pram on a road test and try out the brake several times: it should be very hard to move the pram when the brake is applied. At the same time, check that the wheels haven't lost any spokes and that they don't wobble or squeak. The tyres may have rotted or worn away. Local pram shops can normally supply replacement wheels or tyres and cope with minor repairs. Repairing damaged pushchair wheels is a tricky job for the amateur, but squeaks can usually be quite simply oiled out of prams by a little cycle oil on the axles.

The attachment points for harness straps should be checked. The pram hood should be manoeuvred up and down, as the hinges are often rusting away. The hood fabric may have hidden holes, particularly along the folds, where incorrect folding can lead to fraying. Hoods often fray after repeated rubbing against a wall, but if the damage this has caused is not extensive, sew-on-metal shields can be bought from pram dealers to halt the fraying.

The fabric on the rest of the pram should be checked over for tears, patches and signs of wear, which are most likely to show on exposed corners. Small tears are not hard to patch over, but should knock the price down. Any mattress or cushions should be taken out— they often cover up true filth.

Folding prams and pushchairs must be folded up and tried for ease of carrying. Check out the locking devices carefully. Prams don't have log books giving details of previous occupants, but it is useful to know the pram's history. If it has carted the numerous offspring of a family of trampoline artists, the springs may be suffering badly.

Local playgroups are a good source of information and hardware. Prams also figure regularly on cards in the newsagent's window. You could try your own cheap ad in there. Parents of grown children often sell redundant prams by using the free advertisement service for small items in the local press.

Babies under one year old don't normally have pillows in their prams or cots. Pillows designed for older children are protected by British Standards: BS1877 covers airflow through pillows, insisting on the importance of adequate airflow. British Standard recommendations also cover carry-cot stands.

Strict legal force applies to the 1978 Babies' Dummies (Safety) Regulations, which effectively destroyed the very limited and rather distasteful market in secondhand dummies. The regulations state that dummies must be made of rubber and/or plastic and must be sold in a clean condition in a closed container, with a notice about cleaning and hygiene. Few junk shops can comply.

PRESERVING JARS

Fruit preservers and onion picklers usually hate waste. As they are often cost-conscious too, they provide a steady buying pubic for secondhand preserving jars. Demand peaks in the summer when the fruit bottling season begins, and urgent appeals for 1lb jam jars go out from the nation's Women's Institutes as they prepare jam for the winter's jumble sales.

The classic preserving jar, with its airtight system invented by Mr Kilner, was almost by definition made to keep, and ancient Kilner jars are still sold secondhand in their thousands, having stored the family food through two world wars. The "Original" Kilner jar gave way to the "Improved" in 1948, but rubber rings can still be bought to fit the "Original". However, spare screw-on metal tops become available only as salvage when an "Original" jar smashes. As rust attacks old tops, this can be a problem. Screw bands are still sold for the later Kilner with the name "Improved" proudly embossed on its side. The supply may not last long, so prudent preservers buy when they can. Rubber sealing rings and spare metal tops are also available.

The latest metric "New" model has a wider body and neck, square sides and a plastic screw band. Spare rubber rings are easy to find.

If the tops have disappeared and no replacement can be found, the jar can't be used for preserving, but for jam and pickle making a Porosan fruit preserving skin will cover jars of any size. The same company makes more sophisticated recycling of the family's empty jam jars possible by producing caps and rings to fit standard 1lb jam jars to be filled by home-made jam.

PRESSURE COOKERS

The operating principles of the pressure cooker have not changed for decades. A pressure cooker combines a heavy pan and a sealed lid. The seal keeps the steam inside, and this builds up pressure. A safety device stops the pressure rising too high. This pressure regulator must be cleaned out before any secondhand cooker is used: running water and a pipe cleaner

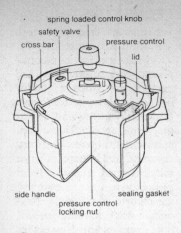

spring loaded control knob
safety valve
cross bar
pressure control
lid
side handle
sealing gasket
pressure control
locking nut

should clear any blockages. A spanner can tighten up the nut holding the regulator in position to prevent steam leaks.

Pressure cookers make alarming hissing sounds, and nervous cooks fear for their safety even with a brand-new one in the kitchen. Oddly enough, a secondhand pressure cooker should be even safer than a new one. This is because pressure can only build up if there is a tight seal between the base and the lid. The seal is made by compressing a rubber gasket (the rubber ring round the lid), and in time the gasket will perish or go hard. The result is escaping steam and a fail-ure to build up pressure. Manufacturers can supply cheap and easy-to-fit replace-ments, although parts may be hard to find if the manufac-turer has ceased trading.

Any pressure cooker is confusing without proper in-structions, which vary from one manufacturer to another. Any cooker on offer without an instruction book is there-fore potentially problematic, particularly as the instruc-tions give the correct cooking times. Manufacturers can normally supply substitutes.

A damaged or missing reg-ulator can also be replaced by reputable manufacturers. The regulator is backed up by a safety valve set in the lid. This blows open if pressure is excessive. However, it will open before cooking pressure is reached if the rubber part has perished. This is very easy to replace.

If the spring in the top knob has weakened, even a new gasket will not hold the steam in. A service will be needed.

Steam leaks around the lid seal could need more than a new gasket if the rim itself has been damaged. This oc-casionally happens when rims are repeatedly battered by serving spoons. A visual check should locate dents and nicks. The entire pan can be distorted if the cooker has boiled dry. As the water is not visible during cooking, this can easily occur. While discoloured aluminium is nothing to worry about, a distorted base is more serious. Such a fault is probably not beyond repair, but a dented pan is not worth buying secondhand. Distorted bases on Prestige and Skyline cookers can be flattened at their repair centre in Derby, where the service manager will have the necessary information on spares availability for any model. Manufacturers can often supply replacement handles and screws, besides the trivet and food containers without which some food cannot be cooked. The trivet keeps the food off the pan bottom during cooking.

If replacement parts for the lid are not available, a pressure cooker need not be discarded. The base on its own makes a very sturdy saucepan. Aluminium is the commonest material, but stainless steel is even more durable.

PROJECTORS

Secondhand cine projectors are often a disappointment. They are complex mechanisms, very similar to a cine camera, in which a shutter opens and closes for every frame as it is clawed between the lamp and the lens. Not surprisingly, breakdowns are common, and there is little the buyer of a secondhand projector can do to increase the chance of buying a good one. A brief examination will not even establish whether the all-important gate mechanism is missing. If the projector lights up and whirrs, that merely proves that it lights up and whirrs, not that it works. It is desirable to run a film through any used projector before buying it, to check that the image is steady and the background noise level acceptable. Automatic threading is a feature of most modern Super 8 projectors, and this is a feature that should be tested, by feeding it with a film in good condition but of little value just in case the projector chews the film beyond repair. If the film snarls up, don't buy the projector.

Serious problems with jammed claws are common,

but even such a routine event as a burned-out lamp can be troublesome with an old projector, as the powerful lamps many old projectors need can cost £20, compared to about £4 for a modern version. Moreover, the right fitting may be hard to trace. The instruction manual should say which type is needed and how it is fitted and will often contain useful lubrication instructions. Incorrect or excessive oiling can clog up the works. Few diy repair jobs are possible. Even replacing a broken or overstretched drive belt can be very awkward, and professional repair services are usually expensive.

Slide projectors Primitive slide projectors are simple and sturdy objects. The major drawback with an old machine is usually the extremely high cost of replacing a lamp. The high wattage lamps for old projectors can still be bought, but more recent models can prove cheaper to run. Modern quartz iodine and quartz halogen lamps give a whiter light and better highlights than the old tungsten type. The superior coated lenses in modern projectors also contribute to the sharpness of the slide show.

Magazine designs become obsolete remarkably quickly. It is wise to buy as many as possible while you can. They rarely break, and thirty or forty should hold the average family's lifetime slide collection.

Any secondhand projector should be put through its paces before a penny changes hands. Before plugging in, inspect the flex for obvious damage, and reduce the risk of electric shock by inviting the seller to handle it before you do. When the projector is switched on, listen for a rowdy fan, and check its cooling power by leaving a slide in the hot seat for several minutes to see if it scorches or melts. Some recent slide projectors are automatically self-focusing; leaving the slide in position for a while should give this feature a chance to work. Remote focusing and automatic feed systems should also be checked out for efficient functioning.

R

RABBITS *see* Pets

RACKETS (badminton, squash, tennis)

Modern rackets are technically superior to old ones. They are stronger, less likely to lose their shape and less prone to cracking up. However, a carefully chosen old racket should be perfectly serviceable for the average player who doesn't combine the strength of King Kong with a volatile temper.

Secondhand badminton rackets are hardly worth consideration, as basic new ones cost so little. The finest new tennis rackets, on the other hand, are extremely expensive, fully justifying a hunt for good secondhand equipment. Even a racket with a broken or shoddy shaft may be worth buying if the head is good and the price is low, as a new shaft can be fitted for a few pounds. Finding a repairer willing to fit a new head onto an old shaft is much harder, although some manufacturers are prepared to tackle the job.

As long as a repairer can be found whose charges are reasonable, a racket sold cheap because of a bent frame may be a bargain, as frames can be straightened out if they are made of metal. Warped wooden rackets are useless, so it is crucial to check the straightness of the frame by looking at the racket from the side. Wooden frames twist when the racket is left out of its press, so a press is a valuable part of a second-hand deal.

If the frame passes the straightness test, continue the examination by checking for hairline cracks. Squash rackets have a hard time on court, and cracked frames are therefore common. Most tiny cracks can be repaired by binding and glueing, but they all shorten the racket's life, and this fact should be reflected in the price. Avoid all cracked rackets if repair facilities are not locally available.

The great debate rages concerning the rival merits of natural gut and synthetic strings. Synthetic strings are better in wet weather conditions, as they do not need to be stuffed up your white woolly at the first sign of rain. But gut can hit much harder. String tension can be tested by banging the edge of one racket against the centre of another. The higher the ping, the tauter the string. If possible, make a comparison with the ping from a good new racket. Broken strings can be replaced individually or as a complete set. If all the strings are looking frayed, with tattiness increasing towards the racket centre, the racket will soon need restringing. Restringing with gut costs approximately twice as much as synthetic strings.

Repairs can be arranged through most shops, which may repair rackets on the premises or send the work out to a home-based specialist. Londoners can benefit from the very knowledgeable proprietor of Gefen Sports, 114 Longstone Avenue, NW10. Besides selling secondhand sports equipment, and running an extensive racket repair service, Mr Gefen sells the simple tools for restringing rackets and will give individual tuition in racket restringing. It takes three to four hours to run through the tricks of the trade. A shortage of stringing services has grown with the popularity of squash.

Balls Traditional wisdom insists that the bounce in tired tennis balls can be improved by gentle heating in the oven. Nearly-new tennis balls are put on sale at the end of most small tournaments, but the balls struck by stars at Wimbledon and other major events are not to be had. All depends on the club's arrangements with the supplier: if the club has bought the balls, they sell them off, but if not, they are returned to the supplier. A list of tournaments can be obtained from the Lawn Tennis Association, Palliser Road, London W14, together with the names and addresses of the club secretaries who handle sales.

RADIOS

Brand new portable radios have become so cheap that there is little point in looking for a secondhand one. Bulky bakelite radios with their glowing valves and muffled sound have begun to appeal to the wealthy collectors' market, and prices have risen rapidly in recent times, a sad blow to the secondhand listener. Bakelite's humble place has been taken at the cheap end of the secondhand market by the tinny trannie. A number of good secondhand radios lacking long wave reception came onto the market when the BBC reorganised its wavelengths in November 1978 and moved Radio 4 to the long waveband.

Fully-transistorised radios should last well. Transistors are more durable than valves, and hot valves always tended to overheat all the radio's other components. Unfortunately, transistor radios eventually break down, and repairs are normally too expensive to contemplate. Only a well-equipped enthusiast would be wise to consider buying a broken transistor radio. The average buyer should hear the radio in action before the sale goes

through. It is unfair to judge the radio's performance using an old battery—well-prepared buyers take their own new battery to the market place. Check for corrosion caused by leaky batteries.

Listen to the quality of the sound on stations on every waveband. The judgement will to some extent be subjective, but a rattling speaker should deter all buyers.

Press all the buttons and twiddle all the knobs, listening for alarming crackles and hums or a lack of response. Valve radios can still be repaired by specialists and enthusiasts such as Morgans of 5 Leigh Street, London WC1. Most repairers are unwilling to touch them, and even the willing remainder are unlikely to have the circuit diagrams needed for diagnosis. Although the larger valves are no longer manufactured, a couple of far-sighted companies have built up formidable stockpiles which should last the repairers for decades.

The problems of overheating inside a valve radio can be aggravated by old and faulty wiring. The rubber sheathing on cable is likely to be perished and should be replaced. The flex on most ancient radios is threadbare and flimsy. The desire for a completely authentic period piece should not deter you from renewing dangerous flex.

Traces of overheating can often be detected by sniffing around the back panel without even switching the radio on. Inside the set, overheating could have caused scorching on the cabinet or bubbling on the varnish. A hot transformer can drip molten pitch onto the bottom of the cabinet.

Although secondhand radios are covered by the electrical safety regulations, which make it illegal to sell an electrically dodgy set, very few dealers are aware of this. Most wrongly believe that secondhand goods are excluded, and as a result large numbers of lethal radios are up for sale.

RAILWAY CARRIAGES

Railway enthusiasts can shunt their own genuine BR railway carriage into the back garden. The trains now standing on private property include several conversions into living accommodation, while others house the very youth clubs which were once put forward as the solution to the problem of youthful railway vandalism.

When the legendary Brighton Belle was sold off in 1972, the hotel and catering industry moved in at express speed. Allied Breweries bought the second class parlour cars, while first class parlour car Moira was coupled to a Surrey restaurant and Mona moved to a Cheshire pub.

Old coaches are sold by the Director of Supply at British Rail's Railway Technical Centre in London Road, Derby. Some 90 per cent of those coaches deemed too damp and draughty even for commuter services are sold as scrap. All condemned coaches are sold by competitive tender to the highest bidder, but BR make considerable efforts to give all railway preservation societies and individual enthusiasts a chance to bid for glory. The price fluctuates wildly with the volatile scrap metal market, where prices can double or plummet in any twelve month period. Besides the value of the metallic content, the type and condition of the carriage will influence price.

In 1980, most redundant coaches were sold for £500–£2,500 each. At present, the secondhand market is dominated by pre-1960 non-passenger carrying stock. Most passenger vehicles are recycled by British Rail, who convert them for further life on the railways, as Engineers' Service Vehicles or as Carflats.

Transport can, paradoxically, be the major problem with a used railway carriage. The buyer has to pay the cost of moving the carriage from the point of sale to final destination, although BR's rail network will normally be put at the buyer's service to get it as far as the nearest rail point, where a road transport company will take over.

RECEIVERS see Audio equipment

RECORD PLAYERS see Audio equipment

RECORDS

You can't judge the condition of a record without playing it all the way through on good equipment. Most record shops won't allow customers to listen to a single track even on a brand-new record. The chances of hearing a second-hand record before buying it are minimal, and the quality of sound on a secondhand record may be very poor.

On average, secondhand records cost about half as much as new ones, but cheap imports of brand-new rock and popular albums have been undercutting even this price, much to the chagrin of Britain's established record dealers and record companies. In 1981 cheap new records manufactured in Italy, Portugal, Canada and the USA were on sale all along Oxford Street, London, making a mockery of the capital's record industry.

With every rise in the price of oil, records get thinner, and many emaciated new records don't stand up well to the strain of life under the needle. The quality of manufacture is often so awful that a thick old secondhand record may be no more likely to send the stylus skipping and jumping like a high school hop. However, there are some undeniably dreadful secondhand records on sale. One dealer in the north of England seems to specialise in selling library rejects, which are in a condition beyond belief. A damaged LP can be hard to spot just by looking at it. Besides obvious scratches and warps, signs of play may show around the centre hole where the player has been trying to locate the turntable's spindle.

Modern hi-fi stereo systems don't damage records, but heavy old mono machines can hurt a stereo record. The groove of a stereo record has two separate tracks, one moving the stylus from side to side in the traditional manner, with a "hill and dale" track undulating along the bottom of the groove. A stereo stylus will trap both signals, but heavy mono equipment will just plough through the hill and dale, flattening it out and leading to a dreadful sound over one of the speakers. The only visible sign of the damage will be a slight greying at the bottom of the grooves. If you have the chance of listening to the record, play each channel in isolation to check for damage.

Cleanliness is not necessarily a virtue. A filthy and fingermarked record may play perfectly well, whereas overzealous polishing of the surface can cover it with audible scratches. Most cleaning devices can harm records. Washing is worthless, as the streaks sound as crackles. Some hi-fi dealers own a machine costing as much as the average stereo system which will safely clean the dirt from the grooves of a 33 or 45. The fluid it uses dissolves 78s. 78s can be cleaned with warm, soapy water, but a dip in overhot water will warp them. Warp spoils the sound quality, and serious warps can send the needle flying off the machine.

A scratch-free surface obviously puts up the value of a record, and the condition of the sleeve is also a significant influence on the price of an LP. This is because many people buy them as gifts, and a dog-eared cover gives the cheap origin away. In the USA, record sleeves are sold without any record inside, as part of the general rise in the value of rock paraphernalia.

The price of early rock 'n' roll and pop records has rocketed in recent years, led by the Beatles and Elvis Presley. Collectors will pay £100 for a copy of a 78rpm Beatles single manufactured in India. Collectors prize publishers' demos and DJs' promotion copies above the regular releases. Demand is truly international, with Britain's major collectors' magazine (*Buygone Record Sales*) going to subscribers in the USA and Yugoslavia, Australia and Japan. Buygone operate a classification system for secondhand records, and this method of indicating a record's condition has become fairly commonplace in shops, market stalls and sales lists.

The classification begins at "Mint", which means the record, cover and any additional material such as a lyric sheet are in perfect condition. A "Very Good" record will have been played several times, and the cover may be vaguely grabby. A "Good" record and cover will be worn but without serious defects, whereas the sound on a "Fair" one will have deteriorated noticeably. A "Poor" record will be barely playable, and its cover could be torn or defaced. "Bad" records are not worth having, and their price should reflect this.

Secondhand rock 'n' roll records are advertised in *Not Fade Away,* the official magazine of the Vintage Rock 'n' Roll Appreciation Society, edited by the dedicated Neil Foster. Rock On, 3 Kentish Town Road, London NW1 compile irregular catalogues on special subjects, which they send out to collectors. Jazz enthusiasts will find thousands of secondhand records at Mole Jazz, 374 Gray's Inn Road, London WC1 and in Honest Jon's three London branches.

London is the centre of media coverage of music in Britain, and the West End is littered with review copies. Many of these go straight from the reviewer's desk to the secondhand shops, often completely unplayed. Cheapo Cheapo's grubby shop in Rupert Street, London W1 is renowned for its stock of secondhand rock, but rivals are now sprouting all over Soho. The famous Record and Tape Exchange is located at 90 Goldhawk Road, London W12, very near the BBC building, where a lot of review copies circulate. The Exchange carries all kinds of records from pop to classical, and all are classified. Even the most reputable of dealers can't be expected to play their stock through before selling it, but the best dealers will happily take a record back if you have legitimate complaints. The problems are maximised with a mail order operation.

Britain's best established specialist record shop dealing in 78s is the 78 Record Exchange, 9 Lower Hillgate, Stockport. A clue to their vast stock is given in their three extensive catalogues of records for sale. Each one is updated every three years. The first, reissued in 1981, covers classical orchestral and instrumental records, the second (1980) personality and dance bands, with vocal and operatic records in the third. Other occasional lists appear, covering for example brass and military band music. The Exchange also supplies 10 inch or 12 inch cardboard sleeves for a few pence each, steel needles, secondhand books and magazines, and their own record cleaning materials.

Scratches alone don't usually spoil the pleasure in listening to a 78. The human ear can attune itself to ignore the sound of scratches. In fact surface noise can be an essential part of the pleasure of a 78, whereas the identical sounds reissued on an LP are unbearably bad.

Far more serious than scratching is overall wear. A record groove is a wiggly line, with the most intense wiggling on the high notes. As a steel gramophone needle ploughs its way through, it tends to wear away the walls of the wiggle, straightening the line out. The result is the muffled sound known as "blast". Blast can be seen without playing the record, as a greyness in the grooves, most noticeably on the high notes.

Only in exceptional cases does the sleeve affect the price of a 78. About 1902 a number of records by such 78 superstars as Nelly Melba and Caruso were issued with a picture sleeve. Collectors value these. Besides the demand for a particular musician's records, the main factors affecting price are the scarcity of the recording and the condition of the record. Records which originally sold well tend to continue to sell strongly, although popular "personality" singers command on average only half the price of the early operatic stars. There is a steady demand from overseas for rare early recordings. The USA

275

used to be the major destination, but it has been replaced rather surprisingly by Japan, where there is a growing passion for early operatic, violin and piano recordings.

REFRIGERATORS

Fridges are reliable machines, with a basic design which has not changed dramatically since the first fridges appeared in British kitchens in the 1920s. The enormous growth in freezer ownership has led to the marketing of the new "larder fridge", which has no ice box, but with this exception the layout of an old fridge should be very similar to the most modern models. Storage facilities will include individual egg spaces, milk rack and dairy shelf. The most significant improvement of recent years has been the introduction of automatic defrosting, a feature found on few secondhand fridges and one which can't be properly tested until a fridge has been installed at home for a week or so.

A similar length of time may be needed to discover whether the fridge is keeping cool efficiently. You can tell whether a compression fridge —the commonest type— is working at all merely by switching on and listening for the motor cutting in and out as the thermostat controls it. Turning up the thermostat should immediately bring the motor into action. After a few minutes' operation, the condenser on the back should begin to warm up: if it doesn't, there's a serious fault in the refrigeration system.

The usual explanation for a failure to refrigerate is a leak somewhere in the sealed system, allowing the refrigerant to escape. The first indication of such a problem may be the compressor running for long periods without stopping, even when the thermostat is turned down low. The evaporator (see drawing), which in normal operation is cold, may feel warm to the touch. Leaks can sometimes be located by the bubble test. With the fridge switched on, dab diluted washing-up liquid on the pipes, especially at the joints, in the part of the system including the compressor, condensor and capillary. Any bubbling indicates a leak. The rest of the system—the low pressure side—can be tested when the fridge is not running.

Leaks must be repaired before the fridge is recharged with refrigerant, and this calls for expert knowledge, specialist tools and major expense. This "regassing" is a simple enough operation, but the special equipment needed is heavy and expensive, involving high pressure bottles. Because of this, only specialist dealers find it worthwhile to recharge fridges. They are usually the best source of guaranteed fridges.

A properly sealed system is the key to a fridge's efficiency, and also the reason why repairs are so expensive: a breakdown of any element usually means replacing the entire system. A burned-out motor, for example, is the most common cause of fridge failure, but it cannot usually be replaced in isolation. Replacement could consequently cost as much as a

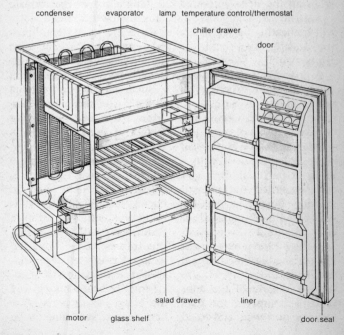

condenser   evaporator   lamp   temperature control/thermostat
chiller drawer
door
salad drawer   liner
motor   glass shelf   door seal

completely new fridge, for the rest of the appliance apart from the sealed system is basically a very cheap box with a bit of insulation.

Few repairs are worth carrying out. Exceptions are thermostats, which occasionally go wrong and which are easily and cheaply replaced. A broken internal light bulb is another quick and easy replacement job. On second-hand fridges check that the internal light doesn't stay on when the door is closed by pressing the door-activated switch inside. If it does, it will be heating up the fridge and wasting fuel until the faulty switch is replaced.

A poor door seal will make the fridge more expensive to run by allowing warm air to enter. It will also cause excessive build-up of frost. The standard test for a sound seal is to close the door onto a piece of paper: if the paper can be pulled out without meeting some resistance, the seal should be replaced or built up with a silicone sealant. The problem may lie not in a perished or flattened seal but in the door hinges: excessive loading of the door storage compartment puts strain on the hinges and could

have distorted them. Ice-box hinges are often damaged by being forced closed against solid ice, and these should be checked out. At the same time, check that the ice-cube tray is not missing and that shelves are neither missing nor broken.

If a fridge is unplugged and left with the door closed without first defrosting and mopping up all traces of moisture, a musty smell will almost certainly have developed. This can be cleared by leaving a dish of bicarbonate of soda in the fridge for a couple of days. Cleanliness is important. Dirt and dust should be wiped off the condenser before the fridge is pushed into position against a wall. Moisture cannot escape from self-defrosting fridges if the drain hole is bunged up: a prod with a pipe cleaner will normally clear a blocked passage.

The fridge could easily be damaged during delivery. It is not essential to keep a fridge absolutely upright during transportation, but the exposed parts at the back should be protected from accidental impact damage. Let the fridge stand for twelve hours before switching on, to give the refrigerant time to settle.

Don't dump a dead fridge. Broken fridges in the street are a menace to children, who can end up trapped inside with the door closed and friends gone home. The number of fridges littering the streets has fallen recently, as secondhand fridges have become valuable scrap, with dealers fighting over them at jumble sales. The struggle is for the copper in the condenser coils at the back, which is both accessible and valuable. Of course getting the refrigerant out safely can be a problem, as the chances of explosion are quite high. Dealers are prepared to try. If asked, the electricity boards will "render an old fridge safe" for nothing, but one of their informal surveys revealed that they had *never* been asked for this service. Gas boards will provide a similar free disposal service for gas fridges.

Good discount prices can undercut secondhand. In London, check out prices of fully-guaranteed, new, "near perfect" fridges and freezers at Buyers and Sellers before deciding on a used machine which may involve servicing problems. Shops are at 120 Ladbroke Grove, W10 and 72 Uxbridge Road, W12.

RUCKSACKS

Old-fashioned rucksacks can be a bargain. Since the new ultra-lightweight models are so very expensive, a lot of people prefer to carry a few extra lbs to save a few extra £s. Points to look for are straightforward—frayed or torn material, broken or missing buckles, loose straps and fastenings. Try the rucksack on to feel if the frame is bent or uncomfortable.

Well-travelled rucksacks rarely make the classified columns of the camping magazines, though one or two appear for sale in the Youth Hostelling Association members' free quarterly magazine *Hostelling News*. More are advertised in the Camping Club of Great Britain's monthly magazine.

S

SAWS *see* Tools

SCISSORS

Scissors are badly-abused tools, which rarely reach the secondhand shop before being ruined. When the tips or blades are bent after prising cans open, the damage is usually permanent. Since only low-grade untempered steel blades can be straightened, bent scissors are a bad buy. Bear in mind that scissors are traditionally designed to bow slightly. Sharpening is possible to a limited extent, but it is neither easy for the amateur nor cheap by the expert. Sharp scissors should cut a sheet of newspaper or a strip of linen along the entire length of the blade.

Cheap but high-quality scissors may be a good gamble even if the blades have worked loose at the pivot, as long as they are rust-free, straight and sharp. A loose pivot can often be tightened up simply by putting the pivot screw head on a hard surface and hitting the other side with a hammer. Wilkinson rivets need special attention.

SCREWDRIVERS *see* Tools

SECATEURS *see* Garden Tools

SEWING MACHINES

The most expensive modern sewing machines can produce a miraculous array of tricky stitches, most of which are completely useless to all but the virtuoso sewer. For simple repairs, curtain-making and basic dressmaking, much cheaper machines are adequate. The most basic machines are limited to straight, forward stitch; others also have reverse which is useful for finishing off seams. Some models will take extra attachments to increase their scope, such as a zipper foot. However, even the unambitious sewer will save hours by owning a machine with an inbuilt zigzag which prevents fraying by finishing raw edges, attaches patches, applies appliqué and sews elastic on, as well as being the only stitch which can be used on stretch fabrics. Satin stitch will prove handy for buttonholes. Some zigzag machines will even take two needles to sew double rows. Beyond the zigzags come the more complex semi-automatic, automatic and electronically-controlled machines which few normal humans can need.

A flat-bed machine can happily cope with most jobs, but for patching trousers or sewing up armholes, one which converts to free-arm is a good idea. Free-arm machines tend to cost more than those which have just a flat bed.

Secondhand sewing machines are often very good value, but it is easy to waste money by choosing an over-complicated machine. As with other electrical appliances, such as toasters or coffee grinders, once you have lived with an electric sewing machine, manual operation seems impossibly primitive. Nevertheless, many people swear by the old treadle-operated Singers. Both treadle and electric machines leave two hands free for sewing, unlike hand-operated machines, which can now only be bought secondhand in the UK.

Old mechanical machines have lasted well, and many are still on sale secondhand. A cheap, hand-operated machine may be worth having. Successful conversion to electricity is possible, giving variable speed control and greater speed. However, conversion can cost as much as a new machine, and it may throw an old machine out of balance, causing bad vibrations during operation. Old treadle machines don't take kindly to electric conversion—they were designed to run slowly, and the extra speed caused by electric power can result in too much friction. The cast-iron frames of old treadle machines have a certain antique value, and this has pushed the price up in recent years. Sewing machines are sturdy, serious repairs are rarely needed, and repair costs are usually low. The motor and speed control are the most likely parts of old machines to pack up.

Both are replaceable.

Never buy a used machine without trying it out yourself for ease of operation and overall efficiency. The seller can usefully start it up to prove it is safe to touch, but no salesperson should be allowed to put a machine through its paces on your behalf, as he or she will be able to camouflage faults and inconveniences. A fifteen minute trial is reasonable to reveal any problems. Even a little-used old machine must be tested, as long periods of idleness can damage the machine. A machine can be rejected without seeing it at work if it is too bulky, ugly or heavy for the circumstances in which it will be used. A light portable may slide alarmingly around the work table. If the weight seems right, look at the supply cord on electric machines for signs of fraying, and check the foot control box, as plastic ones are easily cracked.

Examine the case; a damaged one can be very difficult to mend. Check that any carrying handles and catches are secure. Be alert for rust chewing away a cast-iron treadle and the surprisingly common woodworm eating its way through the wooden frames of treadle machines. The accessory box should at least contain several bobbins and a screwdriver for adjusting tension. If all seems satisfactory, set the machine up for action, taking care to thread it properly and if possible using different colours of thread for top and bottom, to simplify identification. If the thread keeps snapping during operation and adjusting tension doesn't cure the problem, avoid the machine, as an expert repair may be needed to correct the timing.

The machine must be capable of sewing a perfectly straight seam with stitches of absolutely uniform length, the length varying only when the setting is altered. If the stitches are uneven or the line wanders, these faults are very hard to rectify.

Tension should remain steady once it is set. If there is a sudden rush of thread, the tension is suspect. If the material gathers up, reject the machine and take the test no further. Try the machine at various speeds, and put it into reverse: poor operation in reverse is an early warning of approaching collapse through overwork.

No machine is worth buying if it makes a lot of noise or vibrates during use, as these faults will get worse in time. After the test is over, feel the motor, if it is accessible: it should not be hot to touch.

On a simple machine doing only straight stitch and perhaps zigzag, an instruction booklet is not absolutely vital for an experienced operator, but it is indispensable on complex machines. Instruction leaflets for current models can be obtained, at a price, from the manufacturer. Singer can also supply leaflets for many, but not all, obsolete models. As a rule of thumb, booklets are unobtainable for the old black and gold models, which are still sold, reconditioned, in Singer shops, where a full demonstration is given before sale. The same shops can supply the cheap and very handy *Manual of Domestic Sewing Machines* (60 pence in 1980), which gives a useful rundown on how older machines work. If an instruction booklet is being offered with a secondhand machine, make sure it is the right one! It should explain what extra attachments can be fitted to the machine to exploit its full potential. These attachments may not be available for obsolete models.

Spare parts for many ancient machines can still be found. For example, the handles for obsolete Singers are still being made, and old machines have many individual parts in common with new models. Even if the manufacturer has disappeared, parts may be obtainable from specialist dealers. For instance, Sewcraft of 150 King Street, London W6 (tel: 01–748 5511) may be able to satisfy owners of broken Cresta machines.

Besides repairing machines ancient and modern, Sewcraft also sell secondhand sewing machines, offering a very reassuring two-year guarantee on parts and labour. Their willingness to do this reflects the high reliability of sewing machines, and points to the good sense in buying a used machine from a specialist dealer. There are unfortunately some secondhand sewing machine sharks trying to stitch up the public. They place ads in the classified section of newspapers offering enticingly cheap machines, then turn up on enquirers' doorsteps with a car bootful of new machines, a fistful of hire purchase agrrements and a hard line in sales talk. It is much better to buy from an established shop offering reconditioned machines, guarantees and repair facilities if things go wrong.

SHEARS *see* Garden tools

SHEETS *see* Cloth and household linen

SHOES *see* Clothes

SILVER

The secondhand silver market went through a curious frenetic lurch in late 1979, when a rapid rise in the world price led to a rush of eager fools all anxious to sell off the family silver before the metal price dropped. The world's silver dealers were equally eager to take advantage of this mass folly, as the price offered reflected only the value of the metal content, taking no account of the value of the workmanship. While the weight of metal remains the only legitimate criterion for silver dealing in North Africa, antique or not, much of the value of European silverware lies in the craftsmanship. An artefact is not just a lump of used metal to be melted. The hallmark is the buyer's clue to a piece of silver, guaranteeing the purity of the metal and giving the year in which the assay office put it to the test.

Only the most idiotic secondhand dealer will fail to spot and interpret a hallmark, but customers make regular mistakes in identifying the meaning of the marks. Counterfeit hallmarks have been rife since the earliest days of hallmarking in the 12th century. Although the 1973 Hallmarking Act outlaws any pseudo-hallmarks designed to confuse, they are still common. Each British assay office has its own symbol: London has the leopard, Edinburgh the castle, Sheffield the crown (the rose since 1975) and Birmingham the anchor. Sterling silver (925 parts silver to 75 parts other metal, mainly copper) is distinguished from even purer "Britannia" silver by the lion or the thistle. Silver of foreign origin is given its own symbol: the leo sign, the cross of St Andrew, Libra or the triangle. The meaning of each individual mark, together with year of manufacture, can be worked out by using one of the reference books to the subject such as *English Silver Hall-Marks* edited by Judith Bannister, a pocket-sized paperback published by Foulsham.

Silver tarnishes but it comes clean. Goddard's are the traditional experts in the silver polishing trade, and their products are easy to find. The astonishingly effective Silver Dip is the fast way to fight back against the effects of sulphurous egg yolks, fish, lemons, salt and open fires. If the surface is pitted, complete cleaning is probably impossible. Repairs and replating usually prove too expensive unless the article is of vast historical or emotional significance.

A high world market price for silver encourages recycling schemes. Enterprising recyclers have turned to photographic processing as a curious but lucrative source of silver. Silver is washed off the film and into the developer during processing, and usually the silver baby is simply thrown away with the fixing bath water, dispersed in the sewers and lost forever. This silver is easily recovered by electrolytic plating. In this process two electrodes are

 Leopard
London

 Castle
Edinburgh

 Crown
Sheffield (before 1975)

 Rose
Sheffield (after 1975)

 Anchor
Birmingham

Assay Office Marks

 Britannia
Silver

 Sterling
Silver (marked
in England)

 Sterling Silver
(marked in Scotland before 1975)

 Sterling Silver
(marked in Scotland after 1975)

 London

 Edinburgh

 Sheffield

 Birmingham

Marks on imported Silver

dangled in the silver-rich solution and an electric current is passed between them; the dissolved silver solidifies on the cathode. The metallic replacement method is cheaper and simpler to set up and needs no electricity, but the silver recovered is less pure.

X-ray film is a particularly rich source, as it is silver-coated on both sides, whereas the film for the family snapshots has only one coated side. The recycling of both X-ray developer and redundant film could make some contribution to inadequate hospital funds.

(*See also* Cutlery.)

SKATES

There are multiple objections to rolling around on a pair of secondhand skates. Artists on wheels wear roller skates with the boot attached like the traditional ice skate. After a few sweaty sessions speeding around the floor, the boot moulds itself to the skater's foot and will fit no other. A secondhand pair of skates is no healthier than other used shoes, and there is a further problem with well-worn skates: the leather around the ankle softens up and stops providing support. Boots in this condition should always be rejected, however well they fit.

Changing fashion or broken bones may make a roller skater sell an expensive pair before they wear out.

Precision-made modern roller skates can be a very expensive pleasure, but the price of the traditional rattling metal roller skates remains low. These are fully adjustable, as long as the key can be found, and the curious shape of the previous owner's feet presents no problems. Worn bindings can be replaced, but if the wheels will not spin freely the skates are probably about to roll to a complete halt.

Putting the word around the rink or the local sports centre could turn up a bargain, but this is not a lively market. Never buy skates in a darkened disco. You could miss scuff marks on leather and torn satin. Heavy falls can even rip the sole from the roller plate, although this is less likely with the best skates, whose sole is sandwiched between two plates. Spin all the wheels to test the bearings; they should be almost friction-free.

Unwanted ice skates are sometimes offered for sale at the ice rinks. Skates are very personal, but children grow out of them quickly, and the ice rink's notice board is often found to be a cheap and effective way of buying and selling skates. Look out for chipped, snapped or bent blades, which make the entire boot useless.

SKIS

A ski's life is short. The serious skier changes skis annually, believing that a solid season on the slopes makes even a good pair too tired. However, most ski enthusiasts take five years to clock up the fifteen weeks or so which make up the fanatic's average season.

The sensible novice skier postpones any buying decisions until at least the first two skiing holidays have passed by on hired skis without broken legs or other disasters putting him or her off the sport for ever. Only the rashest novice would buy skis without taking expert advice on the most suitable length for his or her particular ability, height and weight, although the short and stiff "compact" type of ski is widely advised as the beginner's best buy. A visit to a ski shop is useful to learn about the wide range of skis on offer.

Skis are traditionally made of wood or metal, but both materials have become outmoded by the rise of fibreglass and plastics. Some skis offer a compromise, with for example a core of metal sandwiched between fibreglass layers. Fibreglass is generally considered the toughest material. Metal tends to bend and is hard to straighten out; even if straightening is successful, the ski will remain weak afterwards.

Metal skis lose their flexibility, and the curve flattens out. Wooden skis also flatten in time, but problems often show suddenly and dramatically, when a perfectly sound ski becomes unusable overnight.

Besides looking a second-hand ski over for such obvious signs of damage as scratches, chips and deeply-scored soles, there are specific tests to reveal its condition. To check how much flexibility is left in the ski, hold it at both ends, place your knee in the centre and flex it. It should compare favourably to a new one.

Place the ski on a flat surface to see how much of a curve is left. If there is no natural arch, don't buy it. Put the skis side by side to check that the arch on both is identical. Don't buy warped skis. If the skis have metal strips along the edges, check them carefully for signs of damage. Avoid all damaged skis, as damp—in the form of melted snow—may have penetrated the ski, rotting the insides which you can't see. The area around the bindings should not be full of old bore holes where past owners have changed the bindings. The slightest sign of bore holes, no matter how well plugged, should deter the cautious buyer, as damp could have penetrated. The wise buyer will also be wary of skis where the laminations have come adrift and been glued back in place.

Keen skiers often sell their skis after only a year's use. Without competent advice, a beginner who buys them could end up with quite unsuitable extra-long racing skis. Advice is usually obtainable free of charge from specialist ski shops, where ex-hire skis may also be on sale. At the end of the skiing season these shops usually run genuine sales of new skis, unloading their old stock to make way for the new season's models. Ex-hire skis can often be bought in the ski resorts—it may even be possible to buy a pair after using them successfully on hire throughout a skiing holiday. One less obvious source well worth exploring is the notice board in any squash club, as people who sweat in squash courts are also likely to fly down snowy slopes in winter.

Even a beginner could benefit from joining the Ski Club of Great Britain, 118 Eaton Square, London SW1. Besides having a club notice board useful to anyone wanting to buy or sell equipment, they produce a magazine five times a year which is sent free to members. This magazine—*Ski Survey*—has pages of advice on choosing equipment. During the skiing season a skiing adviser sits in a room at the club on two days a week, dispensing sound advice.

SLATES *see* Building materials

SLEEPING BAGS

Let sleeping bags lie. They are rarely a good buy and often an unpleasant one, as they tend to be used on camping holidays when washing facilities are minimal and body odour at its most powerful. Any secondhand bag must be thoroughly cleaned before you surround yourself with it. This can be pricey. Although polyester-filled sleeping bags can be pushed into a washing machine at the launderette, feather or down bags are better dealt with by an expert dry cleaner. The very helpful Drycleaning Information Bureau can provide the names of your local members of the Association of British Launderers and Cleaners who are capable of carrying out the work. Send a large sae to them at 178–202 Great Portland Street, London W1. Check out the cleaners' current prices before you buy a bag.

SPANNERS *see* Tools

SPECTACLES

The country's finest legal minds have puzzled over the legality of secondhand specs. According to the 1958 Opticians Act, it is illegal for any-one but a registered optician or medical practitioner to sell "optical appliances" to the 24 million wearers of spectacles in Britain, and the legal eagles have deemed that even an empty frame is an optical appliance. The innocent junk dealer with a drawer full of old specs is kept out of prison by s.21 (4) of the Act, which offers the let-out: a seller is in the clear if he can "prove that he sold the appliance as an antique or secondhand article and that he did not know, and had no reason to believe", that the appliance was bought to be used. The buyer need have no qualms, as it is no offence to *buy* secondhand glasses. The buyer should be more concerned with the practical and aesthetic problems of spec evaluation.

Only the luckiest lookers find a pair of secondhand spectacles with the right lenses to correct their personal sight problems. New lenses will normally have to be fitted. It is perfectly normal for opticians to fit new lenses in old frames. Fitting suitable lenses in secondhand frames is in effect no different from having a broken lens replaced in your own old pair. However, opticians make a large part of their income by selling new frames at a mark-up as high as 400 per cent, and may be less than enthusiastic about your moneysaving idea. If you don't want the optician to know the glasses were not originally yours, smash the incriminating lenses.

Problems can arise when age has wearied the old frames. Plastic frames must be heated to remove the old lenses and fit new ones. Since old plastic grows brittle, frames often disintegrate during the operation. Even an optician may not be able to spot a dud frame, and may therefore not accept the job or quote a price before the lens grinder has examined the frame at close quarters. Metal frames—such as the ever-popular round antique "granny specs"—are therefore a better bet.

Wearing ill-fitting specs of any material is a miserable business, and it is worth paying considerable attention to the comfort of the glasses before you buy. Metal frames are often bent beyond repair during their brief passage through the junk shop, especially if there are no lenses to help keep the frame rigid.

As the lenses will probably distort your vision enough to turn the flattest of mirrors into a surface worthy of the Hall of Mirrors, you will need a trusted friend to tell you how they look on your face.

A sympathetic optician may replace the lenses in old NHS specs at NHS rates. Where the shape of the frame is non-standard, the cost of lens replacement can be very high, justifiable only if you really like the frame better than new models or you happen to have picked up a pair of rejects from Elton John's spectacular specs collection.

If you don't need glasses to sharpen your eyesight, but your keen eyes spot a nice old pair you would like to use as sunglasses, an optician can fit plain dark glass into an existing frame. However, it is rarely worthwhile on purely financial grounds. The cost of lens replacement is often more than the price of a new pair, as the unit cost of the new sunglasses is reduced considerably by mass production methods. Individual attention costs money.

The converse conversion—

turning an old pair of sunglasses into an ordinary pair of glasses—will often be possible, but always bear in mind the risk of a plastic frame disintegrating during the changeover. Costs of conversion will be higher for large and unusual shapes.

SPIN DRIERS

Spin driers spin clothes drier than automatic washing machines can, and make a mockery of a mangle's efforts. Zipping around at over 2500rpm, the belt-driven drum flings the water out by centrifugal force; the force of gravity or a belt-driven pump carries the water to the outside world. Anyone who does a lot of washing by hand at home or who owns a washing machine that doesn't spin or doesn't spin fast enough, can cut drying time dramatically by using a spin drier. Costs can also be cut if the drier is secondhand. Buying secondhand makes particular sense if the machine is intended for intensive but only temporary employment, for example when a baby means a lot of nappies around the house for a while.

The presence of young children makes it particularly important that the machine's lid should be impossible to open before the machine stops or is running too slowly to cause injury to the hands of the inquisitive. British Standards now make this feature mandatory, but the rule only came into force in April 1975, and many secondhand machines were made before such regulations were thought of. Others will once have complied, but time will have made their once-efficient braking system ineffective. The braking system which stops the drum is similar to a bicycle brake: cables go slack and brake linings wear down. The mechanically-minded owner can easily adjust a drier's brakes, but professional repair will cost pounds. Call-out charges are of National Debt proportions.

The only way to test the brakes properly is to plug the machine in, switch it on, lift the lid and see if the drum has stopped. If there is no chance of plugging it in, a secondhand drier is hardly worth gambling on. It is less crucial to fill it with sodden clothes for the test, but as the cycle is so brief (typically one to ten minutes) and water is almost invariably available, such a test is worthwhile. Provision should be made to catch the water as it pours out or the seller may become irate.

With the drier switched on, the faults begin to show. A burnt-out motor should be plain, as nothing will happen; check the plug, because a broken fuse or bad connection will lead to a similar lack of action. If the motor sounds active but the drum refuses to turn, there could be clothes caught inside or a broken/slack drive belt. Belt adjustments and replacements are simple jobs on most driers, although new belts may not be available. The belt driving the pump should be even simpler to replace, as the motor mountings shouldn't even have to be slackened off to slip a new belt over the pulleys. An instruction manual may explain the procedure.

Squeaks are a sign of lack of lubrication. Signs of age will be visible without even plugging the machine in. Cracked or hardened rubber seals will need replacing, and jammed or missing wheels will make moving the drier more awkward. Rust can break out anywhere on the metal, especially down below where water can be left swilling around by negligent owners. Feel around the drum for any sharp edges which might lead to snagging. Frustrated owners often cause damage to the drum by prodding violently with pointed objects when the drum gets jammed. A pump blocked by socks can cause the drier to flood. Obstructions in the pipe can usually be felt.

A long hose can be useful, and some come bent at the end to hook handily over the edge of the sink. A long flex can save a buyer having to spend more money on an extension lead if the socket outlet is remote from the spot where the drier is to be used. Standard features of the machine should be explained in the instruction manual, which may still be available.

STOVES

Interest in the classic "bar-rack-room" cylindrical stove has risen with coal costs, because enclosed heaters of this type are very efficient users of fuel, twice as efficient as an open coal fire. Some households are heated even more cheaply if there's a ready supply of free wood to put on a woodburning stove, but smokeless zone regulations make wood burning impractical in many places. Both wood and coal stoves need storage space for the fuel and a chimney or flue for the fumes.

The stoves' decorative steel outer casing covers extremely heavy cast-iron innards, which should be checked carefully for cracks in secondhand models. Godin stoves are still made to very traditional designs, and design of the cast-iron insides of the famous Pither has remained unaltered for decades. Spare parts for the earliest stoves are available from the manufacturers. In old Pither stoves the firebricks may have cracked up or disappeared, but replacements can be bought from the makers. A stove used without firebricks will soon be damaged.

The fumes from the burning anthracite in a Pither are toxic, and airtight seals are therefore crucial. The lid of the stove is bedded in sand to seal it. Best quality silver sand is the grade to use, as ordinary builder's sand can corrode the rim. Corrosion may also have attacked the fuel container if it has been filled with wet fuel. Corrosion grips an old Godin stove when the enamel is chipped.

Check that the combustion controls at the back still move freely on old stoves. The cast-iron fire bars and the ash tray are loose and may therefore have vanished.

Informative installation and operating instructions are available from the manufacturers.

SUB-AQUA EQUIPMENT

Secondhand sub-aqua equipment is scarce and desirable. New gear is dear and demand for used equipment strong. Hordes of eager divers pounce on a piece of good used gear faster than piranhas on a prime steak.

Advertisements for secondhand items occasionally appear in the diving magazines, but most equipment is sold as soon as word moves around the club house that a member is giving up underwater sport and putting his equipment up for sale.

Joining one of the 800-plus branches of the British Sub-Aqua Club is the best way both to learn the sport and to locate well-maintained secondhand equipment. Safety is of course the major consideration, and no-one should buy the sophisticated equipment for deep water exploration without proper training. The club's instructors will teach the safe way to dive, but there are surprisingly few regulations covering the safety and performance of equipment. Only high-pressure air cylinders are subject to legal requirements. They are made to Health and Safety Executive specifications and must be given a hydraulic test every two years. The month and year of test will be stamped on the cylinder, together with the code number of the specifications. The two essential considerations when buying secondhand cylinders are that the code number of the specification must be current and the cylinder still in test. Buying an untested cylinder is a pointless gamble, as old ones often fail the test. Insist that the owner has out-of-date cylinders retested before you buy. Most diving dealers can arrange tests.

The test is vitally important, as a bad cylinder can go off like a bomb. With a pressure of up to 3,000psi, a rusty part can cause considerable damage. If a cylinder fails the test, it is common practice to render it useless by drilling holes in it and hacking it into pieces. The specifications to look for on aluminium alloy cylinders are HOAL 3, HOAL 2 or HOAL 4. On steel cylinders the latest code is BS5045/1/CM/S, but HOS and HOT are acceptable. Certain foreign specifications are technically unacceptable in the UK, but they are perfectly safe and are on open sale. Buyers may experience problems having them tested and filled.

The dangers of using inadequate cylinders were exposed in the mid-1970s when a bunch of submarine cowboys illegally bought, stamped and resold a number of low-pressure aluminium brewery cylinders. As a result, divers were maimed.

New specifications require a visual examination of the cylinder every year. Only cylinders stamped with the new specification number are forced to comply, but the BSAC recommends an annual check for all cylinders.

Cylinders are filled with compressed air, which is released through a demand valve when the diver inhales. There are no specifications for demand valves, and inexpert buyers face possible pitfalls with ancient valves, which can be hard for the novice to spot. The problem is that the maximum pressure inside a cylinder has increased during the past decade from some 2000psi to 3000psi, and further increases are likely. An old demand valve will not work well at the higher pressure and could easily suffer from mechanical failure. No valve should be bought unless it has been recently serviced. A reservice costing about £20 can rejuvenate even very jaded valves, but caution can save money. A good indication of overall condition is the metal filter on the pressure inlet. This should be shiny, brass or copper coloured. Beware of rusty, green or filthy filters, as the insides of the valve are almost certainly in a worse state.

The main cylinder decants air into the cylinder feeding the life jacket. This smaller cylinder is not subject to the same rigorous specifications, but it works at high pressure and requires regular maintenance. Cylinders can be tested in the same way as main cylinders. If there is any suggestion of water, or rust, or a tinkling noise when the cylinder is shaken, beware. Examine the life jacket carefully, paying particular attention to the rubber bag.

Deep water divers and even serious snorkellers will want a neoprene wet suit complete with gloves and hood. Every square inch of a used suit should be scoured for holes. The seams are usually the first spot to show damage. The more basic snorkelling equipment—mask, fins and snorkel—is not often bought secondhand. A face mask should fit snugly over eyes and nose, leaving the mouth uncovered. A simple test for a proper fit or rotten rubber is to place the mask in position and breathe in through the nose: if the seal is air-tight, the mask should stay on without support. Avoid snorkels with a valve on top, as these are dangerous. An open J-tube with a mouth piece is a safer design.

The British Sub-Aqua Club can be contacted at 70 Brompton Road, London SW3 (tel: 01—584 7163).

SYNTHESISERS

Music has embraced the electronic revolution, and pride of place among electronic instruments goes to the synthesiser. Bargain buys are not rare even in these relatively early days of development, as the secondhand value of a good instrument can plummet when the model is discontinued after a very brief concert career.

Synthesisers are complex and unreliable machines, and problems are unavoidable. If electronic wizardry is not your talent, it is very important to know where a used synthesiser can be repaired. Modified synthesisers are especially dodgy.

Many of the checks for a synthesiser are the same as for a used piano. Every key must be tried, and every control operated. As with a piano, tuning can be a real problem, and tuning on a secondhand instrument will almost certainly be wrong. The high frequencies are the most likely to be out. On models with two or more oscillators, they should track each other consistently without too many beats. Have any faults rectified before you buy.

Turn up the output volume fully without playing a note: background noise on a good machine will be somewhere between minimal and non-existent.

T

TAPES *see* Tools

TAPS *see* Bathroom fittings

TELESCOPES

A telescope is like a one-eyed binocular, and the pre-purchase examination of both instruments will be almost identical (*see* Binoculars). The secondhand telescope is a safer buy insofar as there can be no awkward problems with double images. However, the image in an ill-treated telescope can be distorted. A good case will protect the instrument.

Wobbling tubes can be an irritation with old telescopes, when the pads between tubes flatten or wear down. These can be replaced with new felt or cardboard pads. The lenses should never be removed even for cleaning. Secondhand telescopes are sold by the same dealers who handle used binoculars.

TELEVISION SETS

A one-year-old colour television will probably have depreciated by a full third, and each passing year chops a further quarter off the price. This suggests that television buyers value the "New!" label as much as television advertisers do.

Buying a used set is often an alternative to rental, as both markets appeal to viewers short of ready cash. Old tvs can't be counted on for long, but a very cheap secondhand set may be worth buying even if its Coronation Streets are numbered. If the price of a working used set is less than the deposit on a rented set (six months' rental was payable in advance in 1981), buying is probably preferable to rental. This is particularly true if the dealer offers a warranty covering repairs for at least part of the period. Repair of rented sets is entirely free, and rental companies tend to act faster than secondhand dealers, who have little to gain but a bit of goodwill.

A deposit equal to one month's rental may be enough on "decontrolled" rental sets, which are sets too old to be covered by the government's Control of Hiring Order. This is an economic regulator manipulated by the chancellor. In 1980 the age limit stood at two years. Old rented sets may be sold to the secondhand trade, but they will be reconditioned, reboxed and rerented when demand is high.

Before deciding to buy secondhand rather than rent, consider the cost of installation. The average televiewer is incapable of installing a colour set at home, balancing the colour and adjusting the aerial. A visit from an engineer could add considerably to the overall cost. It is useless, incidentally, to pay for any engineer who installs a set without using the test card for fine tuning.

A colour tv is an extraordinarily complicated piece of equipment. Do-it-yourself tv repairs are generally impossible. Amateur attempts at adjustments inside the set are quite likely to ruin the tv or electrocute the examiner. Many modern sets are designed to be impenetrable.

Although repairs are more likely to be needed on old sets, repair costs should not rise with the set's age, although the major expense of replacing a tube in a colour set grows in probability as the set passes its fifth birthday. The industry places great faith in the durability of the modern in-line tubes. It is often possible to spot a tube which is "going soft" and about to fade away for ever. Avoid any set with the contrast control turned fully up, especially if the picture is still grey, as this indicates a dying tube. No control on the set should have to be turned up to its maximum, as this rules out the possibility of further adjustments if matters deteriorate.

A colour tv picture is made up of red, blue and green pictures fired at the screen from separate guns. When one gun goes out of alignment, a red, blue or green ghost shadows the objects on screen. Repair can only be carried out by a professional.

The picture on a colour set will probably look dreadful if no adequate aerial is fixed. Room aerials are seldom satisfactory, and a good aerial fitted on the roof or in the attic improves reception on most sets. Aerials are expensive: it is therefore handy if one is included in the price. The ideal aerial varies from place to place, and they travel badly, so there is little point in buying one in a Cornish auction for use in the Scottish highlands.

Without an effective aerial, ghosts often creep into the picture as the signal bounces off a nearby building or hill. A snowy screen could also be due to aerial inadequacies.

Even without an aerial, the picture should fill the entire screen unless you are lucky enough to tune in to a cinemascope movie. The picture should not roll or flick around.

Fiddle with the tuners to check that they work positively and easily on every channel. Tuners wear out after years of use, so the most reliable sets will probably be sold by ITV addicts or committed BBC watchers who would never think of channel hopping. The best sets will probably come from Japanese manufacturers, whose reliability record is vastly superior to the British.

It is rarely possible to see a set working in street markets or auction rooms, where only gamblers will pay high prices. You really cannot tell much about a set without switching it on; the set should be left working for at least twenty minutes, which gives problems time to show. Sets with signs of physical damage are not worth gambling on, as knocks harm sets' insides. The function of the controls may also reveal something about the set's age. No set receiving on 405 lines has been made in the UK since 1969.

Dual-standard sets adapted for both 405 and 625-UHF transmissions were manufactured during the period between the start of BBC2 on 625 lines in April 1964 and the completion of the switch to colour by all channels in December 1969. A lot of these sets are found on the secondhand market. After the complete shutdown of 405-line transmissions, the 405 sets made before the BBC2 era will not pick up a thing. Their only interest will be to the antique dealer and collector. The demand for valve sets is becoming increasingly specialist. Valves can still be found to replace burned-out ones in ancient sets. A plan showing how to locate the valves should be pasted on the back of the set or inside the rear panel. Solid-state sets are less liable to break down. They are also considerably less bulky, which is a significant factor in most homes. Large old models are often very ugly lumps of furniture whose absence improves the look of most rooms.

Facilities for the fourth channel will be built into all but the oldest sets with preset push-button channel selectors. Sets with a rotary tuning control will pick up all channels. Older sets are unlikely to have facilities for teletext reception, and sets built before 1974 will need a simple adaptation before video recordings can be played through them. Only modern sets offer battery-powered operation and true portability.

Secondhand sets rarely come with a guarantee, and maintenance contracts — which are an expensive form of insurance — are equally hard to find for used sets. As things can go wrong, the safest source of secondhand sets is probably the specialist selling reconditioned sets, who can carry out repairs. Old sets are often taken by retailers in part exchange, but buyers should remember that the previous owner must have had good reason to trade a set in.

There is no point in importing a secondhand set from another country. Each country's sets are made specifically to prevent interference from foreign stations. In Germany, for example, you can receive pictures but no sound with a British set, which limits viewing to silent movies.

TENTS

After years of humiliation as the poor man of the European campsites, the traditionally ill-equipped British camper is beginning to erect the family tent with pride, matching the smartest continentals frame for frame, kitchen for kitchen, curtain for curtain. Those families who grow to love life under canvas or whose love life under canvas makes the family grow, periodically upgrade their tents, selling off the redundant tent secondhand.

Springtime is the start of the season for buying new tents. In October and November, on the other hand, after a dismally damp summer, unhappy campers who have sworn at each other throughout the summer and sworn to heaven never to camp again, sell off the symbol of spoiled holidays.

Inexperienced, infrequent or unconvinced campers may be well advised to hire equipment in order to sample camp life before buying even a secondhand tent. Hire companies are themselves a source of secondhand tents. They renew stock after the summer and sell off bedraggled items cheap. Prices can be cut to 60 per cent of the new price, with even larger discounts for people who have hired the equipment. Ex-hire tents may have been ruined by a series of clueless campers doing a Laurel and Hardy erection and demolition job, but major hire companies such as

Rentatent offer long guarantees. Camping shops often sell off display tents cheap in the autumn.

Only the foolish or clairvoyant should buy a second-hand tent without seeing it erected. Fabric rot could have taken a strong grip. All-important frame sections could be missing from an expensive frame tent package. Frame parts for old and discontinued tents are particularly elusive. Check on availability or substitutes with the manufacturer before committing yourself to an irksome purchase. Poles could be severely weakened by rust, bends and buckles. Mild rust can be cleaned away by steel wool or rust-removing liquid, and bends can occasionally be straightened out by firm but careful levering, but kinks are final. Kinked poles will need replacements, and the right sort could be hard to locate.

Accept no excuses by a shifty seller for not putting the tent up. If he claims that it will take too long to erect, don't buy: such a difficult job is not one you want to face when you arrive at a wet campsite on a wild night. It is important to erect the tent yourself, taking note of any tips from the experienced seller, which could save you hours of frustration and the mockery of fellow campers later on. The ideal arrangement is to have the tent on approval for a few days, even for a brief holiday.

Do not let trifling problems worry you, such as broken spring links on poles — these do not last long, and replacements are cheap and easy to fit. Dirty marks are insignificant, and even tiny tears in the canvas itself need concern only the very nervous or inept; they provide the perfect haggling point to force the price down.

The main strain on tent fabric occurs where canvas touches the framework. These stress points should be protected by an extra thickness of canvas. Only the most sieve-like of tents will reveal leaks without a battering from heavy rain. Easy diy reproofing is possible using a can of proprietary reproofing treatment, but if damp storage has caused rot and mildew, reject the tent. The signs of irreversibly damaged fabric are dark marks and a musty smell.

Eagle eyes should scan seams for weak or rotten

stitching where leaking will be likely. The stitching often starts to break away at the end of seams, but the proverbial stitch in time usually rectifies the problem. Seams should be at least double-stitched. Rub-on proofing solutions are on sale. Turn up an unexposed part of the fabric, perhaps under a seam. If it is noticeably darker in colour than the rest, the tent has been bleached under a fierce sun and the fabric may be suffering from terminal sun-stroke.

Check that zips work smoothly and guy attachments will hold the tent steady. Stiff old zips can often be freed by rubbing them over with a candle. Canvas loops or D-rings where the pegs are driven in can absorb a lot of moisture if they are unproofed, and this leads to rot which can even spread to the rest of the tent. Feeble loops should be replaced using sail twine as sold by yacht chandlers. A good stretch unmasks perished rubber loops, which reveal more cracks than the walls of Jericho. Plastic doesn't perish but it does go brittle with age.

Holes where poles pass through the tent material can be troublesome when they tear and fray. Only skilled sewers should apply for the job of mending them. Vanished eyelets are equally tricky.

If you view the tent by day or by bright light, crawl or walk inside and look up for signs of holes in the roof. The roof may be hidden by a useful roof lining, designed to hide ugly framework, increase insulation and reduce condensation. This inside view should reveal the adequacy and condition of windows. A sewn-in groundsheet should also be inspected for holes needing repair.

Outside again, check the number of tent pegs and the state of the bag in which it must travel. Part of the bargaining over price could include an enquiry about any other equipment which may be included. Owners determined never to see the inside of canvas again may be willing to part with other aspects of the outdoor life—folding tables and chairs, camp beds, cooking equipment and other picnic items. Don't accept these without examination. A camp bed, for example, may have missing parts, torn canvas or a devilishly complex assembly sequence. Used sleeping bags are not recommended.

TIMBER *see* Building materials

TOASTERS

Broken toasters can usually be repaired, but are not worth paying any money for, as a brand-new toaster can be bought for only twice the price of a typical repair. Ancient toasters may be troublesome, with parts hard to find if anything but an element needs replacing. The only practical solution in such circumstances may be to cannibalise parts from another broken toaster, though diy repair is really only for the confident and reasonably competent.

Traditional toasters are very similar to each other, but all are slightly and irritatingly different. If you need spare parts from an electrical shop, take the old part with you and use only an exact match. Many modern toasters have their components fused in a single block—if one part goes, the whole lot must be replaced.

If an old toaster's earth terminal has been corroded by the heat of a thousand slices, it can burn people as well as toast. If you can't afford a funeral, you can't afford an unearthed toaster. An untested toaster should not be plugged in without an earth continuity test to verify the existence of the earth circuit. The test is to fix one end of a multimeter on to the earth pin of the plug or the earth core in the flex, and the other end on any metal part of the toaster casing. This should complete the circuit.

It may be necessary to lift the casing off to have a look inside: four screws normally hold it on. Always unplug the toaster before you do anything to it. Once open, the horror of unsecured wires and bare wire poking through burned insulation should be on view. Removing the crumb tray may reveal worn parts and poor connections. If the crumb tray is packed with enough damp crumbs to make a whole slice of toast, this could have caused an electrical problem.

Most premises boast an electricity supply, but spare plugs are rare, so it may be wise to take one with you: it only takes two minutes to fix and allows you to examine

303

the condition of the flex, which may have been left trailing over hot cookers, and the state of the insulation, which may be hard, rotten and ready for renewal. Fitting new flex takes time and money. The flex to use is 0.75mm² 3-core, braided and rubber-sheathed.

Trying the toaster with several slices provides the chance to check the thermostat's ability to adapt to different settings, the catch's ability to hold the bread down for toasting, and the pop-up mechanism's ability to fire the hot toast skywards. It will also prove whether the surface the toaster stands on gets too hot.

If the toast turns satisfactorily brown only on the maximum setting, the thermostat is probably about to collapse from metal fatigue. The toast should be browned evenly all over and on both sides.

Two-slice toasters are normal, and these have three or four elements. It is rare for all to burn out simultaneously, so check carefully that every one is a winner. The only possible repair is replacement.

TOOLS

The proverbial bad workman was probably right to blame his tools: the market is littered with lousy tools. Cheap new tools are usually manufactured to low design standards from poor metal, and they don't last long. Good new tools are generally expensive, but they last almost for ever in careful hands.

Some fine old woodworking tools have become reclassified as antiques in recent years and have even been auctioned off as collectors' items at Sotheby's. This trend is causing problems for the nation's handymen, smallholders and craftsmen, because the reclassification has been accompanied by a huge price rise, pushing useful and unique tools beyond the reach of those who actually need them. Whereas only a fanatical collector could claim to "need" an art nouveau vase, a smallholder's need for a cheap scythe to cut his grass is perfectly genuine.

Tools intended for use are more likely to be sold at a general country auction than at Sotheby's. There is usually an enthusiastic huddle of men around the tool box on viewing day, and bidding can be brisk.

Army surplus stores are a good but unpredictable source of cheap old tools, many of which are unused. Tool thefts are a routine part of life on a building site, and stolen tools often turn up in the market place. The stock of general secondhand shops comes mainly from house clearances.

Some tools are better hired than bought. Tool hire companies have flourished with the growth of diy, and they are an excellent source of items like cement mixers and scaffolding for occasional jobs. The hire companies usually provide ignorant customers with a demonstration at the start of the hire period; instruction leaflets may also be available, and these can save days of frustration.

Brace There are two types of jaw design for braces: the Universal type will grip both tapered and straight bits, but Alligator jaws will not grip straight bits. Some braces have a ratchet, which is very useful if it works.

Chisels Chisels are widely abused tools. Wooden handles split when hit repeatedly with a metal hammer rather than the traditional mallet. Cutting edges will be ruined if the tool is used for tack-lifting, and blades get chipped if left loose and unprotected in the tool box. Chisels can be resharpened, but look for signs of sharpening on the bottom face—there should not be any. An oilstone, normally kept lightly oiled in a wooden box, is needed to sharpen the chisel. A second-hand oilstone must be flat: flatness can be checked by laying a straight edge across the stone and looking for light between the two. Slight imperfections can be flattened out of the stone by rubbing it with water and jeweller's carborundum on a sheet of smooth float glass. Hollow oilstones are best thrown away. A combination oilstone—medium on one side, fine on the other—allows you to rub away the chips from a chisel and then hone it sharp. A grindstone wheel will cope with badly-chipped chisels.

Clamps Clamps are strong, though the frame can be distorted by repeated over-tightening. As absolute precision is rarely needed in a clamp, and new ones can be ludicrously dear, they are often good secondhand buys. Avoid a G-clamp if the swivel shoe on the screw jaw is missing.

Cutting knife   Usually known as the "Stanley" knife, a used cutting knife should be satisfactory, though it is worth removing the side screw to check that the thread is not stripped and to see if there are any spare blades stored inside. Replacement blades are sold in diy shops.

Drill bits   Used bits will almost certainly need sharpening, and sharpening a twist drill is a job few amateurs enjoy. Spade-shaped flat bits are easier to tackle. Blunt countersink bits cannot be sharpened. Tool shops will usually run a sharpening service, and manufacturers will resharpen the tungsten carbide tips of masonry drills. A masonry drill will overheat if it is forced through wood: any drill which has turned black and blue through overheating has lost its temper and is useless. Check the bit's straightness. Bits for braces and drills are not necessarily interchangeable. A wide range of engineering twist drills are made in metric

sizes. Number (gauge) and letter size have been obsolete for years, replaced by metric equivalents.

File   Files are made of very hard steel, but in time they wear out. Once a file's teeth are chipped and blunted, it is ruined. Clogged teeth can be brushed clean with a wire brush or a special file card. Handles to fit file blades can be bought for a few pence and can save hands from vile cuts.

Hammer   Loose heads are dangerous when they fly off the handle, but they can be secured with wedging pins bought from a tool shop. Forged steel heads are more desirable than cast iron, which can shatter. Traditionalists prefer the ash handles found on old hammers to the more recent leather- or rubber-covered steel. The claw side of a claw hammer should taper to a fine "V", but the "V" is sometimes sheared open after a long life. Clean up the face of an old hammer with emery cloth before putting it to use.

Hand drill   A broken handle on a hand drill is obvious, but buyers are less likely to notice that the removable handle—which is taken off for jobs in tight corners—has disappeared. A dose of oil will normally improve a hand drill's performance, but in time the jaws may wear out and fail to hold a bit securely. New ones are easy to fit but add to the cost. Bits are unlikely to be included in the price, but fit a bit (or failing that even a pencil will do), to check that the jaws work.

Nail punch Even cheaper than a secondhand punch is a nail with a blunted head.

Plane A modern metal plane is a piece of precision engineering, easily damaged by protruding nails during use or by mishandling in the junk shop or auction room. Wooden planes are rarities with some antique value. Certain patterns of moulding plane are no longer in production and can only be bought secondhand. Blunt blades can be sharpened on an oilstone at home or sent to the diy shop. Replacement blades can be found for secondhand planes.

Pliers Apart from blunted or damaged cutting edges on the jaws, poor alignment and

problems at the pivot, used pliers present few difficulties.

Plumb line A plumb bob's life should be almost eternal, but a handyman trying to save money can just tie a piece of string to any weight. Mind you, with the price of string today ...

Saw The shape of a saw's teeth betrays its function. A rip saw—designed for cutting *along* the wood grain—has chisel-like teeth, and not many of them; teeth on the commoner panel saw, which is happier cutting *across* the grain, are cut at the same angle on both sides of the point. On both types teeth are bent alternately away from the blade to left and right. Once the teeth are flattened, they will no longer clear sawdust, and the saw will stick. Most old saws can be reset and sharpened, a job most amateurs leave to the expert in the tool shop. Long-lasting hard-point saws cannot be sharpened: the old teeth have to be cut off and a new set cut into the blade. Look out for saws with a bent blade— they are useless. Rust can be cleaned off with steel wool and rust remover.

Screwdriver Screwdrivers are the most abused of all tools, and once the blades are bent they rarely bend back again. The tip of the blade must be square and even; chipped and rounded blades can be filed sharp, but are rarely worth buying. The tip of a small damaged screwdriver can be filed into a chisel shape and used as a bradawl.

Cross-head screwdrivers come in two patterns—for Posidriv or the old Phillips screws, which have differently shaped slots. A screwdriver can be damaged by use in the wrong slots. Yankee screwdrivers are designed to take a variety of bits, but the interchange mechanism often fails; check that the bit can be removed and refixed securely in position. An old Yankee will probably need oiling. Ratchet systems crack up in time, and should be tested in working conditions. Check also that the collar is securely fixed.

Spanners Confusion is rife in a box of secondhand spanners. They could be sized according to the metric system or in fractions of an inch. Imperial spanners could be "A/F", on which the stated size is measured across the flats, or British Standard Whitworth, sized according to bolt diameter. Whitworth sizes are common on older machinery. Metric and imperial spanners are not interchangeable. Sizing an old open-ended spanner can be complicated as they often open out at the end after years of abuse. The wrong size of spanner can quickly damage a bolt.

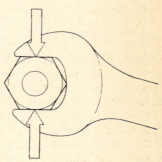

distance between arrows is "across flats" (A/F) measurement

Adjustable spanners are very subject to wear, but a secondhand adjustable self-grip (Mole) wrench is a good buy if the spring is still powerful. These are easily tested before you buy, but be careful not to pinch your fingers.

Socket sets vary too widely in quality and price to be considered a good buy if they are unidentified.

Spirit level   Test a spirit level by placing it on a surface, checking where the bubble lies, then turning the level through 180°—the bubble must be in the same place if the level is accurate. Adjustment is usually possible, and a small level can always be mounted on a longer piece of straight timber to improve accuracy.

Square   A try square is traditionally a tempered steel blade gripped in a wooden stock, but modern stocks are usually plastic. Check the square's accuracy by laying the stock against the edge of a piece of straight timber and drawing a pencil line across the timber. Flip the square over so the stock points the other way: the square edge should be parallel with the pencil line.

Tape   The popular retractable locking steel tape is most versatile in the 3m/10ft metric/imperial combination. Withdraw the whole length of tape, as it may have been trodden on, bent and rendered useless. The numbers commonly wear off near the beginning of the tape, which is the most useful part. The thumb lock should work and the little hook should not be missing from the end.

Vice   The traditional vices have proved to be very durable. Secondhand ones offer good savings.

TORTOISES *see* Pets

TOYS

Adult collectors squabble over old toys more than children ever could. Competition is always fierce at auctions of obsolete electric train sets; antique dolls and early mechanical toys light up many an adult eye; even cheap post-war Asian tinplate space monsters are prized by a limited band of enthusiasts. Tinplate toys are probably safer in a collector's showcase than in a child's hands, as old clockwork tinplate toys often have dangerously exposed sharp edges. Others have excessive doses of lead in the paintwork. Sharp edges and lead paint were outlawed by safety regulations in 1974, when arsenic, cadmium, barium, antimony and mercury joined lead on the list of banned paint additives. Sheet metal edges of tinplate toys should now be covered or folded back to prevent nasty cuts.

Toys with pointed ends are also outlawed by safety regulations, but are often seen on sale secondhand. Arrows for spring-loaded guns and pistols, cross-bows, long bows and pea shooters must not be made of metal. Their ends have to be blunt and protected by flexible tips, but these are often missing from old arrows. The points of toy darts can't be made of metal.

The regulations apply equally to toys made before and after 1974, but in practice protection is very limited for buyers from secondhand shops. The regulations don't apply to private sales between private individuals. Despite the regulations, the secondhand market is still littered with grossly unsafe toys made before the regulations came into force. Unsafe modern rejects are often unloaded through market stalls. Buyers need to be unusually aware of the pitfalls of dud toys before venturing into buying secondhand goods for children.

It is perhaps fortunate that toys normally have a very brief life with children, who tend to see a working toy as a challenge to their destructive powers. Modern mechanical toys are rarely worth buying secondhand if they are not in working order, as the typical methods of manufacture — welding and stamping — make many of them irreparable. Older toys can normally be dismantled by an adept adult and some sort of repair improvised, even if the manufacturer can't supply replacement parts.

Plastic parts are notoriously hard to mend. Despite the claims of the glue manufacturers, glueing remains difficult, as you need to know precisely which type of plastic you are dealing with before you have much chance of success. The manufacturers will often refuse to divulge the information you need, even if they know.

Certain repairs are possible and worthwhile. Very valuable old dolls can be taken to a Dolls' Hospital such as the one at 16 Dawes Road, London SW6 (tel: 01–385 2081). They will also repair cheap dolls which are still in use, but replacement is often cheaper than repair with modern dolls.

Manufacturers make no

provision for spares, but the Dolls' Hospital has wigs for sale. It is normally a simple diy job to reattach a vinyl doll's amputated limbs using a new piece of elastic. A loose-limbed teddy bear can be tightened up by opening his main seam and twisting his metal clips. The facial features of a teddy bear, say the safety regulations, must be very firmly fixed or so deeply embedded that they cannot be gripped by fingers or teeth.

Teddy bears, like other soft toys, are probably ready for a thorough cleaning after a journey through the secondhand world. They could, after all, have been cuddled through disease by pox-ridden children, and the filling may be filthy.

Some toys are designed to be abused. Violent impact is, for example, part of everyday life for a pedal-driven car. Scratched paint and dents are to be expected in a secondhand car and are unimportant. Serious rusting underneath is more worrying. Look for buckled drive rods, which run between the pedals and the axle. They can normally be taken out and straightened or replaced, but removal will often involve drilling out rivets and replacing them with nuts and bolts. On any secondhand toy, the nuts, bolts and screws should be tightened and the moving parts lubricated before it is handed over to a child.

Secondhand electric cars are too unpredictable to recommend, though a good cleaning by an electrically competent person can often improve performance considerably. Faults may be caused just by dirty brushes, a smutty commutator or faulty contacts. Model shops can often carry out more complex repairs. It is best to leave electric train repairs to the experts. Even lubrication is tricky without the manufacturer's instructions, which may no longer be available.

Fire is a hazard to children, and the British Standard for the Safety of Toys BS5665: Part 2: 1978 attempts to stamp out fire in the toybox. Secondhand fireworks and chemistry sets are obviously a bad risk. Beware also of inflammable nurses' uniforms, cowboy outfits, wigwams or toy tents. If a child can go inside a toy, he should be able to open it from the inside.

TRACTORS

The used tractor salesman does not share the hard-won reputation for low cunning of his colleagues in the motor trade. Nevertheless, a tractor shares complexity with the motor car, and mechanically ignorant buyers would be unwise to buy without the advice of a more knowledgeable friend. It can be very awkward to break down hopelessly in the middle of a soggy, half-ploughed field miles from help. This makes it important to check that the tractor is likely to last and that, in case of breakdown, the manufacturer and his servicing organisation have a good local spares and repairs service.

Head-on collisions between drunken tractor drivers are infrequent, but dangerous driving can lead to bad accidents when tractors rear and topple, squashing the driver in his beetroot. Since 1977 a safety cab has been fitted to all new tractors over 11cwt, but it is quite legal for a pre-1977 tractor to be sold secondhand without a safety cab. A protective roll-over bar is better than complete exposure, and these can be fitted around unprotected drivers.

Inexperienced drivers should beware of dangerous cabs in secondhand tractors. The pre-1977 category embraces the thousands of classic "Fergies", the last sturdy examples of the half million built in Ferguson's Coventry factory after World War 2. The Ferguson lacks the sophistication of the modern Japanese mini-tractors which most smallholders lust after. Whereas most modern tractors run on diesel, the Fergie burns paraffin or tvo, but it has to be started from cold with petrol. The highly-praised Japanese models are recent arrivals in European fields, and few have yet reached the secondhand market.

TUMBLE DRIERS

Enthusiastic users of tumble driers have very high electricity bills, which may cause frugal housekeepers to sell off perfectly good machines and buy a more economical spin drier. Chances of finding a good secondhand tumble drier are high, as these are reliable appliances, simple in operation and simple to repair. They need little maintenance apart from a quick clean of the filter after every use to remove the accumulated lint.

Some signs of damage can be looked for before a secondhand machine is plugged in and put through its paces. Rust should be clear to see and could be just as clearly seen on clothes in future if damp garments come into contact with rust marks. Chipped paint on the drier's casing may be Phase One of rust damage. A look for rust and missing screws around the back should provide the opportunity to check that the wheels are working well.

Drop-down doors may squeak—a drop of oil should sort that out—or be hanging loose with strained hinges if heavy wet clothes have been dropped on the door over a period of years. This is not a serious fault, as long as it has not affected the cut-out switch which must stop the drum turning once the door is open. There must be no bodged override bypassing this safety switch.

A broken or overstretched belt is a particular feature of tumble driers. Spares are in-

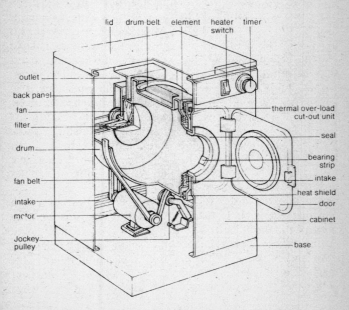

expensive but manufacturers' at-home repair services cost a lot. Typically there are two belts, one driving the fan, the other turning the drum. The fan belt is usually very simple to adjust or replace, the drum belt considerably harder. A cross-head screwdriver is often enough to remove the back panel of the machine; cracked or broken belts should then be very visible. Belts should have half an inch of play at the centre. If they are too loose, they will slip, too tight and they can strain the bearings and cause vibrations.

Excessive vibration could also be the result of a damaged fan. The fan draws air over the heating elements and into the drum. It rarely goes wrong, but if it is chipped it can throw the motor out of balance. Even without excessive vibration, most driers are noisy and should be heard before buying. Internal problems will show up during a test drive when a buyer can verify that the drum turns, and that warm air is forced through the drum.

Lint can catch between the drum and its casing. With the machine unplugged, removal of a pane in the drum may reveal a sock; another test for a lint blockage is to remove the drive belt from around the drum and turn the drum manually, feeling for resistance. Only the skilled or foolish gamble on being able to free a jammed drum at home merely by dragging out a ripped sock, as the bearing may be damaged beyond easy diy repair. Lint can clog the vent and reduce drying efficiency. A common indication of this problem is overheating of the top of the drier, and a noticeable failure of the machine to dry clothes. Clothes will also be left damp if a heating element breaks. Most machines have two heating temperatures and two elements: it is essential to test at both settings and to be certain that the hotter one is in fact hotter. A thermal overload cutout unit stops the machine overheating. These eventually break, and the machine will no longer heat up. Cutout units can be replaced.

A hot smell is not a sign that the machine is working well—it is more likely to be the smell of hot insulation from a burnt-out motor. This is not a job for the amateur to tackle without experience and supervision. Repairs to the elements and thermostats are best left to the professional, and unless the machine is very cheap, the need for professional attention will put off the prudent buyer.

If everything works, the final round of pre-purchase negotiation will establish whether a venting kit is included to carry damp-laden air directly to the outside, and whether the instruction manual is available.

If you buy from a specialist dealer in electrical goods selling reconditioned machines, you may get a wide choice of models as well as a warranty. There is a possiblility of finding a drier to stack on top of the same maker's washing machine.

TUNERS *see* Audio equipment
TURNTABLES *see* Audio equipment

TYPEWRITERS

A faulty typewriter would be worth buying only if it was very cheap, as repairs cost a lot. Even a very basic service for a portable typewriter needing no repairs will cost over £10. Full overhaul of a neglected five-year-old office electric could cost £200.

Luckily, typewriters are relatively easy to test—all you really need is a piece of paper, a new ribbon perhaps, and a plug and socket for an electric machine. Before putting the typewriter through its paces, look for signs of damage on the casing, indicating that the machine has been dropped. A typewriter with a badly damaged case is a bad buy, as typewriters are not like cars, which can have a perfectly sound engine inside battered bodywork. If the casing of a typewriter is damaged, vital internal parts will most probably also have suffered. A cracked or distorted main casting frame will affect general alignment so badly that repair costs will be too enormous to contemplate. The machine is effectively a write-off.

Try every key, with and without the shift. None should stick or jump, and spacing between the letters should be even. The top of the 6 is normally the highest type and the underlining __mark the lowest. See if the ribbon will catch them both. Note how freely the roller turns: it should move easily but without any free play at all. A loose roller will make the type waver.

315

A worn typewriter may have a general alignment problem due to misshapen type bars (the part which comes up when you press the keys). If the type wanders up and down, the machine needs an overhaul. The central bars around the letter N are straighter and therefore lose their shape less quickly than outer ones such as Q, which come under greater stress. Realigning any typewriter is a long and costly job, and poor quality typewriters will be hard to realign at all. A single letter badly and consistently out of alignment is cheaper to repair.

Examine the impression made by the lower case o and the full stop—if they make holes in the paper, the roller has gone hard and must be replaced. The rubber roller wears out like a car tyre. Pitting can to some extent be eliminated by rubbing down the roller (called a platen), but it will have to be replaced eventually. A commercial typewriter in heavy daily use will need a new platen every two or three years; a new one should last for ever in light domestic use. Replacement is no problem for a competent repairer even on an ob-

solete typewriter, as the new rubber is simply cut to fit around the existing cylinder. The job costs upwards of £20, but is worthwhile if a badly-pitted and shiny roller is allowing the paper to slip.

Any external part of the typewriter may be hard to replace, and that includes the case. Visible stylistic features are changed frequently to stimulate sales, without changing anything inside the machine. Mechanical parts for obsolete machines are reasonably easy to find, especially if the production run ended within the past ten years. A repairer should be able to tell the date of manufacture from the machine's serial number.

Old black and chrome models are likely to be at least 40 years old. Worn parts will be a problem, but such machines can be cleaned up and made to work perfectly well. A general cleaning includes blowing and brushing out the dust, lubricating the moving parts and rubbing down the platen. A pile of rubber dust inside the machine is a sign that it hasn't been serviced recently.

If there is any doubt about

the availability of spares or the cost of repairs, try to buy the machine on approval and get a repair estimate as soon as possible. Office equipment suppliers are major sources of used typewriters, and they will normally offer a guarantee of at least three months on used machines. Some of the typewriters will have been thoroughly overhauled, even completely rebuilt, and these are likely to be expensive. However, they should still be cheaper than a new machine and just as reliable.

Electric typewriters Typewriters have been affected by the micro-electronic revolution, and the very latest electric typewriters are radically different from manual machines. However, traditional electric typewriters of the type commonly on offer secondhand are fundamentally just manual typewriters with a motor and drive mechanism. An electric machine's innards are in many cases identical to those inside an equivalent manual model. The electric machine will therefore be prone to the same mechanical faults, and the same costly repairs, as the manual.

The electrical system inside a typewriter consists of a motor driving some form of power roller, and this in turn operates a cam which is normally made of plastic. Damage to the cams is the commonest fault exclusive to electric typewriters. Although neoprene cams are in themselves inexpensive to replace, the labour involved in fitting them can push the repair cost up dramatically. Damaged cams can be hard for the inexperienced buyer to diagnose. They are seen by removing the inspection cover underneath the machine; look for general signs of wear and lumps gouged out of them.

A less common but extremely expensive fault is a burnt-out motor. Motors are replaced, not repaired, and even the trade price is over £50 before the labour and profit begin. Luckily, motors rarely go wrong, so if the motor on a secondhand machine works, it is likely to go on working well for years. Reject any machine with a damaged motor.

The casing may help betray the age of a machine, as the metal cases of early electric typewriters have been largely replaced by plastic. Age is less important than the degree of use the machine has had and the standard of maintenance. For this reason, the best buys in second-hand electric typewriters are often arranged through work.

Companies usually have a maintenance contract with a repair organisation, and the machines are overhauled regularly. When the time comes to renew office equipment, redundant electric typewriters are often sold off to employees, with relatively few being returned to the dealers in part exchange. The maintenance contractor will often continue to repair the machines at a discount rate just as a goodwill gesture to the customer, even after they have been sold off second-hand.

Without such an arrangement, repair costs can be astronomical. Buyers should therefore be wary about buying damaged machines in a private sale. It is better to buy from a reputable dealer who will offer a guarantee of at least three months. The length of guarantee will vary from machine to machine in the same shop, giving some indication of the dealer's confidence in their chances of lasting.

TYRES

Tyres are perhaps the most vital part of a car. They are, after all, the car's only contact with the road. Running on bad tyres increases the risk of a blow-out at high speed, and the consequences can be horrible. Only a lunatic tired of life would try to save a few pounds by buying used tyres from a dubious source.

Good tyres may be salvaged from scrapped cars. The simplest way for the ill-equipped motorist to fix a salvaged tyre on his or her car is to swap the whole wheel. Struggling with hefty car tyres makes childhood battles with bicycle tyres seem insignificant. Make sure all four tyres are the same model from the same manufacturer, and don't buy any which are worn down to the one millimetre legal minimum tread thickness. Avoid tyres with irregular tread wear, bulges on the carcass, cracks in the rubber or scuffs on the sidewalls.

The market in used tyres is dominated by retreads, a term covering various practices which prolong the active life of a tyre. Techniques regulated by British Standards range from "remoulding", in which new rubber replaces the old over the entire tyre, to "top-capping", where only the worn tread rubber is renewed.

Retreads can be a very good buy for the motorist who uses a car only for pottering around locally. Major tyre companies make reliable retreads, and it is wise to stick with known names, as bad remoulds are a real hazard. Driving long distances on retreads is unwise, and covering any distance at over 70 mph on retreads is a dangerous practice, besides being against British law.

A British Standard, BS AU 144b:1977, covers retreads made for speeds up to 70 mph, and this number should appear on all tyres which conform. Other markings on the tyre wall give the retread manufacturer's name and/or trade mark, the tyre size (or a code mark), and the ply rating (or a code mark). Tubeless tyres will be marked "tubeless", and radial tyres will be marked with the word "radial" or the letter R. The word "retread" or "remould"

should also be there.

The grubby back-street shark selling suspiciously cheap tyres is to be avoided, as you are at the dealer's mercy. Unfortunately it is often impossible to spot a dangerous tyre until it is too late. Prices may be higher from the specialist dealer, but standards will be higher too. The tyre specialist will probably be a member of the National Tyre Distributors' Association, whose headquarters is at Broadway House, The Broadway, London SW19 (tel: 01–540 3859). Association members conform to British Standards for retreads and represent the safest source.

Britain's motorists get through some 25 million tyres a year, some of which find interesting alternative employment once their travelling days are done. Some are used as flower containers, others are stacked up and used to construct cheap, long-lasting and effective walls, perhaps as a barrier against drifting sand or incorporated into a landscape design. The tyres are stacked several wide at the base, the number reducing towards the top. The tyres can be filled with rubble or with earth if vegetation is to be encouraged. Worn tyres may become part of the roads they have rolled over, if they are ground into the "crumb" which is used in surfacing roads and tennis courts. Decomposition by pyrolysis turns tired tyres into fuel.

An old tyre's life on the road is also prolonged in Morocco, where shoemakers have for many years used discarded tyres to provide soles for high-mileage sandals. Other unroadworthy tyres are cut into strips and sewn together to make watervessels which are slung over the backs of Morocco's beasts of burden.

U

UMBRELLAS

Umbrellas should be the symbol of the lost property business. Fine brollies are sold at lost property auctions, but secondhand umbrellas too often act just as misshapen filters for the rain. The weakest part of a brolly is normally the frame with its eight ribs, as this is exposed to rough treatment by both the user and the weather. Metal ribs must be rust-free, with stable linkages. Rust will not be a problem with truly antique umbrellas, made before the metal-framed Paragon's virtues made the traditional whalebone or bamboo frames obsolete. The Paragon was followed by two famously reliable frame names: Hoyland and Fox.

Unusually shaped antiques are hard to re-cover when the fabric rots and tears, as the old wooden templates for cutting the "gore" (the triangular piece which fits between each pair of ribs) will have disappeared. The pagoda shape of the nineteenth century umbrella can no longer be reproduced.

Patching is a poor way to deal with a torn cover, and re-covering will put extra strain on old ribs. Few cover makers will work with silk, but the choice of modern nylon fabrics is admirably wide.

Handles were once made with the lovely lancewood, but softer woods and plastic now rule. Even relatively recent handles and tips can be troublesome to mend as certain diameters of dowel disappeared with metrication. Parts availability for old and foreign brollies is unpredictable. The finest resting place for an irreparable brolly is James Smith & Co., whose magnificent umbrella shop claims to be Europe's oldest, having stood in New Oxford Street, London since 1867. They follow the laudable policy of never throwing umbrellas away. In consequence, their cluttered basement contains the skeletons of hundreds of brollies, with drawers full of thousands of salvaged ribs and handles, all waiting to be used by the repair shop on the premises.

V

VACUUM CLEANERS

Portable electric vacuum cleaners have been sucking up domestic dust since 1904, and Hoovers began beating and sweeping the USA clean in 1908. Some very old appliances are therefore lurking in attics and likely to find their way into secondhand shops. Luckily vacuum cleaners are sturdy machines built on a simple principle: an electric motor turns a shaft which turns a fan, and the fan pulls dirt-laden air through the machine, where the dust is filtered out in the bag.

The commonest faults are also the easiest to rectify. Number one problem is neglect. If a vac stops sucking, it is probably because the dust bag needs emptying or replacing. Dirt may also have clogged up the filter, but cleaning this is equally easy.

The power of a secondhand vacuum cleaner should be tested by scattering visible filth such as sawdust and bright bits of thread on the seller's floor, and trying to clean it off. It should all disappear with ease.

Before plugging in and

switching on, be sure you are safe. Disconnected wires dangling inside the machine could touch a metal case and lead to shock horrors. You can check that there is a good earth by carrying out an earth continuity test before you plug in (see Electrical Appliances). Look for signs of wear and tear on the flex: any damage makes replacement inescapable, and this can be expensive as vacuum cleaner flex must be long to be convenient.

The machine's mobility can also be checked before plugging in, by just pushing it around the room or the shop floor. Squeaky wheels or difficulty in moving the appliance could be due to poor lubrication. Worn-out beater brushes will also slow you down. These can be replaced simply, but all spares normally have to be paid for.

The condition of a fabric dust bag on an upright cleaner will be apparent before switching on. These wear away after years of rubbing and snagging on the furniture, and a worn one needs replacing.

If the appliance sucks badly when it is switched on, put your hand or a carpet over the suction end: the pitch of the motor should fall as the cleaner is put to work, and rise again when the work is taken away. Then disconnect the dust bag and filter and cover the end again. If suction increases, the bag and filter should be replaced. If the machine seems just as feeble as before, the hoses could be clogged, in which case a quick clean-up should clear the problem. It is a mistake to test pick-up power with the filter removed, as dust is sucked onto the motor where it can cause overheating and eventually lead to a burn-out.

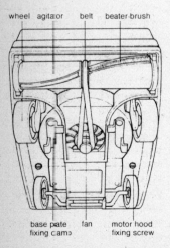

wheel agitator   belt   beater-brush

base plate   fan   motor hood
fixing clamp   fixing screw

vacuum cleaner with plate removed

All the cleaner's attachments should be tested. If one proves poor, it is probably blocked or torn. A good suction hose should lift the corner of a rug or carpet, as long as it is not nailed down!

Intermittent motor activity could mean faulty flex, worn brushes or loose wires which must be checked out. If the motor whirls round convincingly but there is no suction at all, the drive belt on upright cleaners may have perished away, fallen off or been severed when the cleaner swallowed a sharp object. Belts are sometimes jammed when fabric winds round the pulley, and this leads to an alarming smell of hot rubber. Access to the belt is usually given simply by unhooking the cover plate under the appliance. If this plate is missing, be sure spares are available before buying, and be certain the fixing points are intact.

If the noise of the motor is accompanied by metallic clanks, there is either a loose bit of metal rattling around inside or a misaligned fan which needs attention. A rumble from the motor means worn bearings and expert attention.

If the motor will not turn at all, and the fuse, flex and plug seem all right, electrical tests will probably be needed to locate the damage, which might be a damaged on-off switch or a broken motor which will require professional repair.

Spare parts for vacuum cleaners are usually easy to find, either in specialist repair shops or draped like dead snakes over a market stall.

A repair shop may be a good source of complete reconditioned machines as well as spares and the specialist tools which may be needed for successful diy repair. The specialist dealer in spares and secondhand appliances will usually be more willing to offer a lengthy written guarantee than the general junk shop on the corner.

VICES *see* Tools

VIDEO

There is a certain social status to be won from being among the first owners of any new technological toy, but the pioneers' machines normally have teething problems which are ironed out for later models. The first generation of video cassette recorders

(VCRs) has proved to be extremely unreliable; most need a very expensive annual overhaul and are poor buys secondhand. It is crucial to see a secondhand VCR working and to check out maintenance and repair services before you buy it. Reliability and performance can be confidently expected to improve as the market grows, and prices should fall.

At present, secondhand VCRs are worth buying only as an investment in techno-logical curios which may one day be of antique value. Depreciation is rapid, but if a market winner should emerge among the three competing, different and mutually incompatible systems at present widely available, many VCRs will become obsolete, very cheap and of little use.

Secondhand television sets manufactured before 1974 may need a simple adjustment before they will play pre-recorded video cassettes.

W

WCs *see* Bathroom fittings

WASHING MACHINES

A few lucky buyers make a success of secondhand washing machines. There is, for example, the true and inspiring story of the entrepreneur in the Philippines who opened a starch-separation plant built around a $10,000 batch of secondhand washing machines: it soon put a $1.5M, high-technology, supposedly efficient rival plant out of business.

Most domestic buyers are less lucky with old washing machines, which can even present a scrap-metal dealer with problems, as they contain so much junk besides the valuable steel he wants to salvage.

Brand-new washing machines are notoriously troublesome, and old ones are worse. Problems are hard to spot and diagnose, and washing machines are really too complicated for extensive diy repairs. It can cost a lot to get a repairman as far as the front door, and necessary repairs can easily double the cost of a secondhand automatic washing machine within a year.

Most handymen could replace perished or kinked pipes and hoses, fit a new rubber door seal, mend a faulty door catch, remove scale from a blocked pipe, even take buttons and coins out of the filter and adjust the tension of the drive belt, but serious faults can be hidden from view and beyond the handyman's capabilities.

Home repair can leave a machine in a dangerous state. The machine's entire casing must be earthed, and it is simple to break the earth continuity when the machine is dismantled.

Spare parts for old machines can be hard to find. It is worth buying a couple of spare belts for any old machine before the manufacturers stop selling them for ever. Snapped or stretched belts are among the commonest causes of breakdown.

Manufacturers continue to stock spare parts for at least

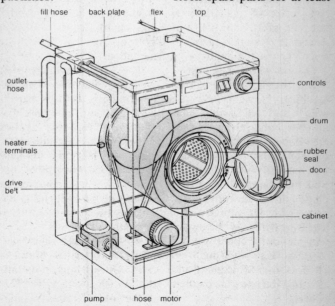

ten years after the date of manufacture; after this time major parts are very hard to track down without cannibalising another similar machine. Some very old machines are still around and working. The first washing machines appeared on the British market in the 1920s, and some of these are still cleaning clothes. Manufacturers change the shape of the cabinet more frequently than the working parts, but it is hard to tell the age of a machine. The serial number will tell the manufacturer the precise week of manufacture, but this information will not necessarily be passed on to a member of the public.

On the whole it is best to avoid secondhand washing machines. However, they are bought and sold in significant numbers, and buyers can increase their chances of a wise buy by exercising caution. Mechanically skilled buyers will find bargains, as a machine may be up for sale because of a very minor fault. The mechanically incompetent majority could find it worthwhile to pay a qualified electrician to come along and examine the machine on their behalf.

Certain sources of used machines are generally more reliable than others. Auctions and small ads are bad sources. Buyers are unlikely to be able to see the machine in operation before deciding whether to buy, so it is important to be able to return the machine if it doesn't work. This is seldom possible with small ads and auctions. Chances are better at established repair shops or manufacturers' agents, who may sell reconditioned machines with a six-month guarantee. A machine whose complete life history is known to have been brief and happy so far could be bought from a friend or neighbour.

The life expectancy of a washing machine will depend on use, but it is usually hard to insure any machine over six years old against breakdown. Any automatic over five years old is unlikely to be a good investment, but twin tubs could continue to work well for longer and are usually cheaper to repair when things go wrong.

A secondhand machine will probably offer as useful a range of washing programmes as a new one. In 1972/3 the manufacturers established the current range of nine agreed washing processes by the addition of programmes 8 and 9 to the seven established in 1966. The nine are now printed on detergent packets and on the machines' control panels. Instruction books are vital to learn how to get the programmes on a foreign machine. Continental manufacturers are not keen on the system.

Rust is a serious enemy of old washing machines. Leaky hoses can lead to rust, which in turn can lead to broken earth continuity, besides putting permanent brown stains on freshly-washed clothes. No rusty machine is worth buying, and it is worth checking out underneath the casing for the first signs of rust.

Chipped enamel can let in water and allow rust to develop. The enamel coating inside the tub can break up if coins, buckles and other hard litter are often included in the wash. Chipped tubs are bad buys.

It can be a very costly mistake to load a used machine up with your best clothes for its first run. There may be all sorts of filth lurking in the drum and waiting to deposit itself on your washing. Before washing anything, load the empty machine with detergent and run it through the hottest wash cycle.

A lot of modern front-loading automatic washing machines can be stacked with a matching tumble drier. This saves floor space, so if the arrangement appeals, check with the manufacturer whether a stacking kit is available for older models.

WATCHES
A traditional mechanical watch movement is delicate and complex; once it is broken, it is usually a very bad buy. A stopped watch is worth considering second-hand only if you understand precisely what has gone wrong and are certain spare parts can be found to repair it cheaply. Watches bearing the scars of unsuccessful diy repair are best rejected. Replacement straps and bracelets are easy to find and fit, as are spare hands and glasses, but diy repair of a valuable watch movement is only for the professional or the skilled hobbyist. Skills may of course be learned by practising on a cheap broken watch!

The manufacturers' habit

of discontinuing lines after a year or two in production makes spares for many modern models hard to trace. Manufacturers cannot be relied on as sources of spares and repairs, as some major manufacturers have disappeared in recent years.

Even a working watch may gain or lose a lot, and be too far out to regulate. The safest way to buy is therefore on a fortnight's approval. Make sure you have a receipt, and take the watch along to a reputable mender for an opinion and a repair estimate.

The king of the spare part sector rules from 35 Caledonian Road, London N1, home of the Obsolete Watch Materials Supply. The proprietor, Mr Bob Szewczyk, stocks literally millions of parts for over 20,000 types of obsolete watch, with a selection of cylinders in over 15,000 sizes, staffs in 8,000 sizes and a further 4,500 stems. If he cannot mend your watch, you are in trouble. Mr Szewczyk's shop aims to do the impossible, and grateful customers are ticking at the wrist worldwide. He still patrols the junk markets of London looking for clocks and watches

spurned by both trade and public. Nothing, he believes, is without value to the person who can recognise materials. He is a true secondhand hero.

The watch mender's traditional skills are threatened by the arrival of the quartz watch. Quartz watches are particularly easy to damage by a clumsy job. Removing a screw can break a printed circuit, and the watch can be short-circuited by touching parts with a finger. Circuits can also be fused if a new battery is put in the wrong way round. Damp can also damage quartz watches. Most traditional watch menders are unwilling to tamper with quartz watches except to change the battery, and broken watches are best returned to the manufacturer or a specialist repair shop, both of whom will have the parts (which are very expensive) and the equipment to do the job. The manufacturer may be hard to find. Without knowledge of the market, money can easily be wasted on a poor watch.

Many attractive old watches are sold as antiques, and the buyer's protection is very limited in the antique world. Antique dealers often disclaim all knowledge of how a thing works, and they can quite legitimately claim to have sold a useless watch as a decorative artefact, not as a working timepiece.

WATER HEATERS

An old and supposedly instantaneous water heater provides one of the daily terrors of life in the average bedsit—the agonising wait between turning the tap on and seeing the gas burners burst into flame. In fact water heaters cause remarkably few accidents. They are reliable and durable appliances, but buying a secondhand one can be risky. Unwanted heaters are ripped from walls by clumsy builders in a hurry and sold to the unwary in junk shops. The customer rarely has a chance to see the heater plumbed in, connected to the gas supply and in working order. The buyer can do little more than look it over for excessive rust, turn the taps, check that the viewing window (if any) is not ruined by heat, and then remove the front panel. This should be easy. Look inside for splits in the heat exchanger—it's a coiled tube—and corrosion around the water pipe fix-

ings. Old heaters may leak water or fumes, the thermostat may have failed, and they will at best be in need of a thorough overhaul after years of neglect.

British Gas recommends an annual service. Filth and verdigris build up inside, and scale can clog up waterways in hard water areas. Proprietary descalers are available, but you may need a technician to use them. To comply with British Standard BS 1250 all the waterways liable to scale up must be accessible, so the Kitemark is worth looking for. The same standard says that there must be a tap controlling the gas supply and that the various tap positions should be indelibly and clearly marked. They are useful guides. The symbols are: a disc for "Off"; a stylised spark for the pilot ignition position if there is one; a large stylised flame for the nominal rate of the burners; a small stylised flame for the reduced rate if there is one.

Some heaters may be sold "reconditioned and guaranteed". It is worth checking out the current cost of a routine service before you make an offer for an old heater which arrives without warranty from a dubious dealer. A competent technician will be needed to install and adjust the appliance. An installer displaying the CORGI sign should be workmanlike, and should have access to the manufacturer's technical instructions. These illustrate the main parts which can be replaced or removed. Without the manufacturer's "instructions for use", routine use, cleaning and maintenance can be very confusing.

Water heaters have improved with technology, and a reconditioned water heater should be of the most recent type. The traditional open flue was made unacceptable for bathroom use by regulations in 1972. A balanced flue became compulsory. Small unflued sink water heaters are not designed to run for more than five minutes and are therefore unsuitable for running a hot bath. Some heaters are designed to be connected to a cistern, others to the main water supply. Water board regulations may dictate which type of heater is acceptable. Proper ventilation is important with all old appliances.

Electric heaters Few secondhand heaters can be viewed wired up, plumbed in and working, and water and electricity is a menacing combination. The heater may turn out to be broken, with its elements burned out. The burns could be on the user's hands if the thermostat has stuck in the "on" position and steam comes rushing from the tap.

An electric water heater must be well earthed, and corrosion or poor maintenance can break the earth continuity on secondhand heaters. After looking for obvious signs of severe rusting on the casing, check out the earth. It must be tested before the heater is installed, and money can be saved by using a multimeter before buying a used heater. The multimeter can also reveal the commonest problem with immersion heaters—a burnt-out element. In a heater with twin elements, one can burn out, leaving just one element and luke-warm water.

A build-up of scale on the elements can cut efficiency noticeably. If the heater has not been given a pre-sale overhaul by a competent electrician, arrange for a service at installation time. The casing will have to be taken off to see inside the heater. Look it over for signs of holes and traces of leaks through gaskets. Badly-corroded metal is not worth buying. The water cylinder should be copper. If rust has eaten away the fixing points, the heater cannot easily be mounted on the wall. A professional installation is always advisable.

WATERING CANS *see* Garden tools

WHEELBARROWS *see* Garden tools

Z

ZIPS

Old zips fail at awkward moments, springing open dramatically or sliding secretly down, never to rise again. Diy zip replacement on a pair of jeans is a really tough job, as the zip is double stitched and set in before the jeans are sewn together. Because of this difficulty, despairing wearers often chuck out perfectly sound jeans when the zip goes. These jeans can be secondhand bargains, as certain dry cleaners can replace zips cheaply. Shops belonging to one of the bigger groups have a central repair point or a visiting outworker who collects clothes needing repair.

Always test a zip on old clothes by running it up and down to reveal broken teeth and trying to tug the two parts apart a little to check its strength. A stiff zip may be evidence of dyeing. Professional dyeing processes demand high temperatures, which make metal zips expand and contract, leading on occasion to slightly bent zips.

Professional dry cleaning should leave zips unaffected, as the cleaner will normally test and oil a zip before pressing the garment. Stiff zips can be lubricated by rubbing them with a pencil or a candle.

Jeans need heavy zips, but light nylon is better on antique clothes. A delicate old crepe, for example, will buckle under a heavy zip. Lightweight zips will be suitable with stretch fabrics. Information on repair services is provided by the Drycleaning Information Bureau.

ADDRESS LIST

Where to find specialist suppliers, services, organisations and societies referred to in the secondhand A-Z

Advisory Board for Redundant Churches
Fielden House
Little College Street
London SW1
advise on uses for redundant churches and issue demolition certificates

Anstey Horne & Co.
Harrow Road
London W2
auctioneer of British Rail lost property

Architectural Salvage
Hutton and Rostron
Netley House
Gomshall
Surrey
clearing house for secondhand building materials; will supply lists of currently available materials and advertise particular needs

Association of Manufacturers of Domestic Electrical Appliances
593 Hitchin Road
Stopsley
Luton
Bedfordshire
recommend minimum periods for maintaining stocks of spares and issue code for sales of new appliances; manufacturers can be traced through them

Bath Services
26 Romilly Street
London W1
will retouch chipped enamel and reenamel baths

Bee Books New and Old
Tapping Wall Farm
Burrowbridge
Somerset
sell books and provide information about bees

Frank Bowen
15 Greek Street
London W1
*fortnightly auctions of office
furniture (Thursdays)*

Bristol Hi-Fi Consultants
28 Upper Handlin Street
Bristol
specialist hi-fi repairs

**British Beekeepers'
Association**
no permanent central
address; the address of your
local branch may be
obtained from the General
Secretary
High Trees
Dean Lane
Merstham
Surrey RH1 3AH
*issue the magazine Bee
Craft*

British Canoe Union
45–47 High Street
Addlestone
Weybridge
Surrey
*supply information on
affiliated clubs; publish
Canoe Focus, free to
members, and the booklet
Choosing a Canoe*

**British Electrotechnical
Approvals Board** (BEAB)
Mark House
9/11 Queen's Road
Hersham
Walton-on-Thames
Surrey KT12 5NA
*operate voluntary
"approved appliances"
scheme for electrical safety
of household appliances*

British Gas showrooms
(address in phone book)
*supply information on
authorised dealers and
registered installers as well
as manufacturers' addresses*

**British Hang Gliding
Association**
167a Cheddon Road
Taunton
Somerset TA2 7AH
*hang glider pilots advised
to join; issue the magazine
Wings*

**British Parachuting
Association**
Kimberley House
47 Vaughan Way
Leicester LE1 4SG
*membership obligatory to
parachutists before jumping*

British Railways Board
Railways Technical Centre
London Road
Derby DE2 8UP
*information on railway
carriages for sale*

British Sub-Aqua Club
70 Brompton Road
London SW3
*has some 800 branches,
where instructors can be
found*

British Waterways Board
Craft Licensing Supervisor
Willow Grange
Church Road
Watford WD1 3QA
*will supply annual list of
canal mooring fees and
houseboat certificate fees;
also information on
houseboats on canals*

Brunnings (Holborn) Ltd
133 High Holborn
London WC1V 6PX
*suppliers of new and
secondhand microscopes
and optical instruments;
reliable repairers*

Bush and Hall
40 Theobalds Road
London WC1
*supply metric and imperial
weights for old balance
scales*

Camera Care Ltd
30 Tottenham Street
London W1
*do fast bench test on
cameras*

**Camping Club of Great
Britain and Ireland Ltd**
11 Lower Grosvenor Place
London SW1
*issue a free monthly
magazine for members;
advise on tent and caravan
selection*

**Carpet Cleaners'
Association**
97 Knighton Fields Road
West
Leicester
*can supply details of
specialist carpet cleaners in
any area*

CEBRA
261 Queen's Road
Halifax
West Yorkshire
*may be able to update old
electric blankets*

China Matching Service
Margaret A Janes
Tamarisk
Warren Road
Kingsbridge
South Devon
*matching service for owners
of incomplete and obsolete
services*

Citizens' Advice Bureaux
see 'phone book for local
office
*give advice on consumer
affairs*

Companies House
55–71 City Road
London EC1Y 1BB
and 102 George Street
Edinburgh EH2 3DJ
register of companies

**Confederation of
Registered Gas Installers**
(CORGI)
twelve branches tied in with
Gas Board regions; *their
register of gas installers
should be available from
local gas showrooms and
local libraries*

Consumers' Association
14 Buckingham Street
London WC2N 6DS
*well known publishers of
Which? magazines and
tireless product testers*

Crafts Council
12 Waterloo Place
London SW1Y 4AU
*supplies details of craft
courses and keeps a
register of craftsmen*

Dowell Lloyd & Co.
4 Putney High Street
London SW15
*Metropolitan Police
bicycles sold by auction*

**Drycleaning Information
Bureau**
178–202 Great Portland
Street
London W1N 6AQ
*will supply name and
address of suitable local
cleaner for specific
problems, including carpets*

Alfred Dunhill Ltd
30 Duke Street
St James's
London SW1
*parts for repairs to old
Dunhill lighters*

Dylon International
Consumer Advice Bureau
Worsley Bridge Road
London SE26
free advice on dye

Early Music Society
62 Princedale Road
London W11
*may be able to advise on
teachers and instruments*

Electric Razor Hospital
491 Commercial Road
London E1
*can repair almost any
broken electric razor and
give service and 6 months'
guarantee*

**Electrical Association for
Women**
25 Foubert's Place
London W1V 2AL
*publications (useful for
everyone) and classes*

Electricity Council
30 Millbank
London SW1
*publish free leaflets on
electricity in the home,
available from local
showrooms*

Ellis Sykes and Co. Ltd
Victoria Works
Howard Street
Stockport
Cheshire
*supply parts for Godin
stoves*

**English Vineyards
Association**
c/o the Merrydown Wine
Co.
Horam
East Sussex
*occasional source of used
wine-making equipment*

Federation of City Farms
12 Wilkin Street
London NW5 3NC
*help anyone wishing to set
up a city farm*

Friends of the Earth
9 Poland Street
London W1V 3DG
*contact the London head-
quarters or any of the 200
local groups for information
on recycling*

Gefen Sports
114 Longstone Avenue
London NW10
*restring tennis rackets and
may give tuition to
customers, also supply
materials for diy restringing*

General Auctions
63/65 Garratt Lane
London SW18
bicycle auctions

German Bedding Centre
138 Marylebone Road
London NW1
*specialist cleaning and
renovation of duvets; will
also convert eiderdowns*

Glass and Glazing Federation
Information Office
6 Mount Row
London W1
register of members able to repair stained and leaded glass, make new glass table tops and undertake resilvering of old mirrors

Glass Manufacturers' Federation
Information Office
19 Portland Place
London W1
firms on their register include those who will grind chips out of crystal glasses and bowls; others recycle glass

Harvester
Maylord Street
Hereford
sell new and used goatkeeping equipment by mail order, also have notice board in shop

Home Laundering Consultative Council
41/42 Dover Street
London W1X 4DS
information for home launderers

Jazz Centre Society
35 Great Russell Street
London WC1
may help find secondhand instruments for sale, and give names of teachers

Johnson & Calverly
Brook Street
Elland
West Yorkshire
may be able to update old electric blankets

Lawn Tennis Association
Palliser Road
London W14
list of club secretaries handling sales of used tournament balls

A T Lee & Co.
PO Box 530
Chester Street
London SW1X 7BH
distributors of bottle choppers for the creative recyclist

Lighter and Shaver Repair Centre
231 Oxford Street
and 4 Lumley Street
London W1
undertake repairs to shavers and lighters; claim to turn down only 5% of damaged lighters

London Bicycle Market and Auction
Bay 49
Westway Flyover
Ladbroke Grove
London W11
auctions on Saturdays, spares and repairs on weekdays

London Pigskin Co.
144a Royal College Street
London NW1 0TA
will tackle dirty pigskins; few others do

London Sound
266 Field End Road
Eastcote
Ruislip
Middlesex
top hi-fi repair specialist

Lord Chancellor's Department
Page Street
London SW1
supplies copies of free leaflet, Small Claims in the County Court

Maisemore Apiaries
Old Road
Maisemore
Gloucestershire GL2 8HT
supply secondhand beehives

Ministry of Agriculture, Fisheries and Food
contact nearest Ministry Divisional Office
(address in phone book under "Agriculture")
for health checks on bees

Morgans
5 Leigh Street
London WC1
valve radio repair specialists

Mutual Aid Centre
18 Victoria Park Square
London E2 9PF
encourage the development of small-scale consumer cooperatives

National Inspection Council for Electrical Installation Contracting
(NICEIC)
93 Albert Embankment
London SE1
their list of approved electricians can be obtained from them or electricity boards

National Institute of Adult Education
19b de Montfort Street
Leicester LE1 7GE
supply list of residential short courses

National Supervisory Council for Intruder Alarms
St Ives House
St Ives Road
Maidenhead
Buckinghamshire
alarms must be approved by them to satisfy most insurers

National Tyre Distributors Association
Broadway House
The Broadway
London SW19
their members are a safe source of retreads

Office of Fair Trading
Field House
15–25 Bream's Buildings
London EC4A 1PR
watch-dog for trading matters, publish free leaflets on consumer matters, obtainable from them (Room 310) or Citizens' Advice Bureaux

Oldtimer Cameras Ltd
14 Gables Avenue
Boreham Wood
Hertfordshire
have microfilm of old issues of Amateur Photographer

Paraffin Heating Advisory Council
121 Gloucester Place
London W1H 3PJ
compile list of appointed service agents

W R Pashley
Masons Road
Stratford on Avon
Warwickshire
manufacture spare parts for old bicycles and will supply name of your nearest retailer

People's Dispensary for Sick Animals
(Head Office)
PDSA House
South Street
Dorking
Surrey
some 30 local branches have charity shops

Photographer's Gallery
5 and 8 Newport Street
London WC2
see their notice board for camera sales etc.

Piano Tuners' Association
c/o 5 Northdown
Eastrees Park
Ashford
Kent
should be able to find you a piano tuner

Pither
Wade Lewis Ltd
Stewart House
Brook Way
Kingston Road
Leatherhead
Surrey KT22 7ZY
*supply parts for Pither
stoves*

Prestige Group Ltd
City Road
Derby DE1 3RL
*repairs and information on
Prestige/Skyline products*

**Queckett Microscopical
Club**
c/o British Museum
(Natural History)
Cromwell Road
London SW7 5BD
*club for amateur and
professional enthusiasts;
publishes Microscopy and a
Newsletter*

78 Record Exchange
9 Lower Hillgate
Stockport
Cheshire
*Britain's best established
specialist 78 record shop;
can supply stock catalogues*

Rentatent
Third Way
off South Way
Wembley
Middlesex
branches in Manchester,
Wakefield and Shefford
*for purchase of ex-hire
camping equipment*

Renubath Services
596 Chiswick High Road
London W4 5RS
bath reenamelling service

**Residential Boat Owners'
Association**
c/o Eridanus
Benbow Way Mooring
Uxbridge
Middlesex
*market information and
advice on finance sources;
publish Newsletter with ads
of boats for sale*

**Royal Institution of Naval
Architects**
10 Upper Belgrave Street
London SW1
*their chartered engineers
are reliable surveyors of
boats*

Royal National Institute for the Blind
224 Upper Belgrave Street
London W1
local branches may be able to give information about craftsmen, especially for recaning furniture

Royal Pigeon Racing Association
The Readings
Near Cheltenham
Gloucestershire
sales and reringing of pigeons

Royal Society for the Prevention of Accidents
Cannon House
The Priory Queensway
Birmingham B4 6BS
information on safety precautions in the home

Royal Society for the Prevention of Cruelty to Animals (RSPCA)
The Causeway
Horsham
Sussex
and local branches
stray pets looking for new homes

Salvation Army
International Headquarters
101 Queen Victoria Street
London EC4
local branches in phone book
inexpensive and variable source of furniture

Sarose Scientific Instruments Suppliers
2 Manor Road
London W13
supply secondhand microscopes and laboratory equipment

Self Sufficiency and Smallholding Supplies
The Old Palace
Priory Road
Wells
Somerset
supplies for the smallholder, backyard farmer and self-reliant householder; mail order service

Ship and Boat Builders National Federation
Boating Industry House
Vale Road
Oatlands Village
Weybridge
Surrey
members operate code of practice for boat sales

Ski Club of Great Britain
118 Eaton Square
London SW1
*publish Ski Survey for
members*

Smallholders' Association
Stoke House
Stoke St Mary
Taunton
Somerset TA3 5BZ
*members operate a barter
scheme for equipment and
produce*

**Solid Fuel Advisory
Service**
Hobart House
Grosvenor Place
London SW1X 7AE
*technical officers give free
advice on installing old
fireplaces*

Suede Services
2a Hoop Lane
Golders Green Road
London NW11
*excellent postal service for
cleaning and restoration of
leather and suede clothes*

West London Auctions
Sandringham Mews
London W5
*for auctions of airport and
airline lost property*

Christopher Wray
600 Kings Road
London SW6
*all parts for oil lamps and
reconditioned oil lamps for
sale, especially antiques*

Woodfit
Whittle Low Mill
Chorley
Lancashire PR6 7HB
*mail order supplies of vast
range of fixtures and
fittings for furniture*

**Yacht Brokers, Designers
and Surveyors Association**
Orchard Hill, The Avenue
Farnham Lane
Haslemere, Surrey
*reliable surveyors of
secondhand boats*

MAGAZINES AND PERIODICALS

Addresses of specialist magazines and periodicals useful to the buyer of secondhand goods. Most are available from newsagents.

Airgun World (monthly)
10 Sheet Street
Windsor
Berkshire

Amateur Photographer (weekly)
IPC Specialist and
Professional Press Ltd
Surrey House
1 Throwley Way
Sutton
Surrey SM1 4QQ

Art and Antiques Weekly (weekly)
Independent Magazines Ltd
Bridge House
181 Queen Victoria Street
London EC4V 4DD

Bee Craft (monthly)
the official publication of
the British Beekeepers'
Association
Bee Craft Ltd
13 Althorp Road
London SW17

British Business (weekly)
Department of Trade and
Industry
Millbank Tower
Millbank
London SW1P 4QU

Building Trades Journal (weekly)
Northwood Publications Ltd
Elm House
10–16 Elm Street
London WC1 0PB

Bygone Record Sales
30 Radcliffe Road
West Bridgeford
Nottingham

Canoe Focus (quarterly)
the official magazine of the
British Canoe Union
Flexel House
45–47 High Street
Addlestone
Weybridge
Surrey KT15 1JV

Car Mechanics (monthly)
Business Publications Ltd
109–119 Waterloo Road
London SE1

Caravan (monthly),
*Caravan Fact
Finder* (annual)
Link House Magazines
(Croydon) Ltd
Link House
Dingwall Avenue
Croydon CR9 2TA

Clocks (monthly)
Model and Allied
Publications Ltd
PO Box 35
13–35 Bridge Street
Hemel Hempstead
Hertfordshire

Commercial Motor (weekly)
IPC Transport Press Ltd
Dorset House
Stamford Street
London SE1 9LU

Cycling (weekly)
IPC Specialist and
Professional Press Ltd
Surrey House
1 Throwley Way
Sutton
Surrey SM1 4QQ

Draper's Record (weekly)
Knightway House
20 Soho Square
London W1V 6DT

Early Music (quarterly)
Oxford University Press
Ely House
37 Dover Street
London W1X 4AH

*Exchange and
Mart* (weekly)
Robert Rogers House
New Orchard
Poole
Dorset

*Flight
International* (fortnightly)
IPC Transport Press Ltd
Dorset House
Stamford Street
London SE1 9LU

Glass's Guides:
to Caravan Values
(quarterly)

to Used Car Values
(monthly)

to Used Motor Cycle
Values (monthly)

(confidential trade
publications)
Glass's Guide Service Ltd
Elgin House
St George's Avenue
Weybridge
Surrey KT13 0BX

Guns Review (monthly)
The Ravenhill Publishing
Co Ltd
Standard House
Bonhill Street
London EC2A 4DA

Hostelling News (quarterly)
Youth Hostels Association
(England and Wales)
Trevelyan House
St Albans
Hertfordshire

The Jewish
Chronicle (weekly)
25 Furnival Street
London EC4A 1JT

Laboratory Equipment
Digest (monthly)
Morgan Grampian (Process
Press) Ltd
30 Calderwood Street
Woolwich
London SE18 6QH

Laboratory
News (fortnightly)
World Media Ltd
40 The Boulevard
Crawley
West Sussex

Machinery Market (weekly)
The Machinery Market Ltd
146a Queen Victoria Street
London EC4V 5AR

Mobile Home and Holiday
Caravan (monthly)
Link House Magazines
(Croydon) Ltd
Link House
Dingwall Avenue
Croydon CR9 2TA

Motor Cycle News (weekly)
8 Herbal Hill
London EC1R 5JB

Motoring
Which? (quarterly)
Consumers' Association
14 Buckingham Street
London WC2

Motorists Guide to New and Used Car Prices (monthly)
B ackfriars Press Ltd
PO Box 80
Smith Dorrien Road
Leicester LE5 4BS

Nature (weekly)
Macmillan Journals Ltd
4 Little Essex Street
London WC2R 3LF

Parkers Car Price Guide (monthly)
Parkers Price Guides Ltd
45 St Mary's Road
Ealing
London W5 5RQ

Personal Computer World (monthly)
Sportscene Publishers Ltd
14 Rathbone Place
London W1P 1DE

Powerboat and Water Skiing (monthly)
Ocean Publications Ltd
34 Buckingham Palace Road
London SW1W 0RE

Practical Caravan (monthly)
Haymarket Publishing Ltd
38–42 Hampton Road
Teddington
Middlesex TW11 0JE

Practical Self Sufficiency
Broad Leys Publishing Co.
Widdington
Saffron Walden
Essex CB11 3SP

Rowing (nine times per year)
official magazine of the Amateur Rowing Association
Aylings Boathouse
Embankment
Putney
London SW15 1LB

Ski Survey (five times per year)
official journal of the *Ski Club of Great Britain*
The Ski Club of Great Britain Publications
118 Eaton Square
London SW1

Sporting Gun (monthly)
EMAP National Publications Ltd
21 Church Walk
Peterborough PE1 2TW

Subaqua Scene (every alternate month)
the official magazine of the Sub-Aqua Association
Ocean Publications Ltd
168 Victoria Street
London SW1E 5LV

*Threestokes Guide to Used
Outboard Motor
Values* (twice yearly)
C & D Partners
145–147 High Street
Kelvedon
Essex CO5 9JA

Time Out (weekly)
Time Out Ltd
Tower House
Southampton Street
London WC2

Waterways World (monthly)
Waterways Productions Ltd
Nottingham House
Dales Street
Burton-upon-Trent
Staffordshire DE14 3TD

Which? (monthly)
Consumers' Association
14 Buckingham Street
London WC2

Which Bike? (monthly)
Sportscene Publishers Ltd
14 Rathbone Place
London W1P 1DE

Wings
the official magazine of the
British Hang Gliding
Association
167a Cheddon Road
Taunton
Somerset TA2 7AH

BOOKS AND LEAFLETS

Recommended further reading for the consumer in the secondhand market

The Art and Antique Restorer's Handbook
Savage, George
Barrie and Jenkins, 1976

The Buyer's Right, a Which? guide for consumers
Consumers' Association, 1978

Buying a House or Flat
Bedford Square Press
26 Bedford Square, WC1, 1977

Buying and selling at Auction (free leaflet)
Incorporated Society of Auctioneers and Valuers
3 Cadogan Gate, SW1

Buying a Secondhand Boat
Gannaway, David
Nautical, 1980

The Care of Carpets (leaflet)
British Carpet Manufacturers
Technical Centre
Ackroyd House
Hoo Road, Kidderminster

Choosing a Canoe (booklet)
British Canoe Union

Common Sense and Electrical DIY (leaflet)
Electrical Association for Women
25 Foubert's Place
London W1V 2AL

The Conveyancing Fraud
Joseph, Michael
Michael Joseph 1976

Dealers in Books: A Directory of Dealers in Secondhand and Antiquarian Books in the British Isles
Sheppard Press, 1978

Electricity for Everyday Living
Electrical Association for Women
25 Foubert's Place
London W1V 2AL

English Silver Hall Marks
ed Judith Bannister
Foulsham

Firearms: What you need to know about the law (leaflet)
Home Office

For Your Protection (series of leaflets)
Office of Fair Trading

International Directory of Book Collectors
Trigon Press
117 Kent House Road
Beckenham
Kent BR3 1JJ

Junk
A Guide to Bargain Testing
Benedictus, David
Macmillan, 1976

Junk Genius (free brochure)
Sterling Roncraft

The Legal Side of Buying a House
Consumers' Association

Manual of Domestic Sewing Machines (leaflet)
Singer Sewing Machines

Pet Care (series of leaflets)
PDSA

Photography: the Guide to Technique
Hawkins, Andrew and
Avon, Dennis
Blandford, 1979

Repair Your Own Home Electrical Appliances
Burdett, Geoffrey and
Mattick, John
Foulsham, 1977

The Retail Jeweller's Guide
Blakemore, Kenneth
Newnes-Butterworth, 1976

Understanding Your Car
Johnstone, Roy
Macdonald Guidelines
(Macdonald Educational),
1977

Which? Way to Repair and Restore Furniture
Consumers' Association and
Hodder and Stoughton,
1980

Wonder Worker
Phillips, Barty,
Sidgwick and Jackson,
1977
Corgi, 1978

Wonder Worker's Complete Book of Cleaning
Phillips, Barty
Sidgwick and Jackson,
1979

Yearbook of Society of Master Saddlers (annual)
9 St Thomas Street
London SE1